Economics and Ethics

AF835305

# Economics and Ethics

## An Introduction

Revised Edition

Amitava Krishna Dutt
*Professor, University of Notre Dame*

and

Charles K. Wilber
*Professor Emeritus, University of Notre Dame*

palgrave
macmillan

© Amitava Krishna Dutt and Charles K. Wilber 2010, 2013

All rights reserved. No reproduction, copy or transmission of this publication may be made without written permission.

No portion of this publication may be reproduced, copied or transmitted save with written permission or in accordance with the provisions of the Copyright, Designs and Patents Act 1988, or under the terms of any licence permitting limited copying issued by the Copyright Licensing Agency, Saffron House, 6-10 Kirby Street, London EC1N 8TS.

Any person who does any unauthorized act in relation to this publication may be liable to criminal prosecution and civil claims for damages.

The authors have asserted their rights to be identified as the authors of this work in accordance with the Copyright, Designs and Patents Act 1988.

First published 2010
Revised and updated paperback edition published 2013
PALGRAVE MACMILLAN

Palgrave Macmillan in the UK is an imprint of Macmillan Publishers Limited, registered in England, company number 785998, of Houndmills, Basingstoke, Hampshire RG21 6XS.

Palgrave Macmillan in the US is a division of St Martin's Press LLC, 175 Fifth Avenue, New York, NY 10010.

Palgrave Macmillan is the global academic imprint of the above companies and has companies and representatives throughout the world.

Palgrave® and Macmillan® are registered trademarks in the United States, the United Kingdom, Europe and other countries.

ISBN 978–0–230–57595–0 hardback
ISBN 978–1–137–34755–8 paperback

This book is printed on paper suitable for recycling and made from fully managed and sustained forest sources. Logging, pulping and manufacturing processes are expected to conform to the environmental regulations of the country of origin.

A catalogue record for this book is available from the British Library.

Library of Congress Cataloging-in-Publication Data
Dutt, Amitava Krishna
Economics and ethics : an introduction / Amitava Dutt, Charles K. Wilber.
p. cm.
ISBN 978–0–230–57595–0 (hardback)
1. Economics—Moral and ethical aspects. I. Wilber, Charles K.
II. Title.
HB72.W54 2010
174—dc22 2010007407

*For Harolyn and Mary Ellen*

# Contents

# List of Figures and Tables

## Figures



## Tables

# Preface

This book focuses on the relation between ethics and economics, both in economic analysis and economic policy. To do so, it makes three simple points. First, economics necessarily involves ethics, and economists cannot engage in economic analysis or giving advice on economic policy without making value judgments. Second, individuals have ethical values that shape their behavior and affect what happens in the economy as a result of their interactions. Third, ethical values are involved in evaluating how an economy is doing and in choosing and appraising economic policies. The rest of this book develops these three points.

Our aim in writing this book is to encourage people who are interested in economic issues – including students and professional economists who are not familiar with ethics – to take ethics more seriously in thinking about the economy. We believe that many people interested in economics, including professional economists, pay insufficient attention to ethical and moral issues, and economics is the worse for that.

Ours is not the first book that deals with the relation between ethics and economics. There are a few excellent treatments of the subject, including a short book by Sen (1987) and the longer work by Hausman and McPherson (1996, 2006). While we have drawn heavily on these and other works, we have tried to make this book different from them in several ways. First, we have tried to provide a fairly comprehensive coverage of the main issues that relate economics and ethics, rather than focus on some key foundational ideas. Second, we have tried to avoid surveying the field with all its complexity and detail, focusing instead on what we believe are some of the central issues relating economics and ethics. Third, we have tried to relate ethical issues closely to economic analysis more narrowly defined – such as microeconomic and macroeconomic analysis and income distribution theory. Our purpose in these decisions is to make the material more accessible to a wider audience than professional economists and philosophers.

The gestation period for this book has been long. The final result has been much enriched by discussion and debate with, and comments from, many colleagues and students. We particularly wish to thank

David Betson, George DeMartino, Georges Enderle, Ronald Hoksbergen, Ken Jameson, Alasdair MacIntyre, Kali Rath, Jaime Ros, Jim Sterba, Jonathan Wight, and many undergraduate students in the economics and ethics course offered at Notre Dame.

We are also grateful to the production staff at Palgrave-Macmillan for their speedy and efficient work in seeing the book to its completion. This paperback edition is a revised version of the first edition with some corrections and a new chapter on the ethics of the global financial crisis. We thank our readers of the first edition and several reviewers for prompting these changes.

Finally, we would like to thank our families for their understanding, good humor and support, and for occasional discussions on the subject of this book and suggestions on the manuscript.

# Part I

# Introduction and Background

# 1
# Introduction

The purpose of this book is to provide a short introduction to the relationship between ethics and economics. It is written by two economists and is meant mainly for readers who are interested in economic issues. In addition it may be of use to those who are interested in ethics, but who have no more than an elementary knowledge of economics.

It is widely believed by economists and noneconomists alike that knowing about and "doing" economics does not involve ethical and moral issues. Economics is sometimes called a science – indeed, the Nobel Prize in Economics is called the Nobel Prize in Economic Sciences[1] – which is interpreted as being based purely on empirical observation and logical analysis for understanding the truth about how the economy works (just like natural scientists do with the natural world),[2] and is sometimes thought of as a form of engineering – engineers learn about how to build bridges and have them built, while economists learn about how to intervene in the economy and then help design policies to actually intervene in it.

It is, of course, well understood that economic activity and policies may have some ethical consequences. For instance, the economy can experience high and growing levels of inequality of income between people, or economic policies may involve giving away money to those who do not work for it, both of which may be considered ethically unacceptable. However, it is believed that economists can only investigate whether inequality is high and growing and, if it is, explain why, and that they can analyze what giving money away to people will actually do, and politicians, other government officials, ethicists, and people in general are the ones who will make ethical judgments about what is going on and what policies should be pursued. This is similar to the argument that scientists can do nuclear physics without deciding whether their country should develop nuclear weapons and nuclear energy, and engineers can build underground railroads without deciding whether a particular city should have it in the first place.

However, it is increasingly being recognized that ethics and economics cannot be kept separate and many economists and philosophers have begun examining their interaction. Before we examine the relation between ethics and economics, however, we need to say a few words about what we mean by ethics and by economics. We do this, in turn, in Sections 1.1 and 1.2. Section 1.3 discusses neoclassical economics, the dominant approach to economics. Section 1.4 then provides a brief introduction to the relationship between economics and ethics. The final section presents a brief outline of the book by stating what is covered in each of the following chapters.

## 1.1 Ethics

Ethics refers to the study of what is morally good and bad, what is right and wrong. It is concerned with questions like the meaning of the good life, what are good and bad actions, who is a morally good person, and how society ought to be structured. Sometimes three concepts central to the subject matter of ethics are distinguished: good (which refers to the ideal, or the thing that is desired); right (what is not wrong); and ought (which refers to obligation, duty, or responsibility, both of the individual and of the society).

Ethics and moral philosophy are often considered to be synonymous in the study of philosophy.[3] For our purposes, however, we may take moral philosophy to be a subset of ethics, where ethics also refers to religious ethics. Thus, moral philosophy or ethical philosophy can be thought of as the study of ethics using reason and arguments, whereas, at least in the Western tradition, religious ethics refers to what is considered good in terms of religious faith, that is, due to divine revelation. It is not necessary to have religious faith to study ethics. In this book we will discuss primarily moral philosophy and not be explicitly concerned with religious ethics as such. We will therefore sometimes use the terms ethics and moral philosophy interchangeably. However, since people's ethical views are frequently shaped by their religious ethics (in fact more so than moral philosophy for most people), in our discussion of how ethics shapes behavior we will examine the role of both philosophic and religious ethics.

It is often believed that ethics and morality are matters of opinion, that arguments about ethics cannot be resolved, and that these issues are relative and subjective, rather than absolute and objective. Thus, examining ethical questions may be useless. It may even be harmful, because it may lead to some people intolerantly imposing their ethical views on others. There may be some truth to these charges. Ethical questions may be relative to what the facts are: for instance, it may be considered ethical to lie to someone if telling them the truth would lead the person to locate his victim and kill her. Well-reasoned debates about ethical issues may lead good and ethical people to disagree with each other. Sometimes the "morality police" can breed intolerance and oppression. But all of this does not make a valid case for rejecting the study of ethics. It does not mean that whatever a person or society believes is right. The issue is not just *what* a person believes but, more importantly, *why* the person believes it. One can formulate arguments, examine premises on which people can agree on, and try to use logical reasoning to come to some conclusions about disputed issues. It even seems to be the case that there is more agreement regarding ethics than there is disagreement, even among people from different backgrounds and parts of the world. There seems to be general agreement that to kill and to torture is bad (especially for entertainment), that an ideal of good behavior is to be kind and charitable to others (especially those who are more disadvantaged than us) even to the point of being selfless, that it is not good to be selfish,[4] and that it is wrong to be intolerant of people with different views.

## 1.2 Economics

A very brief overview of what economics is concerned with and what issues it examines is useful to provide some background for the rest of the analysis of this book. Providing this overview can also make most of this book accessible to readers who have not even read a book on introductory economics. In what follows we first define economics; then discuss its major branches, microeconomics and macroeconomics; and then describe some of its major subfields. Most economists and introductory texts follow what is called the neoclassical approach, and we will make some comments about this approach to economics and its main alternatives in the next section. These sections are somewhat long to provide a reasonably self-contained outline of economics.

It is useful to define economics as studying some activities or some system. The activities definition is used by the British economist Alfred Marshall (1842–1924), who popularized the use of supply and demand curves for studying markets and was a major figure in the professionalization of economics (as a separate scholarly discipline). He defined economics as "a study of mankind in the ordinary business of life" (Marshall, 1920, Part I, Chap. 1, §4). Marshall did not specify what he meant by the ordinary business of life, but we can presume that this business refers to activities such as consuming, producing, working, buying and selling, saving, investing (that is, installing new capital goods for future production), and holding assets such as financial assets.[5] The system definition is used by the American economist and Nobel laureate Paul Samuelson (1915–2009) in his extremely popular introductory economics text (Samuelson, 1948) which has gone into 18 editions at the time of this writing. He defines the economic system as one which answers the following questions about the production of goods and services: what, how, and for whom.

Economics is almost universally divided into two parts, microeconomics and macroeconomics. Microeconomics examines the behavior of individual economic agents or actors (such as producers and consumers) and how they interact with each other, and studies the operation of individual markets (for instance, the market for coffee) and their interaction. Macroeconomics studies the behavior of aggregates, aggregating over both economic actors and markets. Thus, while microeconomics is concerned with the level of production of a firm, and the consumption of apples by an individual consumer, macroeconomics is concerned with the level of aggregate production of goods and services of the economy as a whole and the level of aggregate consumption of all people in an economy without necessarily examining individual actors or individual markets.

Microeconomics studies the behavior of individual consumers and firms and the interactions of these individuals. It examines how consumers choose what and how much they buy, and how their buying plans are affected by the prices they pay and their incomes. It explores how firms decide how much to produce of what goods, and how they produce them under different types of market conditions – for instance, if they are one of a very large number of firms in a market all producing an identical product (what, with some additional conditions, is called perfect competition), if they produce slightly differentiated products, if they are one of a few sellers (what is called an oligopoly), or if they are the only seller in a market (called a monopoly). It also examines how firms change their plans depending on changes in their environment, for instance, in perfectly competitive markets, how their production plans are affected by changes in the price. Interaction between buyers and sellers is used to examine how market prices of goods and services and factors of production, such as labor (that is, the wage), are determined, and how the interaction of different markets in the economy, in what is called general equilibrium analysis, determines the prices and quantities of all goods and resources. Sometimes individual interaction is examined without having markets and market prices, but simply by examining how these individuals affect each other using specified rules of interaction. In all this analysis of behavior, it is almost always assumed that individuals are self-interested maximizers of their profits or well-being (as measured by what is called their utility levels which reflect their preferences). Microeconomics also examines whether the outcome that markets and other forms of interaction may produce[6] – called the equilibrium – is desirable in some sense, usually in the sense of being efficient. Efficiency is defined as a situation in which no individual can be made better off without making someone else worse off (that is, there are no costless – in the sense of making someone worse off – ways of making anyone better off). It finds conditions under which market equilibrium is efficient, and explores how what are called market failures can prevent an equilibrium from being efficient. Market failures include such things as follows:

1. Monopolies and other departures from perfect competition. Monopoly producers may produce less than what is efficient for the economy, because they want to create an artificial scarcity and keep the price of their product high in order to make high profits.
2. Externalities, in which people and firms affect others adversely or positively without either paying or being paid. Firms may emit too much pollution which makes other firms and people worse off because the latter, rather than they, bear the costs of pollution.
3. Public goods which no private firms will want to produce because they cannot make people pay for them. Public goods are those which can be enjoyed by all at the same time (like listening to radio programs off the air) and which the producer cannot prevent people who don't pay from consuming it (for instance, national defense – a producer of this service cannot selectively protect some people from foreign invasion without protecting others who do not pay).
4. Imperfect information, in the sense that buyers and sellers do not possess all the relevant information to produce efficient outcomes. Imperfect information implies that at least some individuals in the economy do not have complete information that allows them to make appropriate decisions: for instance, if consumers do not have complete information about the properties of medicines, they may

buy those which do not work, or not buy those which actually work but which they think do not (in the latter case, both the consumers will be better off by using the medicines, and the firms would make more profits if they did).

If market failures do occur, microeconomics analyzes how markets can be made to operate more efficiently, for instance, with governments breaking up monopolies, imposing fines for pollution, supplying public goods, and by certifying whether medicines work. Microeconomics is also concerned with the determination of income distribution between people, and if the distribution is considered to be unfair, of how it can be made fairer without creating or exacerbating inefficiencies.

Macroeconomics is mainly concerned with trying to understand how the level of aggregate production in the economy is determined, why aggregate production frequently fluctuates through recessions (and sometimes depressions) and booms to result in business cycles, what determines unemployment (that is, the number of people who want to work but who are not employed), what explains the level of inflation (that is, the rate of increase of the average price level of all goods and services), and what determines the rate at which the level of production of goods and services (at constant prices) grow over time. It examines how financial markets function, for instance, what determines interest rates and stock and bond prices, and how these affect output and inflation. Macroeconomics also examines the trade balance of a country (its exports minus its imports) and its balance of payments (its overall receipts of foreign currency through, for instance, exports and foreign capital inflows due to borrowing and foreign investment less its overall spending of foreign currency through imports and foreign capital outflows) and how these affect the economy as a whole. Macroeconomics examines not only why unemployment exists, why inflation can be high, and why growth can be low, but also how government policy can be used to overcome problems, if and when they occur, through monetary policy (by controlling interest rates and the supply of money) and fiscal policy (by changing government expenditures and taxes). There are differences of opinion within macroeconomics about whether involuntary unemployment exists and what causes it, and what policies to adopt when unemployment is high. Macroeconomics is also sometimes concerned with income distributional issues, for instance, looking at the relative income of the rich and the poor (as broad groups), and examining the relation between income distribution and growth.

One can, in principle, examine these macroeconomic issues by examining the behavior of individual agents and particular markets and then putting all this together. Indeed, a few economists argue that this is the only way to understand issues such as unemployment and growth, usually with the argument that people (and not aggregates) act and make decisions based on individual reasons, and call for the abandonment of macroeconomics altogether.[7] A less extreme position insists on having microfoundations of macrobehavior, that is, basing macroeconomic behavior on the behavior of individual economic agents, usually with the use of what is called a "representative agent." In terms of the real world, can one analyze how many cars will be produced without analyzing the behavior of the firms which produce cars and the consumers who buy them? However, it is possible that one may lose sight of the forest by focusing on the trees – individuals and particular markets – and even more seriously, analyze how the economy operates inadequately by leaving out important issues that depend on how macroeconomic factors affect individual behavior. For the real world, can one analyze how many cars a car producer will produce without understanding whether unemployment is going to rise or fall since people may be unwilling to buy cars if they feel insecure about their jobs? Thus, some economists insist that there should be appropriate macrofoundations of microeconomics.

In addition to working on general aspects of microeconomics and macroeconomics, economists work in a number of subfields of economics which are concerned with the applications of these general ideas to particular aspects of the economy. We will call the study of these particular aspects applied economics.[8] There are many such subfields of economics, of which we will mention only a few as illustrative examples. Development economics is concerned with the economic problems of economically less-developed countries which have low per capita incomes, and examines the problem of how economic growth can be increased in these countries and how well-being can be improved. International economics deals with issues concerning the interaction of economies with the rest of the world and with the global economy. It examines the implications of free trade without government restrictions on it, and whether government protection is bad for the economy. It also examines what effects foreign borrowing, foreign investment, and the exchange rate (the domestic price of foreign currency) have on the economy. It also explores the implications of the interaction between rich and poor countries, and what this implies about international inequality. Environmental economics examines, for instance, how pollution can be controlled when it occurs due to externalities, how economic activity affects the environment, and how environmental degradation affects economic growth and well-being. Labor economics is concerned with wage determination, the determination of employment and unemployment, the role of labor unions, and the effects of education and minimum wages on unemployment and wages. This is just a small sample of subfields of economics, which also includes, among others, public economics (economics of government activity), economics of poverty and income distribution (the determinants of poverty, income distribution, and policies which affect them), and industrial economics (the economics of firms and industries, market structure, industry performance, and antitrust policy).

## 1.3 Neoclassical economics

Since economics – as is widely acknowledged – is dominated by the neoclassical approach (and indeed, for many it is synonymous with economics itself), and since we will have much to say about it in the rest of this book, we will briefly discuss the nature of this approach to economics. In doing so, however, we face the problem that there exists no generally accepted definition of neoclassical economics. We will discuss two specific definitions which are in relatively wide currency. One definition, which relates to method, is that it analyzes the economy by examining the behavior of individual, self-interested, optimizing agents and how they interact with each other. The second is a narrower definition related to how the economy operates which, in addition to the assumption made in the first definition, assumes that the economic agents interact with each other in smoothly functioning markets in which all resources are being fully utilized and in which there are no distortions such as imperfect competition.[9] We consider four different aspects of the approach and then return to these two definitions.

First, neoclassical economics tries to explain all behavior in terms of the optimizing agent. The optimizing agent is assumed to have preferences over possible "states of the world";[10] in the case of consumers this usually refers to alternative bundles of goods and services they can choose to consume. Given constraints such as income and prices that they face, consumers are assumed to buy bundles that are most preferred by them, and this is usually represented by assuming that bundles which consumers prefer give them higher utility, and that they, thus, maximize their utility. This assumption is often justified on the basis of the rationality of economic agents.[11] However, it is often criticized because it is pointed out that individuals are in fact not rational in this sense, and that they in fact cannot be rational in this sense. Because they do not have all the relevant information, they can obtain information only by incurring costs, and there is no way to obtain the optimal amount of information without obtaining even more information. The assumption is sometimes defended by saying that it is not necessarily connected with the rationality postulate, but is simply a way of organizing analysis about behavior on the basis of individual decision-making. Yet the assumption does involve a specific view of human behavior, that is, individuals maximize their utility with given preferences and, moreover, that they are self-interested in the sense that they are concerned about their own levels of consumption, and that they believe more is better in the sense that they are better off if they consume more of a good or service.

Second, neoclassical economics often, but not always, assumes that individual consumers and firms interact through markets and buy and sell at market prices which are the same faced by all agents. The goods and services are typically assumed to be what are called private goods which are competitive in consumption (that is, more than one individual cannot consume the same unit of output: if one person consumes a bowl of rice another person cannot consume that same bowl of rice) and excludable (that is, sellers can exclude people from consuming goods if they do not pay for them). Often it is assumed that the markets are perfectly competitive, so that there are many buyers and sellers and there is complete information, that the plans of buyers and sellers can be represented by supply and demand curves, and that prices are flexible in the sense that if there is excess demand (that is, market demand exceeds market supply) for a good or service its price increases. Some neoclassical economists believe that these assumptions are reasonable descriptions of the real world. However, not all neoclassical economists believe that markets are perfectly competitive or free of distortions (such as the existence of externalities and public goods), and many devote a great deal of time to analyzing the consequences of departures from the assumptions of perfect competition.

Third, the neoclassical approach shows that under certain assumptions – that is – under conditions of perfect competition and the absence of distortions, individual optimizing behavior leads to efficiency, or the state described earlier in which no one can be made better off in terms of the utility they obtain without making someone else worse off. In this sense, competitive free market outcomes have a desirable property. If, as some neoclassical economists believe, the economy actually has perfect markets, then the free market will actually bring about an efficient outcome, so that if efficiency is the desirable goal of policymakers, the best policy is one of laissez-faire, or of minimizing the role of the government in the economy. If, as other neoclassical economists believe, there are market imperfections, even if efficiency is the goal of policymakers, the government needs to adopt policies which bring the economy nearer to the competitive markets, by encouraging competition in imperfectly competitive markets by breaking up monopolies and regulating firms, developing markets where none exists (for whatever reason), providing public goods, and imposing taxes or providing subsidies to firms whose activities create externalities. In some cases, it is even possible that unequal income distributions and the existence of poverty can lead to market failures – for instance, poverty may make some people less productive than they otherwise would be, which implies that the economy could produce more and increase people's utility by making people less poor. In this case, even if the society does not intrinsically care about income distribution issues, it may try to improve distribution instrumentally to increase efficiency. Some neoclassical economists argue that the existence of these market failures does not necessarily make the case for government policy interventions, because private individuals may often spontaneously develop arrangements which will overcome these distortions (for example, with appropriate agreements which protect individuals against negative externalities imposed by others, if the costs of enforcing these agreements are low), and governments may not have the knowledge or the ability to improve on market outcomes.

Finally, many neoclassical economists take the view that it is desirable not only to promote efficiency, but also to promote fairness. Efficiency says nothing about whether what different people get in terms of goods, and hence, utility, is fair: some might get a lot and others very little. If it is believed that a particular competitive outcome is unfair (even if it is efficient), there is a need to change the distribution of income, and hence utilities, so that the outcome becomes fairer. However, in improving fairness, neoclassical economists worry about increasing inefficiency.

The discussion of these four aspects of neoclassical economics allows us to clarify the implications of the two definitions of neoclassical economics. The first definition, which stresses the maximization assumption, does not imply that free markets will result in efficient outcomes and therefore does not necessarily advocate government nonintervention in markets. However, to the extent that this approach values efficiency, economists who accept this approach are in favor of adopting policies which move the economy closer to the perfectly competitive distortion-free situation. The second definition implies that the economy is usually efficient and that if all that is important is efficiency, they are in favor of free market, laissez-faire policies. However, if they care about fairness issues, then government intervention may be acceptable.

Neoclassical economics, especially in the first sense, dominates economics. But there are other approaches to economics. Rather than taking the view that all economic analysis must be based on individual, self-interested, optimizing behavior, some economists conduct analysis by examining the behavior of groups (for instance, the Marxian approach focuses on the behavior of classes, such as workers and capitalists), some by focusing on institutions rather than people, some by viewing individuals as not being only self-interested, but as having a variety of motives and following societal norms even if doing so seems to be against their own interest, some by recognizing that people are not optimizers, but that because they lack perfect knowledge, and because the future is uncertain, they often follow rules of thumb (such as following the opinions of others, or those that they consider to be experts, or continuing to do what they are doing unless things go terribly wrong). Many economists take the view that the economy does not normally produce desirable outcomes, or even can be made to achieve such outcomes by appropriate government policies, and rather focus on trying to improve how society functions and what outcomes it produces, such as fairness rather than just efficiency. These ideas can be illustrated by considering a few examples of approaches other than the neoclassical one. The Marxian approach focuses on the behavior of classes of people, such as workers and capitalists, whose interests are opposed. The institutionalist approach focuses on institutions and social norms and how they affect individuals rather than on the individual as such, and take into account that people have many different, often conflicting, motives. The post-Keynesian approach focuses on how rules of thumb, which pattern the behavior of groups in an uncertain environment, typically result in unemployment and low growth and how that can be improved upon by active government policy. Behavioral economists examine how people actually behave in reality; drawing on psychology and other disciplines, and with the use of experiments and survey information, they try to understand the social outcomes resulting from such behavior, and how these outcomes can in some sense be improved upon. Feminist economists look at differences in the motives and behavior of men and women, and how the economy affects men and women differentially, rather than relying on the apparently gender-free (but actually male) individual optimizing approach.

## 1.4 Relation between economics and ethics

The relation between economics and ethics arises for at least three separate reasons.

First, when economists study the economy they necessarily make value judgments, that is, judgments which involve ethical or moral issues, whether they do so consciously or not. The distinction between scientific (or engineering) economics and ethical issues is not as clear-cut as is usually thought, and ethical issues cannot be kept separate from the study of economies. The strict separation between positive economics and normative economics, and the claim that positive economics is value-neutral, does not withstand careful scrutiny.

Second, economics studies people and groups of people, how these people and groups interact, and institutions such as markets, firms, labor unions, and even religious organizations. The people and groups have ethical values which shape their activities and their institutions, and their economic activities and the outcomes that these activities produce in turn can affect their ethical values. Economists need to understand ethics if they are to understand better how individuals, groups, and institutions behave and operate.

Third, economists often have to make policy decisions, and their work influences policy decisions. It is in fact to evaluate what is going on, and what should be done about it, that many of them study the economy. Evaluating what is happening – that is, whether it is good or bad – and devising appropriate policies for improving on what is happening obviously require ethical analysis. Given the close connection between economic analysis and policy evaluation, even those economists who do not directly make policy proposals or changes need to be aware of the ethical implications of their work.

## 1.5 Outline of the book

The rest of this book examines these three issues in more detail.

Chapter 2 focuses on the first of the relations mentioned in the previous section, that is, how economics cannot avoid making value judgments. It asks whether economics can ever be value-free by examining the popular distinction between positive and normative economics and the supposed value-neutrality of positive economics based on the fact-value dichotomy. It argues that although the distinction between positive and normative economics can serve some useful purposes, the supposed value-neutrality of positive economics, and the argument that economics as a whole can be value-neutral, cannot be sustained. It also provides a brief discussion of the value judgments implicit in the dominant approach to economics, that is, neoclassical economics.

Chapter 3 then provides a brief introduction to ethics and ethical reasoning by reviewing approaches to ethics at the individual and societal levels. At the individual level it discusses virtue, deontological, and consequentialist ethics. At the societal level it distinguishes between alternative theories of justice, such as those based on egalitarianism, utilitarianism and related approaches, and rights and desert views. The chapter cannot claim to provide anywhere near a comprehensive review of ethics, confining itself to a few issues relevant for the rest of the book.

The next three chapters examine the fact that individuals have ethical values and the implications of that fact for individual behavior, and for society as a whole.

Chapter 4 focuses on the individual decision-maker, starting from the neoclassical conception of the self-interested, optimizing economic agent; situating it within alternative approaches to ethics; and then introducing ethical considerations into individual behavior. It examines how and why individuals have ethical values, what form these ethical values take, how neoclassical economics is affected by the existence of these values and norms, and the consequences of these norms for societal outcomes.

Chapter 5 turns to how individuals interact with each other in general terms and addresses how ethical beliefs of individuals affect the outcomes of these interactions. To do so, it utilizes the commonly utilized technique of game theory to discuss the problems which arise from the so-called prisoner's dilemma, and relates these problems to ethical and institutional issues.

Chapter 6 focuses on how the major institution of neoclassical economics, the market, is related to ethical issues. It examines how ethical issues affect markets. It argues that markets cannot operate properly without the existence of individual values and social norms, a view that was taken by Adam Smith, and often forgotten, and it explores how ethical values can also prevent the smooth functioning of markets. It also examines how markets affect ethical values that individuals have.

While chapters 3 through 6 together address the second of the two aspects of the interaction between economics and ethics mentioned in the previous section, the next four chapters address primarily the third aspect, that is, how economic outcomes and policies can be evaluated.

Chapter 7 discusses the question about whether markets and other institutions are moral and in what sense. It first examines the moral standing of the market and then turns to the morality of different kinds of markets; it follows with an examination of some examples – markets for blood, body parts, and surrogate motherhood. It also discusses the morality of the government and government intervention.

Chapter 8 examines the individual utility view of evaluating economic outcomes, the main approach taken in neoclassical economic theory and many policy applications. It raises questions about the assumptions that make evaluations based on individual utility possible, that is, the exogeneity of preferences, perfect knowledge, and questions about the preferences of future generations. It also briefly discusses the method of cost-benefit analysis which is often used for evaluating economic policy initiatives.

Chapter 9 turns to the approach to evaluating economic outcomes which is usually adopted in practice, one which is based on the income or production approach. It examines this approach and compares it to other ways of evaluating outcomes, including the utility approach discussed in Chapter 8 and the rights and capabilities approaches. It discusses the problems that arise from issues such as poverty and income distribution considerations and from environmental problems.

Chapter 10 focuses on the question of income distribution and inequality. The utility and production perspectives provide the means of evaluating economies not only in terms of concepts of efficiency and average well-being, but also in terms of fairness and equality. This chapter focuses on these issues, examining the determinants of distribution, and why we should be concerned with fairness and equality, equality of what and between whom.

Chapters 3 through 10 address the relationship between economics and ethics in general terms, and consider examples from different aspects of the economy. Chapter 11 provides a brief discussion of the relationship between ethics and the issues discussed in some sub fields of economics, such as development, international, environmental, labor, and business economics (or the study of business behavior), and chapter 12 an analysis of ethical aspects of the global financial crisis of 2007–08, to address ethical considerations that arise in real-world applications of economics.

Finally, Chapter 13 summarizes and makes a few concluding comments.

# 2
# Economics Without Ethics?

## Introduction

Some economists believe economics is a value-free science, with no place for ethics. A larger number of economists believe that although it may not be possible – or even desirable – to exclude ethics from all of economics, there is a large part of economics in which value judgments play no part. There is a growing minority, however, which argues that economics cannot avoid making value judgments right from the start, and therefore, that economic theory cannot be disentangled from ethics. This chapter examines this debate and argues that economics and ethics are so closely interlinked that it is not possible to have an economics divorced from ethics (Wilber and Hoksbergen, 1986).

To understand these opposing views, it is useful to distinguish between three types of issues economists study: first, what actually happens in economies, why they happen, and what will happen in the future; second, what should happen in the economy, and how what is happening compares to this ideal; and third, if what is happening is not what should be happening, how to go from what is to what should be, or at least, closer to the ideal. The first involves description, explanation and prediction, or what is the subject of positive economics; the second is called normative economics; and the last is the subject matter of economic policy analysis.

Many economists believe that positive economics does not incorporate value judgments because it examines what happens in the real world without trying to evaluate it, while normative economics and economic policy analysis do involve value judgments. Some even argue that some issues in normative economics and economic analysis do not involve value judgments, and take the view that economists can be involved in economic policy analysis while leaving decisions involving values to government officials or to members of society as a whole. If these views are correct, there would be significant parts of economics that are independent of ethics. This chapter will argue against both these views.

The rest of this chapter proceeds as follows. Section 2.1 discusses the distinction between positive economics and normative economics and summarizes the claim that positive economics does not make value judgments, that is, it is value neutral, because it is based on facts about the economy. Section 2.2 critically analyzes the validity of the claim of the value-neutrality of positive economics by reviewing arguments made for and against it. Section 2.3 addresses whether values can be expunged from economic analysis by subjecting it to empirical testing, that is, in terms of the world "out there," making a brief excursion into the methodology of economics. Section 2.4 discusses some of the value judgments made in neoclassical economics, which – as discussed in the previous chapter – is the kind of economics on which most introductory texts in economics and mainstream economic analysis are based. Section 2.5 turns to the relation between values and normative economics and policy analysis. The chapter ends with some concluding comments.

## 2.1 The positive/normative dichotomy and the value-neutrality claim

Most introductory books in economics distinguish between two kinds of economics. One kind, called positive economics, asks questions about what is happening in the economy, why it is happening, and what may happen in the future, and the questions usually start with: "what *is*. . . ." The other refers to what ought to be, and the questions it is concerned with usually start with: "what *should*. . . ."[1] For instance, according to a recent introductory text coauthored by the American economist and Nobel Laureate, Paul Krugman, "Analysis that tries to answer questions about the way the world works, which have definite right or wrong answers, is known as positive economics. In contrast, analysis that involves saying how it *should* work is known as normative economics. To put it another way, positive economics is about description, normative economics is about prescription."[2] This dichotomy is rooted in what is called the Humean guillotine, named after the British philosopher and economist David Hume (1711–76), which separates fact ("what is") from value ("what ought to be").

It is then pointed out that positive economics can be conducted in a value-neutral, purely scientific manner, without making any value judgments or taking any ethical positions. Thus, it is claimed that scientific economic analysis can be completely separated from ethical issues. This view does not deny that ethical questions are relevant for normative analysis or for choosing among policies. For instance, the economist needs to be clear on his or her ethical stance, or know the policymakers,' before making pronouncements on such issues as: Should the minimum wage be raised or should it be abolished? Should foreign aid to poor countries be increased or reduced? But even for such questions positive economics can get us quite far in analyzing what effect an increase in the minimum wage has on employment and on poverty rates, and what effect increasing foreign aid has on economic growth and on the distribution of income in poor countries. Once these kinds of positive questions have been answered by scientific economic analysis, it is argued, we can introduce ethical considerations (such as how much importance should be given to poverty reduction as compared to economic growth) and our policymaking experience, to decide on which policies to adopt.

The value-neutrality argument is based on the claim that since we have objective access to the empirical world through our sense experience, we need not be concerned with questions about "what ought to be" when we are concerned with "what is." In economics this view was championed by John Neville Keynes and later popularized by Lionel Robbins (1932). Robbins argued that the claim that economics is a scientific discipline rests in its positive aspects and in its being neutral as between ends.

## 2.2 The debate on value neutrality

Is positive economics able to expunge ethical considerations by being concerned solely with facts "out there"? There are good reasons to doubt this.

First, there is a very wide range of empirical questions economists may consider and facts they can potentially examine. How does one choose which ones to focus on? How does one decide what the important questions are? Is it important to ask by how much the consumption of apples will fall if the price of apples increases by 10 per cent? What economic value to place on a national park? What determines the rate of growth of per capita income of a country? What is the level of income inequality between the rich and the poor in a country, and how is it changing over time? Is it important to focus on the rate of growth of the economy or the poverty rate or the distribution of income within the country? If inequality across countries is to be measured, how should one do it? It can be argued that which questions one focuses on reflect one's value judgments about what issues are important. The questions we ask will affect what facts we examine, but value judgments also need to be made in choosing and perceiving these facts. Blaug (1975, 406), who is overall supportive of the value-neutrality position, argues that "no doubt Hume's Guillotine tells us that we cannot logically deduce ought from is or is from ought. We can however, influence ought by is and vice versa: moral judgments may be altered by presentation of the facts, and facts are theory-laden so that a change of values may alter our perception of the facts." For instance, the moral judgment that economic growth is good may be altered by the presentation of facts which show that high rates of growth are accompanied by a worsening in the distribution of income, or in the level of happiness or subjective well-being people report in surveys. A change in values which places more emphasis on distributive justice between countries may change our perception of the fact concerning whether the income disparity between countries has been growing or falling.[3] Thus the strict value-fact dichotomy seems to break down in practice, and values permeate into positive economics.

Second, what we can say about the external world depends not only on that world, but also on how we, as observers, perceive it. An economic model is not something one can obtain just from facts about the real world, but is shaped by the lenses through which we look at it. The Austrian economist Joseph Schumpeter (1883–1950) wrote in his classic book on the history of economic analysis that "analytic effort is of necessity preceded by a preanalytic cognitive act that supplies the raw material for the analytic effort. In this book, this preanalytic cognitive act will be called Vision" (Schumpeter, 1954, 41). Schumpeter describes the process by which scientific propositions are produced as follows: "Factual work and 'theoretical' work, in an endless relation of give and take, naturally testing one another and setting new tasks for each other, will eventually produce *scientific* models, the provisional joint products of their interaction with the surviving elements of the original vision, to which increasingly more rigorous standards of consistency and adequacy will be applied." He continues: "Now it should be perfectly clear that there is a wide gate for ideology to enter into this process. In fact, it enters on the very ground floor, into the preanalytic acts of which we have been speaking. Analytic work begins with material provided by our vision of things, and this vision is ideological almost by definition"

(Schumpeter, 1954, 42). Although Schumpeter is not explicit about his definition of ideology, it seems from his usage of the term that he thinks of it as a collection of value judgments. Thus, depending on his or her preanalytic vision, an economist chooses which facts to focus on and how to put them together in an economic model and all of this, especially the preanalytic vision, involves making value judgments.

To summarize these two points, while economics as a science may be driven by a search for truth, it is not interested in just any truth. The relevant truth must be both "interesting" and "valuable," and in this sense economic science is a goal-directed activity. Further, the criteria for a "good" or "acceptable" scientific theory cannot be ranked in terms of their intrinsic importance, but only in relation to the degree they serve particular goals of a scientific community. Theory choice is not, therefore, based objectively on non-controversial criteria (that is, degree of verification or corroboration), but on criteria that are inevitably value-laden (that is, the extent to which each theory serves specific ends). Economists' search for "valuable truth" is directed by what they think society (and science) ought to do. The notion that facts are in some sense "out there" for all to see just doesn't stand scrutiny. It is generally recognized by philosophers of science that facts are theory laden in the sense they become facts of interest only because the theory says so.

Third, the terminology that is used in economic analysis is not free of value-judgments. The Swedish economist and Nobel Laureate Gunnar Myrdal (1898–1987), in his well-known attack on implicit values held by economists, emphasized values hidden in the terminology of economics. Terms such as "economic integration," "productivity," "equilibrium," "balance," "rationality," "optimality," "utility," "development," and "efficiency" have at least two meanings, one which is a seemingly value-neutral and precise one in economics, and another which is less precise, which is used in general parlance, and which has favorable connotations. Myrdal argued that the terminology of economics was permeated with "involved structures of metaphysical ideas, which are now firmly anchored in our tradition of thought" (Myrdal, 1954; 1984, 256–7). It is not necessarily the case that economists insert these value-laden terms to deliberately slip in their value judgments about the desirability of equilibrium or balance, of increasing productivity, and so on – although sometimes this may indeed be the case. However, it more likely that they innocently use this value-laden terminology. But having have done so, some theories may be more persuasive because of the ideological content embodied in their terms; thus, these theories may become more popular, other economists may build on them and the approach may develop over time as the preferred one. The fact may be that the popularity and dominance of this approach is not because of its empirical content, but because of its implicit or explicit value judgments.

The root of the problem – which affects the questions economists ask, the facts they select for examination, the preanalytic vision they employ in their empirical analysis, and the terms they use – is the value judgments they consciously or unconsciously (by following the leads of others) make. It may be argued, however, that this problem is not really a serious one, for two kinds of reasons.

First, it can be claimed that although value judgments are involved in examining and explaining "what is," the value judgments that are made in this stage are not the same kind of value judgments made in normative analysis. Indeed, it is argued that scientific analysis in economics involves three separate components: prescientific decisions, scientific analysis, and post-scientific application. While value judgments are made in both the first and last stage (and not in the second), Hume's guillotine may be protected, following Nagel (1961, 492–5), by distinguishing between two types of value judgments, characterizing value judgments and appraising value judgments. A *characterizing value judgment* concerns judgments about what is to be investigated, the mode of investigation, what features of the real world are to be included in the investigation, and criteria for judging the validity of findings such as levels of statistical significance, standards of data selection, and so on. An *appraising value judgment* expresses approval or disapproval either of some moral (or social) ideal or of some action (or institution) because of the commitment to such an ideal. Some value judgments are thus not really value judgments of any ethical significance, but judgments that merely allow one to carry on the scientific enterprise.[4]

To appreciate how the preanalytic vision affects economic analysis in ways that not only involve characterizing value judgments, but also appraising ones, consider the vision that underlies the simplest of macroeconomic models, that is, the income–expenditure model. This model shows how, given the consumption function which relates consumption expenditure to income, and autonomously given planned investment expenditure, output is determined by the condition that output is equal to aggregate demand (that is, the sum of consumption and planned investment). The preanalytic vision behind this simple model is often depicted with the circular flow diagram of income and expenditure. This approach distinguishes between households and firms and visualizes how money and goods and services flow between households and firms in the form of expenditures and income, factor services (such as labor), and final goods and services, and how there are leakages and injections to this circular flow in the form of saving and investment. This simple framework and the resulting income–expenditure model is recognized as being oversimplified, and the government and the rest of the world are subsequently incorporated into it, as are asset markets and other complications. Something that is typically *not* incorporated into this vision is the distinction between different types of households, that is, high-income and low-income (what can be called rich and poor) households, despite the fact that in the real world there are vast differences in the levels of income among households. These different households in many cases obtain income mostly from different sources – rich ones from profits and high wages, and poorer ones from low wages – and have different spending patterns out of their income – the poorer households typically spend a larger proportion of their income on consumption, saving very little, and the rich ones save a higher proportion. These differences have important implications for the functioning of the economy. For instance, output is affected by changes in the distribution of income between the rich and the poor. One may argue that neglecting the distinction between rich and poor households is just a simplification, like ignoring the distinction between large and small firms, for instance. But every simplification has implications, and there is no obvious best level of simplification for analyzing the issues one is interested in. By adopting the simplification that there is only one kind of household – a representative one – one is implicitly taking the view that income distribution is not an important issue in evaluating the state of the economy, unlike the level of income or output, which is. It is not explicitly being stated that income distribution is not important. But the effect on the model is the same: income distributional considerations are ignored.

This has a number of implications for the questions that macroeconomists typically raise and try to answer. First, they take the objectives of macroeconomic policy to be, typically, to reduce inflation and unemployment and increase growth. They do not explicitly consider the goals of macroeconomic policy to be to improve the distribution of income and to reduce poverty. Second, they do not take into account the fact that the distribution of income may well affect the level of output and growth, thereby impoverishing their examination of output and growth determinants. If, as noted above, higher income groups have a lower propensity to consume than lower income groups, a worsening in the distribution of income will reduce aggregate consumption demand, and thereby possibly reduce output, especially if the reduction in output also has a negative effect on investment, because firms plan to invest less when their sales are reduced. This reduction in investment may possibly reduce the rate of economic growth of the economy as well.[5]

Second, even if economic analyses and models involve preanalytic visions and value judgments, does that really matter? Can we not subject the analysis and models to empirical testing, and see if they conform to the evidence? Isn't that the way that economics as a science should, and does, progress? Many scholarly papers in economics are written along the following lines: a problem is discussed and shown to be empirically relevant and interesting; a theory is developed to analyze this problem; and the implications of the theory are tested against empirical data, usually using statistical techniques in economics, called econometrics. Some papers just develop theories and modify other theories, while other papers test these theories, finding them consistent with the evidence or not. These studies typically do not worry about their preanalytic vision, but even if they did so, that vision would be irrelevant: what matters is whether the theory is consistent with the facts "out there."

## 2.3 Falsification, scientific progress in economics and value judgments

The account just presented accords well with ideas about scientific progress as espoused by the Austrian philosopher, Karl Popper (1902–94), based on the development of falsifiable theories and subjecting them to falsification (rather than verification, as proposed by earlier logical positivists). According to Popper, scientific progress should occur with the accumulation of falsifiable theories that are not falsified.[6] Some of it also is in accordance with American economist and Nobel Prize winner Milton Friedman's (1912–2006) instrumentalism (see Friedman, 1953), which argues that what positive economics should do is not explain, but only predict, and that the realism of theories is to be empirically investigated by examining whether its implications and predictions fit the facts, and not on the realism of its assumptions (which are supposed to be unrealistic in order to abstract from the real world). In fact, Friedman is arguing not only about the unimportance of the preanalytic vision behind a theory, but also about the theory and its assumptions as well. Nothing matters apart from the theory's predictions.

Popperian ideas, while initially influential, and while they continue to influence how many practicing economists do their research and write their scholarly contributions, are not very popular among those who are scholars of epistemological issues in economics or economic methodology. These scholars tend to subscribe more to the ideas of the philosophers of science such as the American Thomas Kuhn (1922–96) and the Hungarian-born Imre Lakatos (1922–74).[7] Friedman's methodology has found even fewer takers, because he does not adequately distinguish between different types of unrealistic assumptions; for instance, those assumptions which have a negligible effect on the main implications of the theory, versus those which affect the implications in a major way, but which may either have a heuristic role (and which require modifications to make them more realistic),[8] or which may be assumptions which restrict the domain in which the implications of the model follow (see Musgrave, 1981).[9] Kuhn's objective is to describe, rather than prescribe, how changes in science occur, and he argues that scientists in fact work within a particular research paradigm. Normal science, according to Kuhn, involves preserving the status quo within a given theoretical framework and defending it against critics using a variety of defensive mechanisms. Revolutionary changes may occur when there is a paradigm crisis due to an increasing recognition of the problems from an accumulation of falsified theories. Lakatos takes the view that individual theories are not the appropriate ones for scientific appraisals, but what does and should take place is the appraisal of clusters of interconnected theories, or what he calls scientific research programs, which have a "hard core" which is irrefutable in the view of those within the research program, and a "protective belt" which consistent of hypotheses which are in fact tested, possibly to be discarded and replaced by others. Research programs can be judged to be progressive if successive versions of it generate additional empirical implications and theoretically explain previously unexplained phenomena, and if the implications are in fact corroborated; otherwise they are called degenerative. Whether one finds these approaches to how scientific work occurs useful or enlightening, they do imply that there is considerable room for ideology and value judgments to have a major role in scientific activity. For instance, followers of Kuhn's approach may take the position that a world view greatly influences the scientific paradigm out of which one works; value judgments are closely associated with the world view; theories must remain coherent with the world view; facts themselves are theory-laden; and therefore, the whole scientific venture is permeated by value judgments from the start. This world view, or *Weltanschauung*, shapes the interests of the scientist and determines the questions asked, the problems considered important, the answers deemed acceptable, the axioms of the theory, the choice of "relevant facts," the hypotheses proposed to account for such facts, the criteria used to assess the fruitfulness of competing theories, the language in which results are to be formulated, and so on.

An important reason for the dissatisfaction with Popper's falsification approach is that it is very difficult, or in fact practically impossible, to falsify a theoretical hypothesis. When a particular version of a theory appears to be falsified by empirical evidence, its adherents can use myriads of ways to change some of its assumptions to modify it, or change the way the empirical data is measured, and find suitable modifications of the theory which are not falsified by the data as measured. The crux of the idea can be described in terms of the Duhem–Quine thesis, named after the French physicist Pierre Duhem (1861–1916) and the American philosopher William Quine (1908–2000). The thesis states that it is not possible to falsify a single hypothesis of interest, because only collections of hypotheses – this hypothesis and a large number of auxiliary hypotheses – can be subjected to empirical testing. This implies that if a particular hypothesis is found to be in conflict with a particular collection of empirical data, we can only conclude that the entire collection of hypotheses, and not just the hypothesis of interest, is being falsified, that is, we cannot conclude whether the hypothesis we are interested in, or one or more of the auxiliary hypothesis, is being rejected. This problem can be illustrated using the case of monetarism, an influential thesis in macroeconomics, which seeks to explain sustained variations in the rate of price inflation in terms of sustained variations in the rate of growth of money supply (see Cross, 1982).[10] It would seem that this hypothesis can be readily tested by collecting data on the supply of money and the average price level, and examining whether, when the rate of growth of money supply increases, the rate of inflation in subsequent periods also increases. However, despite the fact that there have been a very large number of attempts to test this hypothesis without a conclusive result, the hypothesis continues to find adherents and opponents. This can be explained by the fact that, rather than just the hypothesis of interest (that inflation is explained by monetary growth), a large number of hypotheses (including many auxiliary hypotheses) are being tested jointly. These auxiliary hypothesis include: definitional hypotheses (the appropriate definitions of money supply and inflation);[11] auxiliary assumptions from the theory concerning what other factors that affect inflation by affecting the demand for money, such as real income and institutional changes that introduce new forms of making payments, and how these are measured; hypotheses about time periods and lag structures (are the data being used monthly, quarterly, annually, and how much time is being allowed for the change in money to affect inflation); statistical hypotheses which enter into the selection of the method of econometric estimation; the level of statistical significance used for the non-rejection of the joint hypothesis; the hypothesis which identifies causality with precedence in time; and the country and time period examined. If someone likes (or dislikes) the monetarist hypothesis, and an empirical test seems to reject (not reject) it, there are a myriad possible ways of changing the auxiliary hypotheses to get the result he or she wants. Of course, better empirical work does make an attempt to examine what happens when some of the auxiliary hypotheses are varied, through what is called sensitivity analysis, but it is clearly impossible to enumerate and test for all possible variations! Consequently, hypotheses are seldom disconfirmed and general theories seldom if ever falsified. So, one may ask, how do people in fact accept or reject the hypothesis, given the evidence? Although the answer is not obvious, it is very possible that what clinches it are ideology and judgments involving what people believe is the appropriate role of the government. People who believe in monetarism usually take the view that activist government policy (for instance to counter unemployment) is a bad idea, while opponents usually believe that governments should intervene in the economy actively.

Some economists, such as McCloskey (1985), argue that that economics is best understood as a rhetorical activity – as a form of argumentation or persuasion – rather than the value-free scientific endeavor that logical positivists would have us believe. The effort does allow economists and other social scientists to "make knowledge," but it is a contingent knowledge which depends greatly on factors such as the operation of the scientific community of economists, the times, the biases or ideologies of researchers, the historical development and context of the issues, and the technical capacities of the scientists. Rorty (1987) describes this as "pragmatism" and suggests that the aspiration of scientists should be to find mechanisms to bring about "unforced agreement" among themselves, rather than to reach the Truth. Examination of the main economics journals indicates that McCloskey's perspective is gaining a very slow and gradual acceptance by its utilization in professional articles.[12] McCloskey's claim that this type of conversation, with morally constrained "honest" behavior among economists (like not sneering, being open-minded, and not lying), will eventually lead economists closer to truth (not the Truth) in the sense of contingent knowledge, may be wishful thinking (see Mäki, 1995), but more self-awareness about value judgments is likely to make discussion and debate in economics more honest.

## 2.4 Values and neoclassical economics

How values permeate positive economics can be better appreciated by considering the case of neoclassical economics, which – as mentioned in the previous chapter – is the dominant approach in economics, and one which underpins almost all introductory texts in economics.[13] In examining value judgments in neoclassical economics, we must be sensitive to the fact – also noted earlier – that all neoclassical economists do not make the same assumptions about the economy and its inhabitants, and that at least two versions of neoclassical economics need to be distinguished, one that examines the behavior of optimizing agents, and the other that makes additional assumptions which produce equilibrium outcomes which are efficient.

First, consider the values implicit in the neoclassical conception of individuals. As noted in the previous chapter, individuals in neoclassical theory are rational in the sense that they optimize subject to the constraints that they face (as specified in the model), they are self-interested, for instance, in the sense that the utility consumers obtain depends on what *they* consume, and that their utility increases with what they consume, that is, more is better. This means that individuals do not follow rules of thumb, they are not creatures of habit, do not care about anyone but themselves, and always prefer to consume more to less. Some neoclassical economists will disagree with this account of their characterization of the individual. They may argue that individual optimizing behavior does not preclude taking habit formation, having a person's utility depend on what others consume or on other people's utility levels, and preferring more leisure to less (and that leisure time can be spent with friends and family); and point to numerous attempts to do just these things within an optimizing framework. They may also argue that the optimizing assumption has nothing to do with "rationality" in some general sense but, since the model-builder is free to use any reasonable kind of objective and constraints for their agents, the assumption is simply a way of organizing thinking.[14] While the validity of some of these arguments can be granted, it is still the case that the vast majority of neoclassical models do in fact adopt the assumption of rational self-interested agents and their makers and users – perhaps unconsciously – take these assumptions to represent human nature. Three pieces of circumstantial evidence can be produced in favor of this claim. One, as we shall argue in our next point, the level of utility attained by these optimizing and self-interested agents is taken to be the basis of evaluating the goodness of social outcomes. Two, self-interested optimization is typically a necessary assumption – in addition to others that relate to the economy as a whole – that makes these social outcomes optimal: unless firms maximize profits, how will they produce efficiently; unless individuals work where wages are higher, how will they attain allocative efficiency? Three, there is some evidence to suggest that when students take basic economics courses they become more like the self-interested optimizing agent.[15]

Second, consider the values implicit in the conception of the social good. As noted earlier, many economists take the view that value judgments must be kept out of economics, which means that economists should be concerned about efficiency and not issues about fairness. It is recognized, however that concern with efficiency and the way efficiency is defined are the result of a number of value judgments. First, concern with efficiency implies that it is accepted that efficiency is good. Second, that efficiency is important and fairness can be ignored is a value judgment. Third, we are concerned with efficiency, and not with the kind of society we live in, in terms of what kinds of rights we have, or what kind of people there are in society. Fourth, the specific way that efficiency is defined also involves value judgments. As noted earlier, neoclassical economists typically define an efficient state in which no person can be made better off without making someone else worse off, as measured by their own utility functions. Thus, not only is a particular conception of human beings being assumed (as discussed in the previous point), but it is also considered to be good for society that efficiency is defined in terms of that conception. Thus, for instance, it is accepted that more is better because individuals are assumed to have that view.[16] It should be noted that these value judgments, embedded in the concept of efficiency, are not affected by whether one believes that the economy actually is efficient or not. If market failures prevent the economy from being efficient, efficiency is still the ideal one should strive for.

Third, consider the assumptions made about markets and about interactions between economic agents. As mentioned earlier, many (though certainly not all) neoclassical economists make a number of value judgments: (1) about how individuals interact with each other, that is, through bilateral – usually market – transactions and without externalities which affect other people; (2) about whether or not markets are perfectly competitive; (3) the nature and amount of information – including that about the future – available to economic actors;

(4) the kinds of goods and services bought and sold, that is, whether they are strictly private goods in the sense that they are both competitive and excludable in the senses mentioned in the last chapter; and so on. The point is that *all* of these assumptions, as well as a few others, are required to produce the result that actual economic outcomes are efficient, and that starting from any position the economy will tend to an equilibrium that is economically meaningful, unique, and stable.[17] If some assumptions are not satisfied, it is not at all clear that using policies to take care of only a few of the resulting market failures will make the economy more efficient.[18] What are we to make of the value judgments made by neoclassical economists who argue that free-market economies satisfy all of these assumptions? Can it be said that they are in fact making the value judgment that people should be left to do what they want with no intervention by the government in the market?[19]

We may conclude this discussion of the case of neoclassical economics with three comments. First, as noted earlier, assumptions such as those that assert that individuals are in fact optimizers, that people care only about themselves, and that markets are in fact (close to) being perfect in the sense that is required for market outcomes to be efficient cannot be empirically validated because of the Duhem–Quine problem which, as mentioned earlier, states that it is generally not possible to even in principle "test" hypotheses in isolation. Second, it is not being claimed here that all neoclassical economists have a conscious hidden agenda and are a part of a grand conspiracy to produce a false view of the economy which suits their own vested interests. Many economists may make these value judgments without being conscious that they are, simply because that is how they have been taught, that is what helps them to do well as professional economists, and that is what they find enjoyable and stimulating. Third, the value judgments that are made – consciously or unconsciously – often have clear implications for policies and these policies affect different people in different ways. Thus it is easy for economists to be seen as "hired guns" for one group or another without them necessarily being aware that they are actually in that position.

## 2.5 Normative economics and economic policy analysis

If values permeate positive economics, they *a fortiori* permeate normative and economic policy analyses that are based on this positive analysis. For instance, suppose that our positive theory says that the imposition of a minimum wage reduces employment, and our values tell us that unemployment is a bad thing, our policy prescription will be to remove the minimum wage. If, instead, our positive theory says that the imposition of a minimum wage increases the wage without resulting in unemployment, and our values tell us that unemployment is a bad thing and that changes in income distribution favoring wage-earners is a good thing, then our policy prescription will be to maintain the minimum wage and even to increase it. Values enter for both the positive and normative levels of analysis as well as for policy analysis.

While it is usually conceded by most economists that value judgments do enter both normative economics and policy analysis, it is sometimes claimed that in some cases these analyses can also be value-free. For instance, it has been argued by Archibald (1959) that welfare economics, which typically involves normative economics, does not depend on a foundation of value judgments. However, he confines the meaning of the term welfare economics to analysis in the Pareto sense (in which one person is better off and no one is worse off) which avoids comparing the utility levels of different people. Regarding policy issues, the introductory text referred to above says: "Suppose that policy A makes everyone better off than policy B – or at least makes some people better off without making other people worse off. Then clearly A is more efficient than B. This is not a value judgment: we are talking about how best to achieve a goal, not about the goal itself."[20]

These arguments are problematic for three reasons. First, it is rare for changes in the economy and for policies to make no one worse off – most policy changes hurt some people by their own reckoning. Thus, confining attention to cases in which no one is worse off severely limits the scope of normative and policy analysis. Second, even if changes make no one worse off and at least someone better off, we have seen that the notion that this implies an improvement for society (as is explicitly, or at least implicitly, assumed with the use of the word "efficiency") itself involves a series of value judgments. These value judgments include those which evaluate what is good by outcomes, they evaluate outcomes in terms of what individuals alone think are good outcomes, and that – in most applications – individuals think that more is better. Third, if it is assumed that individuals are better off if they receive more goods and services, it abstracts from potential psychological costs to those who see others gain while they stand still. Neoclassical economists tend to dismiss this argument because "envy" is thought of as an unacceptable value. Here again values slip into economic theory.

For policy analysis there is an additional way in which economists can be argued to be value-neutral: by presenting policymakers and the general public alternative policies among which they may choose based on *their* value judgments, without expressing their own values. This argument, however, is also problematic, for a number of reasons. First, as argued several times earlier, even the examination of the effects of different types of changes on the economy requires a framework of analysis, which requires specific judgments about what is important in the economy, which involve values. Second, economists have to necessarily be selective about the choices that they provide to the policymakers and the public. Sometimes there may be many possible options, and since it is impossible to completely and unambiguously specify the objectives of the policymakers and the public, economists will have to narrow down the choices between these options by using their own judgments. Third, even when there are only a few options which involve tradeoffs, the way economists frame these tradeoffs involves value judgments. If the tradeoff is between economic growth and greater equity, or between inflation and unemployment, economists are using their value judgments which result in analyses that suggest that there are, in fact, such tradeoffs, and the way the analysis is done may even make it appear that it is preferable to emphasize one objective over the other. Fourth, sometimes theoretical analysis is inconclusive regarding their implications for the effects of policy changes, and empirical information is needed. However, the empirical studies are also often inconclusive, some suggesting effects going one way and others some other way, as our earlier discussion of falsification suggests. Economists giving policy advice will have to evaluate these studies to decide which ones are more plausible, and here again, value judgments enter. For instance: Would increased handgun controls reduce crime? Will fiscal stimulus reduce unemployment? Will a tax cut promote growth? Does violence on television increase violence in the real world? It seems that empirical information on these issues is not conclusive enough to make economists decide, and they may have to fall back on their values about the appropriate role of the government, individual rights, gun control, and crime. Thus it seems that we must agree with Machlup (1969, 114–29) when he argues that it is impossible for economists to avoid making value judgments when they give policy advice.

## 2.6 Conclusion

We have seen in this chapter that the sharp distinction sometimes drawn between positive and normative economics and the claim that positive economics can be conducted without value judgments or ethical underpinnings are untenable. Economists, even when analyzing how economies work, that is, doing what is called positive economics, cannot make their analysis value neutral. In selecting what questions to ask and what facts to focus on, in developing their theoretical models, and in appraising and applying their models they must consciously or unconsciously use value judgments.

This conclusion implies that it is impossible to divorce ethics from any part of economics. Economists have value judgments which affect how they understand and explain what happens in actual economies. Of course, when economists discuss what ought to happen, that is, when they do normative economics, and when they suggest policies to change the economy, there is general agreement that value judgments have to be made. Thus, no one would argue that ethical issues are unimportant for *all* of economics. What our discussion implies that it is not possible to divorce even a part of economics, what is called positive economics, from ethics.

To use the language of Kuhn and Lakatos, the paradigm or research program of *any* scientific community is circumscribed by boundaries laid out in a world view which, while not perhaps individually subjective, is nevertheless empirically untestable, or metaphysical as Boland (1981, 1982) would say. How then do value judgments about the good, the just and the right, enter into what is often thought of as purely scientific analysis? Such value judgments are themselves entailed by the same world view which gives rise to theoretical and factual analysis. "What is" and "what ought to be" are thus inextricably commingled in the data, the facts, the theories, the descriptions, the explanations, the prescriptions, and so on. All are permeated by the a priori world view. Making explicit the values embodied in that world view will help keep economics more honest and useful.

However, our analysis does not imply that the positive/normative distinction should be discarded. Although ethical considerations enter both positive and normative economics, they enter them in different ways and this may make it useful to distinguish between them.[21] Some questions are purely evaluative ones which cannot even in principle be decided by appealing to what the real world looks like, and others are primarily about the real world and can in principle be evaluated using empirical information. The positive–normative distinction can be useful because it keeps these questions separate, and because it can make debates about some issues less acrimonious by making it less likely that the debate will focus on raising doubts about the moral character of its participants. Moreover, it can issue a warning to the general public about the relevance of the credentials economists – say those who are experts at mathematical modeling or statistical analysis – have in deciding what is good for society.

Our conclusion that value judgments cannot be separated from economics also does not imply that we may as well stop having reasoned discussions concerning economics and economic policy, and that anything goes. It means that ethical considerations will have to enter the equation in deciding on what should be proper policies. Ethical issues also need not be decided on purely personal beliefs or preferences, but can, at least to some degree, be subject to reasoned argument and discussion. In doing so, it is preferable to acknowledge that ethical judgments enter into all levels of economic analysis, and to try to further our understanding of ethical perspectives and why they matter with careful reasoning (even if they cannot be completely resolved by such a process).

# 3
# Approaches to Ethics and Justice

## Introduction

If, as we have argued in the previous chapter, value-free economics is impossible, what ethical values should inform the discipline? If people do not behave simply as self-interested optimizers, what moral theories might guide their actions? What moral theory should be used to answer public policy questions? Finally, if satisfaction of individual preferences is not accepted as the overriding goal of the economic system, what ethical benchmarks or objectives should take its place? None of these issues can be understood, much less resolved, without some sort of ethical theory as a guide.

The aim of this chapter is to provide a very brief introduction to ethics. There are arguments against attempting to provide an introduction to ethics in the abstract, and much to be said – in a book such as this – about discussing ethics in the context of describing economic problems and issues. Ethical issues may seem dry and irrelevant, and the discussion may appear too pedantic. However, economists and those who study the subject usually do not have a comprehensive perspective on the subject of ethics, and we are attempting such an introduction for them – as well as for us – to explore some of the main relevant issues of the subject. Our discussion will focus on alternative approaches; for an issues-oriented discussion see Blackburn (1981), and for a historical view see MacIntyre (1967).

To place our general discussion in context, however, we may start with two examples about concrete issues. Our first example is about international capital flows, that is, international borrowing and lending. Huge flows of money cross international borders, some in the form of foreign direct investment (mostly to set up, or to obtain, a controlling interest in, firms abroad), but a great deal is in the form of loans to foreign banks and firms, and the purchase of bonds and stocks abroad. Is the free flow of international capital a good thing? Or should it be regulated by governments or international agencies? The answer to this question depends in large part on the effects of such flows on the world economy. How does it affect the rate and stability of economic growth in different countries and the world as a whole? Does it lead to financial and economic crises due to rapidly changing inflows and outflows of foreign capital? Does it improve income distribution between countries and within countries? How does it affect unemployment? How does it affect the income of the lowest income groups in these countries, especially in the less-developed ones? Even after we examine these effects, to evaluate whether capital flows should be free we need to assess the relative moral importance of these effects, and compare them against other ways in which countries, especially less-developed ones, can have access to foreign capital. Apart from these effects, should governments interfere with the rights of lenders to lend their money around the world to reap higher returns and the rights of borrowers to borrow internationally cheaply? If some restrictions and regulations should be imposed, which are ethically better? Similar questions arise about the regulation of domestic financial markets as well. These questions are debated by economists and policymakers, especially in the context of the global financial and economic crisis which spread around the world in 2008. We will treat this in some depth in chapter 12.

Our second example is about business ethics – that is the ethics of a business firm, rather than about the ethics of evaluating public policy – and concerns a recent regulatory case in the United States. It was discovered that a particular model of automobile was susceptible to catching on fire in an accident, leading to unnecessary deaths and injuries. The costs of recalling all the vehicles involved and fixing each one would have been high. Finally, the producers of the car agreed to a settlement with government regulators in which they would not be forced to fix the defect, but promised to undertake other safety measures that would save as many lives, but at lower cost.

What moral issues are at stake here? If the company knew of the problem before it sold the cars, did it act improperly in selling them? Once the problem became apparent, did the firm have a duty to fix the defect at any reasonable expense? Did the firm relieve itself of any such responsibility when it agreed to alternative actions that would save as many lives?

Keeping these examples in mind we enter into our discussion of ethics. Since a short chapter such as this can do no more than examine a few issues, we confine our attention to some approaches to Western ethics that are directly relevant for the relationship between ethics and economics. We start in Section 3.1 with a brief discussion of alternative approaches to ethics at the level of the individual, that is, approaches to individual morality. Then we turn to a slightly more detailed discussion of ethical issues relevant for society as a whole (which are sometimes referred to as theories of justice), relating them to the alternative approaches to individual ethics and discussing some additional considerations not emphasized in these approaches. After a general discussion of theories of justice in Section 3.2 we will examine, in turn, theories emphasizing: (1) equality; (2) utility (including utilitarianism and the social welfare approach); (3) rights, liberty, and desert; (4) contracts between individuals; and (5) communities, in Sections 3.3 through 3.7. In Section 3.8 we will discuss another approach to ethics, that is, feminist ethics. Section 3.9 will present some concluding comments.

## 3.1 Individual ethics

Ethical theories are sometimes classified into three basic types: virtue, deontological, and consequentialist theories. This classification may be misleading because of the obvious relations that exist between them (some of which will be discussed below). We believe that, at least for the discussion of ethics at the individual level, it is instructive. These theories can be understood by considering an act performed by an individual, that involves (1) a *person* or agent who performs (2) some *action* that (3) has some particular *consequences*.[1] For instance, if Alex tells a lie to Barbara that causes her to fire Carlos, who is in fact a reliable worker, we can think of Alex as the agent, telling a lie is the action and Carlos losing his job is the consequence. The three kinds of ethical theories differ according to which of the three aspects of an event they consider most basic for making judgments. Virtue theories take judgments about persons or agents as the most basic; deontological theories do the same about actions; and consequential theories do the same for consequences. In our example, Alex does not have the virtue of truthfulness, he violates the prohibition against lying, and this leads to the bad consequence of a person getting fired unfairly.

Virtue theories typically try to develop and defend: first, some conception of the ideal person; second, some list of virtues necessary for being a person of that type; and third, some view of how a person can come to possess such virtues. Almost all ancient Greek philosophers, including

Plato (c. 428–348 BC) and Aristotle (384–322 BC, a), developed theories of this type, focusing on a short list of virtues. For Plato (360 BC), justice is the essential virtue, and justice comes from the harmonious functioning of three other virtues: moderation, courage, and wisdom. For Aristotle (350 BC), the good is what we seek. He called the ultimate good, which is sought for its own sake, *eudaimonia*. It is sometimes translated as 'happiness,' but is more accurately described as the lasting good state of the soul, perhaps better defined as human flourishing. Although Aristotle did recognize that this was affected adversely by extreme suffering, it is not a transient subjective feeling, but is chosen by reason, and involves the golden mean between extremes, that is, courage (rather than cowardice and recklessness) and moderation (rather than being too sensitive or insensitive to pleasure and pain). Subsequently, following the rise of Christianity, the Greek virtues of justice, moderation (or temperance or restraint), courage (or fortitude), and wisdom came to be called the cardinal virtues, and were joined by the so-called Christian virtues – faith, hope, and charity (or love) – to comprise the seven virtues. These, with the seven deadly vices, dominated medieval ethical thinking. Regarding how virtue can be acquired, in Plato's view, it came from acquiring knowledge which, in turn came in four successive steps: accepting tradition and authority; from personal experience and using one's senses; through logical reasoning; and finally, through wisdom, that is, understanding the essential natures of things and concepts. For Aristotle, since virtue is chosen by reason, it comes from contemplation. For many later Christian philosophers it came from the devotion to God. Modern adherents of virtue ethics include the Scottish-born American philosopher Alasdair MacIntyre (b. 1929), who attempts to develop a unified approach to virtue ethics drawing on seemingly contradictory lists of virtues proposed in various approaches by defining virtue as "an acquired human quality the possession and exercise of which tends to enable us to achieve those goods which are internal to practices and the lack of which effectively prevents us from achieving any such goods" (1984, 191).[2] Recent work on the capabilities approach to the quality of life by the Indian economist, philosopher, and economics Nobel laureate Amartya Sen (b. 1933) and the American philosopher Martha Nussbaum (b. 1947) follows the Aristotelian approach to human flourishing in an objective sense by focusing on substantive freedoms such as the ability to live in good health to old age, be educated, engage in economic transactions, and participate in political activities.

Deontological theories regard the fundamental ethical task of a person as one of doing the right thing or of avoiding doing the wrong thing. Sometimes the rules regarding acts may be absolute, such as "never tell a lie," and sometimes they refer to particular circumstances, for instance, "never hit a person except in self defense." The main tasks of deontological theory are to develop and defend: first, a set of moral rules; and second, some method of deciding what is to be done when these rules come into conflict. Deontological theories have early roots in both Eastern and Western traditions. In the classic text, the *Bhagavadgita* or *Gita* for short, Krishna – meant to be God in human form – instructs Arjuna to do his duty (based on just cause) irrespective of its consequences, an idea which is of great importance in Hindu theology. The Decalogue (or the Ten Commandments) provides a set of basic rules, in a religious context as commandments of God, or what is called the divine command theory. The most profound and persuasive attempt to defend this view on self-consciously rational grounds is due to the German philosopher, Immanuel Kant (1724–1804), who tried to find the absolute good, what he calls "good will," that is, something which is an unqualified good in itself, solely based on the concept of "pure reason." His celebrated moral law is given by what he calls the 'categorical imperative': "There is only one categorical imperative and it is this: act only according to that maxim whereby you can at the same time will that it should become a universal law." Kant argues that this is good not for what it affects or accomplishes, nor due to feelings or inclinations, but solely due to respect for the moral law or duty, which is under the control of our will. While the categorical imperative statement is abstract, since it does not tell us what to do in a concrete sense, a second formulation, which he calls the 'practical imperative,' is more specific: "Act in such a way that you treat humanity, whether in your own person or in the person of another, always at the same time as an end, and never simply as a means."[3] Contemporary philosophers who follow the deontological approach include Frances Kamm, Thomas Nagel, and Thomas Scanlon, all of whom have built on Kant's approach. Kamm (1996), for instance, has proposed the Principle of Permissible Harm, which states that one may harm people in order to save more people if and only if the harm is an effect or an aspect of the greater good itself, to qualify the principle of doing no harm.[4]

Consequentialist ethical theories hold judgments about the consequences of actions as the most basic. Their main goal is to specify and justify a thing (or a list of things) as good in themselves and to provide a method for measuring and comparing quantities of these things in order to take actions which will do the most good. For example, if pleasure is the only thing that is valuable in itself, one should act to maximize the amount of pleasure. The distinction between things which are good in themselves – or are *intrinsically* good – and things that are good only because they have a role in bringing about intrinsically good things – or are *instrumentally* good – is of special importance. For instance, if consuming goods gives a person pleasure, and only pleasure is good in itself, pleasure is intrinsically good and consumption is instrumentally good. Consequentialism is a key feature of British utilitarian philosophy which, drawing on the earlier British empiricist tradition, claimed that the only intrinsically good thing is human happiness – obtained by increasing pleasure and reducing pain, and subscribed to the moral principle of acting in a way that promotes "the greatest happiness for the greatest number." We will return to utilitarianism as a theory of justice in Section 3.4, below.

We conclude our discussion of these three ethical theories by noting that the idea of a good person, a good act, and good consequences, are not necessarily independent of each other. For instance, one can say that good people are those who do good acts, and good acts are those that have good consequences. The difference between the three approaches can be seen in terms of some examples. An ethical rule may require one not to act in ways that deliberately deceive others, say by telling lies. However, a good person may lie to a person out of compassion. For instance, one might lie and say that a person is a good cook even though one knows that he or she is a terrible cook. Also, a person may lie to prevent a bad consequence. For instance, a person may lie to a serial killer by saying that the intended victim has gone in one direction knowing that he or she has gone in another, to prevent a bad consequence, that is, a death of a person, from occurring. What distinguishes these different perspectives is the point at which the inviolable test of what is good or bad is applied – at the level of the person (for instance, a good person is a compassionate person), at the level of the action (for instance, it is bad to knowingly tell a lie), or at the level of consequences (the death of an innocent person is bad). Despite the analytical difference between them, it is not necessarily the case that the three theories are mutually exclusive. In practice, some of the world's greatest moral heroes like Jesus and Gandhi seem to have combined both virtue and deontological theories in their lives. In theory, in an uncertain world in which the precise consequences of actions are not known, where it is not possible to precisely describe the characteristics of a virtuous person, where the conditions in which actions are considered good or bad are unclear, and where people's characters are influenced by their actions, it would be reasonable not to choose one of the three points – the person, the act, and the consequences – as the basic level at which judgments have to be made. Choosing among them to the exclusion of others, in fact, can lead to various problems. The virtue approach seems to be incomplete as a guide for action, since it is unclear how it can handle cases of moral conflict, such as between being honest and being kind, or in general how one can choose between actions (if one cannot do both) when both seem virtuous – like spending a limited sum of money to help one group versus another group of equally disadvantaged people. The consequentialist approach has the problem that one can justify any kind of action, however heinous it seems to us, with the claim that the end justifies the means. Adhering to a fixed set of rules of action can also be problematic if it leads to the possibility of disastrous outcomes. For reasons such as these many ethicists do not always exclusively follow only one of the three approaches.

## 3.2 Theories of justice

Having briefly discussed ethics at the individual level we now turn to a discussion of ethics for society as a whole. It is meaningful and relevant to examine separately both what is intrinsically good at the individual level – for instance, who is a good person, or what are good actions of individuals – and what is intrinsically good at the social level – that is, what is a good society. Moreover, ethics at the individual level and at the societal level are related in various ways. First, it may be instructive to examine analogies between individual and societal ethics, since such an examination can increase our understanding of both. In the *Republic,* Plato compared the virtuous individual to the virtuous society to understand what it means for individuals to have virtue, but he was also concerned intrinsically with virtuous states or societies. Second, individuals collectively comprise societies, and societies affect individuals and their actions so that goodness at the individual level and at the social level may be instrumental for each other. The consequences of individual actions will depend on what others in society do, social rules and norms can limit or otherwise affect what individuals can do, and the nature of society can have an influence on the kinds of people who live within it. Moreover, individual ethics is likely to affect societal ethics both in the sense of what kinds of ethical considerations will actually be adopted in social arrangements and how society as a whole evaluates the goodness of collective actions and their consequences.

Nevertheless, there are differences between ethics at the individual level and at the societal level, since societal ethics refer not only to the ethics of individuals comprising it, but also ethics regarding the rules and regulations that affect all individuals and govern how individuals interact with each other, how individuals affect each other, and how they fare in relation to each other. For these reasons, it is difficult to have a discussion of justice or ethics at a societal level which completely parallels our discussion of ethics at the individual level in terms of virtue, actions, and consequences. We will organize our discussion of alternative theories of justice in a different way. However, we will be able to find elements of virtue, deontological, and consequentialist ethics in the different theories of justice discussed below.

We divide theories of justice into five groups, that is: those that adopt egalitarian perspectives because of their intrinsic commitment to equality or needs; those that try to maximize some concept of the social good in terms of consequences, as exemplified by utilitarianism; those that focus on individual rights and the notion that people should receive what they contribute or what they deserve; those which base principles of justice on contracts between individuals; and those which stress the role of the community. This classification combines – or arguably confounds – several ways of distinguishing between theories of justice. One focuses on the type of individual theory of ethics on which it is based (as distinguished in the previous section), another on the way in which individuals relate to each other, yet another on their views about social processes and outcomes, and a final one on their relative emphases on maximizing some aggregate good and equality.

## 3.3 Egalitarian theories of justice

The first category of theories we discuss covers approaches to justice which emphasize equality, the well-being of the least advantaged people in society, and focus on the satisfaction of basic needs of all people.

The German philosopher, economist, and general social scientist Karl Marx (1818–83) is usually associated with an egalitarian view of justice. In his terminology capitalists exploit workers by making them work for more hours than needed to produce what they get as wages and what is necessary for them to reproduce themselves and their families. According to Marx, capitalists can do this because of their class monopoly of the means of production (that is, productive assets) which they initially acquired through primitive capitalist accumulation by using legal and extralegal means of taking over assets such as land (through the privatization of common lands in what is called the enclosure movement) and colonial profits and plunder. But Marx wrote fairly little about justice as such, apart from his critique of justice as an ideological apologetic of existing inequalities based on private property rights and incomes proportional to ability, and endorsing the distributive principle, "From each according to his ability, to each according to his need" (Marx, 1878). It should also be noted, as we shall see later, that Marx had another view of justice as well, which based the idea of justice in distribution on the contribution to production.

There are many modern egalitarian conceptions of justice (see, for instance, Miller, 1982; Parfitt, 1984; Cohen, 1989; and Scanlon, 2003), some of which argue that equality is good in itself, especially if inequality is involuntary, and if it concerns the distribution of some broad thing – such as resources – that people value. Other approaches derive egalitarian conclusions based on other starting points, such as the very influential approach of Rawls, to be discussed in Section 3.6, who is a central figure in modern discussions of egalitarian justice.

A focus on equality leads to questions concerning the equality of what. One question is whether what is good is equality of opportunity among people, or the equality of outcomes. If it is the equality of outcomes, how do we measure outcomes? Should our goal be to equalize income across people, or to equalize some other goods that we think are important, for instance, equality of health conditions (which need not involve equalizing incomes because some people may require more resources to overcome disabilities to attain good health). If it is equality of opportunity, how do we create a level playing field to ensure such equality? Should the rules that are in place treat all individuals in the same way, or address problems of certain types of differences, such as handicaps? If large inequalities in outcome persist, how can we be sure that opportunities are actually equal?

## 3.4 Utilitarianism and related theories

Utilitarianism, which was mentioned earlier, is the exemplar of theories that involve the maximization of social good. It was developed by British philosophers in the eighteenth and nineteenth centuries such as Jeremy Bentham (1748–1832), John Stuart Mill (1806–73), and Henry Sidgwick (1838–1900) and has been described as the theory which seeks to achieve the "greatest good for the greatest number of people." More specifically this approach to justice involves the maximization of the sum of utility of all individuals in society. Individual utility reflects the balance between positive and negative feelings of individuals, and is generally taken to be the amount of pleasure people obtain minus the amount of pain they experience. Social changes, such as those involving government policies, are considered to be good if they increase the sum total of individual utility, and the aim of society should be to maximize total utility for society as a whole.[5]

Utilitarianism, as defined above, represents a form of consequentialist ethics, since good and bad are judged in terms of consequences or social outcomes. It also takes a hedonistic approach to the good since it evaluates consequences by summing up the net pleasure (that is, pleasure minus pain) obtained by individuals. However, its proponents do not always espouse such a simple version of utilitarianism. For instance, John Stuart Mill (1863) thought it necessary to distinguish between different types of pleasures according to their quality and argued that cultural, intellectual, and spiritual pleasures are more valuable than physical pleasures. Some utilitarian ethicists also prefer rule utilitarianism to what is called act utilitarianism which, rather than evaluating acts in terms of their consequences, judges the rightness or wrongness of a particular action in terms of the correctness of the rule it exemplifies which, in turn, depends on the goodness of the consequences of generally following that rule.[6]

What exactly does utilitarianism entail and what does it reject? It has implications for acts and rules, and in this sense it is related to virtue ethics. It can also be used as a defense of an egalitarian perspective. Large levels of inequality do not maximize the sum of utility if we assume diminishing marginal utility. More inequality may result in: some rich people whose marginal utility of income is low getting more, which adds little to total utility; and some poor people whose marginal utility of income is high getting less which reduces total utility a great deal. However, it is important to recognize that utilitarianism makes evaluations not in terms of good acts or good rules, or in terms of equality as such, but in terms of the consequences of rules, acts, or income distributions, in terms of total utility for society. Its sole focus on consequentialism can lead it to support societies that do things which are at variance with most people's notions of justice. For example, it can condone slavery if both slaves and slave-owners feel better by being and having slaves. Moreover, it can condone the killing of a few individuals if the rest of the individuals in a society feel better off in their absence (for instance, because they are different from them in some way and do not like them around) or otherwise gain from their death.[7]

A number of problems have been pointed out with utilitarianism in addition to its neglect of freedom and rights. First, it raises questions about the definition and measurement of pleasure and pain.

In consequences, utilitarianism based on pleasure and pain has largely been replaced by using the implications of choice theory. People are assumed to be better off (and therefore obtain more utility) when they choose something over something else when they could have chosen the latter.[8] While this overcomes the problem of measuring pleasure and pain, it has the problem that it assumes that people always find that they experience more happiness or pleasure with what they choose than what they do not, something that is not always the case. This has led some psychologists and economists to distinguish between decision utility (which relates to choices) and experienced utility (which relates to one's subjective feelings which result from making that choice). Second, it has the problem that it requires comparing the utility of different people and summing them up, that is, it involves interpersonal utility comparisons. Even if we can say that a person is better off in one state of the world than in another, can we say that person A is better off than person B in a particular state of the world? This problem can be overcome with the Pareto principle or social welfare function approaches which we will discuss in Chapter 8. The difficulty with the Pareto principle – which states that society is better off with a change in the state of the world if at least one person is better off and no one is worse off – is that it does not rank order all states of the world, that is, those which involve comparisons between states in which some people are better off and others worse off. The social welfare function approach requires us to have a relation between individual utility levels and social welfare (which ranks states of the world for society as a whole), which economists call the social welfare function. Since the approach requires the social welfare function to be externally imposed, rather than be derived entirely from individual utility, it leaves unanswered the question as to where it comes from. Finally, it has the problem that it evaluates consequences in terms of utility, rather than taking into account the goodness of actions or the character of the actor, that is, ignoring the concerns of virtue and deontological ethics.

## 3.5 Equity, desert, and rights-based theories

The approaches to justice considered here are based on the concepts of proportionality and individual responsibility stressed in equity theory. Equity theorists trace the roots of their theory in the *Nichomachean Ethics*, in which Aristotle (350 BC, a) described a theory of justice based on proportionality between a person's contribution to an exchange or interaction, and the outcome in terms of consequences the person receives, positive or negative. In other words, if two people are involved in an exchange or interaction, the ratio of what a person receives to his or her input should be equal for the two people: the one who provides more inputs should get proportionally more output. Difficulties relate to quantification of inputs and outputs, and also what kinds of inputs are considered appropriate in this approach. Some equity theorists argue that the class of inputs relevant to the equity approach should only include those over which the agent exercises control.

The American philosopher Robert Nozick (1938–2002) argues that a distribution of goods is just if it is brought about by free exchange among consenting adults from a just starting position, even if large inequalities subsequently emerge from the process. This approach is concerned with the entitlement, or rights of individuals to what they possess, or their "holdings." At the core of this approach are two principles: first, the principle of justice in acquisition, that is, how things came to be originally owned; and second, the principle of justice in transfer, that is, how these holdings were transferred between people (Nozick, 1974). Nozick argues that these two principles are violated by theft, fraud, enslavement, and forcible exclusion from participating in exchange. This view draws on the English philosopher John Locke (1632–1704) and Kant, but is opposed to utilitarianism (because he takes individual choices to be paramount rather than attempting to promote the social good) and, as we shall see, Rawlsian justice (since he takes historical acquisition into account rather than assume that history does not exist, as in Rawls's original position). A problem with Nozick's approach is that he does not clarify the details about how his theory applies to specific situations or when forcible exclusion from participating in exchange and fraud is taking place. Moreover, he seems to have a very broad conception of choice, and does not explicitly distinguish between the different factors that separate voluntary allocations of goods from encumbered processes.

Theories of desert aim to provide people with their just desert, or what they deserve. These theories usually distinguish between different factors that affect the distribution of claims on income and wealth. The American economist and Nobel Laureate James M. Buchanan (b. 1919), like Nozick, envisions a limited role for state intervention and gives a wide berth to individual choice and action. He specifies four factors which determine income and wealth distribution: luck, choice, effort, and birth. He argues that of these, the relevance of effort in justifying inequality is least controversial, and the only one which conflicts with widely held views of justice is birth (Buchanan, 1986, 129–30).

In this view, inequality caused by effort, choice, and luck would not be considered unjust.

Others may argue that differences in outcomes caused by birth, luck, and choice are all unfair. According to this view, whether or not one has some inborn talent, intelligence, or physical prowess are all matters of luck for which people should not be rewarded, and only effort should count. But these views can be questioned both for being too restrictive and for being too permissive in justifying inequality. On the one hand, it can be argued that even if a person has some inborn talent, he or she has to expend considerable effort to develop that talent and to make it produce rewards. On the other hand, the ability to expend effort may be the result of some inborn trait of a person, so the effort is not something for which people should be held, at least entirely, accountable (see Roemer, 1998). Regarding choice, Ronald Dworkin (2000) proposes a theory which emphasizes equality, but tolerates some amount of inequality to allow rewards to choice. However, the rewards to choice may to some extent be a matter of luck. Dworkin (1981, 293) distinguishes between two kinds of luck: option luck relates to the outcomes of deliberate and calculated gambles which the person should have anticipated and could have declined, while brute luck relates to outcomes which are not deliberate in this sense. Rewards to option luck, because they depend mainly on choice, can be justified as being fair, while rewards from brute luck are not. While conceptually useful, this distinction is often difficult to apply in practice when the two kinds of luck are intertwined: for instance, the amount and quality of one's education are partially affected by the brute luck of the conditions of one's birth, and the rewards to it are difficult to attribute solely to one of the two kinds of luck.

The approaches discussed in this section are usually associated with libertarianism, which assigns a very small role to government, and with an acceptance of inequality, at least when it results from some acceptable causes. It can, however, be rooted in both deontological and utilitarian ethical theories. Thus, the minimal role of government can be advocated because government intervention infringes on some basic rights. Government intervention can be argued to have the bad consequences of reducing people's choices and of lowering levels of production by reducing people's incentives. Similarly, inequality can be justified by an appeal to the natural right to private property, as advocated by the British philosopher John Locke, or in terms of the consequentialist argument that inequality induces people to excel and to increase economic growth.

It is interesting to note that Marx also had a theory of justice based on the contribution people made to society. But for Marx the right people have is to their contribution in terms of labor, which is related to his labor theory of value. He argued that workers were deprived of a part of what they contributed directly and indirectly to production, and this is defined by him as exploitation. This approach has been used by later Marxist writers to develop a general theory of exploitation which examines how different classes in society, or countries in the world, receive as income more or less of the output than the labor they contribute to production (see Roemer, 1982). However, it seems that, late in his life, Marx's views on justice leaned more heavily toward the need-based approach discussed in Section 3.3.

## 3.6 Contract theories of justice

Contract theories take the approach of deriving principles of justice from what individuals in a group would choose voluntarily.[9] The interaction of individuals in a group can involve conflicts of interest, but may overall be mutually beneficial. Contract theories try to derive ethical principles that individuals may choose, given their objectives which may involve solely the pursuit of self-interest. The idea that the principles of justice can be derived from (possibly implicit) contracts between individuals has early roots in the writings of Plato, Hobbes, Kant, and Rousseau. Barry (1989b) distinguishes between two broad categories of contract theories as applied to justice, that is, those based on mutual advantage, in which self-interested individuals agree on a bargain that furthers each individual's advantage, and those based on impartiality, which examine, what individuals who are impartial (about who they are in society) would pursue, given certain ends which may, but need not be, self-interested. A variant of the latter is what the American philosopher John Rawls (1921–2002) calls the reciprocity approach in which individuals pursue the common good provided that others reciprocate, while impartiality may imply an unconditional commitment to the common good.

Rawls is the central figure in modern contract theories of justice. Rawls's (1971) theory of justice has been extremely influential in reinvigorating interest in justice issues among philosophers, and in framing discussions of justice among social scientists, including economists. Rawls's theory is partly a critique of utilitarianism. It builds on the theory of social contract – in which self-interested individuals come together and voluntarily agree upon a social contract – developed by Locke, Rousseau, and Kant. Equality plays a central role in it, including the duty to help people in need. Rawls's principle of justice, which provides a standard against which the distributional aspects of the basic structure of society can be assessed, is one "that free and rational persons concerned to further their own interests would accept in an initial position of equality" (Rawls, 1981, 11), called the 'original position.' This is a hypothetical situation in which people stand behind a 'veil of ignorance' which prevents them from knowing their social status, wealth, abilities, and so forth. Rawls claims that two justice principles would be chosen by everyone in such a position. In his successive writings these principles have changed to some extent. In Rawls (1993, 291) he states these principles as:

a. Each person has an equal right to a fully adequate scheme of equal basic liberties which is compatible with a similar scheme of liberties for all.
b. Social and economic inequalities are to satisfy two conditions. First, they must be attached to offices and positions open to all under conditions of fair equality of opportunity; and second, they must be of greatest benefit to the least advantaged members of society.

In Rawls's view the first principle takes priority over the second, which implies that he is giving absolute priority to liberty compared to other considerations, including social equality: personal liberties cannot be violated for whatever reason. The first part of the second principle is ensuring that public opportunities are open to all; people cannot be excluded from such opportunities on grounds, say, of race or religion. The second part, which has come to be called the 'difference principle' is taken to mean that a social state is an improvement if it increases the amount of "primary goods" going to the least well off. "Primary goods," for Rawls, refers to general-purpose means to meet people's ends such as "rights, liberties and opportunities, and income and wealth." For example, high salaries for doctors may be justified by improved medical care for all other strata of society including the lowest. If such an argument cannot be made then doctors' salaries need not be higher than those for other workers. Rawls's principles of justice are intended to indicate how major social institutions should distribute rights and liberties, or what Rawls calls the "basic structure of society," but does not encompass the formation of government or individual market transactions.

Rawls's approach is appealing for a number of reasons. It is fair and evenhanded in the sense that it prohibits parties in the original position from choosing a society designed to unfairly favor particular parties, for instance, themselves. If there was some chance that you would either be a doctor or be a nurse's aide, you would be unlikely to insist on policies that unfairly allowed doctors to feather their nests at the expense of health care workers who are less well-paid. Moreover, it is related to individual self-interest. People choosing the structure of society behind the veil of ignorance would be risk-averse and since everyone has a chance of being part of the poorest strata of society, the social contract is constructed to benefit the least well-off members. Rawls also justifies his approach to justice by arguing that it represents what he calls a reflective equilibrium. This is a position that is arrived at by working back and forth among our considered judgments about particular instances and principles or rules that we believe govern them, and the theoretical considerations we consider relevant for them, revising these elements when necessary to achieve coherence among them.

However, Rawls's theory has also been subject to a great deal of criticism. Libertarian critics on the right, such as Robert Nozick (1974), who defend a minimalist state, argue that Rawls's theory of justice requires an extensive state which interferes continually in individual free choice and infringes on people's natural rights to private property. Marxist critics on the left take the view that Rawls's approach does not address what they consider the root of the problem of injustice, that is, the capitalist system and the unequal ownership of productive assets, and by giving priority to the first principle over the difference principle limits the extent to which income can be redistributed. Sen (2009) criticizes Rawls's theory for focusing attention on the "basic structure of society," which refers to rules and institutions, and neglecting the actual behavior of individuals and groups which, together with institutions and rules, determine actual outcomes in society. He also argues that Rawls's project – that of finding a unique transcendental conception on which there will be general agreement – is too demanding and unlikely to be found, but also unnecessary and misleading if one is interested in a comparative approach which reduces injustice incrementally by comparing between two different possible states. Yet another critic, Michael Sandel (1982) argues that Rawls has a thin, individualistic, and asocial concept of the self which leads to contradictions if one uses Rawls's reflective equilibrium. Sandel argues, for instance, that if it is said that I "do not deserve" the diligence, intelligence, and other qualities which enable me to become wealthy, what exactly is the "I" who does not deserve? Once the self is seen as something distinct from its virtues, there is not much left in it, to the point of it becoming an incoherent and meaningless notion. Moreover, if we do not deserve the traits that allow us to obtain wealth, neither do we deserve those that lead us to commit crimes. This implies that we do not deserve punishment for crime, a conclusion that is at odds with our considered convictions. Finally, some feminist ethicists have criticized Rawls's approach of using abstract rules and his conception of the self as being autonomous and self interested, rather than one which cares and feels for particular others.

While Rawls's approach is best known among economists, there are a number of other contractarian justice theories which formulate the question differently. David Gauthier (1986) and Ken Binmore (1994) use game theory to examine how justice emerges through bargaining between individuals. Gauthier's approach, which is in the mutual benefit tradition of Hobbes, considers the result of bargaining among expected utility maximizing individuals in which everyone knows everyone's preferences, capabilities, and endowments. In this approach no individual will agree to accept less than they could without any agreement, and gains from the bargain are distributed so that the largest relative concession one has to make in comparison to their maximum utility and their no-agreement utility is minimized, which is close to what is called the Kalai–Smorodinsky cooperative game bargaining solution (see Hausman and McPherson, 2006, 251–4). Brian Barry (1989a) departs from Rawls's approach, in which justice results from individual choice, and from game theoretic approaches, in which it emerges from bargaining, and examines how principles of justice emerge from debate in which people agree about the reasonableness of principles, even if they are against their own interests. Serge-Christophe Kolm's (1997) theory of the "liberal social contract" involves agreement between real people who are aware of their positions in society (rather than fictitious people behind the Rawlsian veil of ignorance), considers people who are not guided only by self-interest (as in Rawls's and most game theoretic approaches), and allows agreements between subsets of people without requiring unanimity.

## 3.7 Virtue and communitarian approaches

Another approach to justice is what has been called communitarian justice which defends the communitarian ideal of the common good.[10] Writers in this tradition often regard their work as being rooted in Aristotelian virtue theory. Some proponents of this approach have defended their approach by criticizing other concepts of justice, such as the welfare liberal conceptions of justice of the utilitarians and Rawls. An example of this is the work of Michael Sandel (1982), who was mentioned earlier, who claims that the western liberal conception is based on an inadequate conception of the nature of the self, according to which none of the particular wants, interests, or ends that we have constitutes who we essentially are. Sandel argues that welfare liberals espouse this conception of the self because it is fundamental to their conception of justice, one that gives priority of the right over the good. MacIntyre also characterizes liberalism as attempting to separate the rule defining right action from conceptions of the human good, and argues that these forms of liberalism fail and are bound to fail because the rules governing right action cannot be adequately grounded independent of a conception of the good. As mentioned earlier, MacIntyre stresses the importance of internal goods generated in terms of practice within communities which generate good qualities in people within that community. MacIntyre's focus on internal goods like achieving high standards of excellence within the practice makes external goods like money and status unimportant to the pursuit of the good. His focus on the community and goods internal to it draws attention to the fact that virtue cannot be defined for individuals alone, but individual virtue depends on the virtues of communities – so that the whole of society is more than the sum of its parts, that is, its members – and that different communities may, in principle, emphasize different lists of goods which represent virtues. However, MacIntyre does not argue that *any* notions of excellence that are developed by a community are virtuous, and therefore does not take the view that communities are intrinsically good.

Sen's approach, in terms of functionings and capabilities in achieving goods that are valued, usually includes goods such as good health, education, and so forth, but Sen argues that the precise content of these goods are to be determined by societies in the process of public deliberation. Others in the virtue tradition, such as Nussbaum, argue for a universal list of goods which are common to all communities, although communities can add additional goods to this list.

## 3.8 Feminist ethics and justice

Having examined some well-known traditional approaches to ethics and justice, we now turn to an approach to ethical questions that has emerged since around the 1980s, that is, feminist ethics and justice. Feminist ethicists start from the claim that the history of ethics has been constructed from a male perspective, with concepts and assumptions which are not gender-neutral. Virginia Held (1990) reviews the history of western ethics and argues that there are three clear trends which reveal the dominance of the male over the female. The first is the association of rationality with the masculine and of unreason and emotion with the feminine, and of the dominance of reason over unruly emotion which needs to be controlled. The second is the association of 'man' with the human and the 'woman' with the natural, which is reinforced by the association of man with public life and the life of the polis and of woman with the private sphere and the household, ideas which reflected the role of men and women in ancient Athens. Childbirth and childrearing have been treated as being in the sphere of nature and their importance minimized as being merely biological, while the male public activities in the marketplace and government have been given a privileged place for the discussion of philosophy in general and ethics in particular. Third, the concept of the human self developed in ethical discussions of virtue, for instance, has been the rational self-interested and individualistic 'agent,' which reflects male conceptions of masculinity, rather than one which incorporates the feminine perspective. These trends, in turn, have been affected by, and exacerbate, the subservient position of women in society.

Held and other feminist philosophers advocate breaking down these associations and patriarchal hierarchies and of developing ethical perspectives which incorporate women's views and experiences.[11] Mirroring the three trends mentioned in the previous paragraph, they recommend three types of changes. First, they argue that the theories of ethics and justice that are so self-consciously based on reason – starting from the Greek philosophers through Kant and modern approaches, including those of the utilitarians and Rawls – have despite their many differences, the common feature of trying to develop an approach to ethics based on abstract rules. They question whether an ethics built on abstract rules, rather than one paying careful attention to actual contexts, especially as experienced by women, is adequate for dealing with moral questions. As emphasized by the American psychologist Carol Gilligan (b. 1936), women tend to be more concerned with preserving actual human relationships and with caring for those for whom they feel responsible, than with abstract logical rules of justice.[12] Second, childbirth and nurturing need to be seen as human activities involving choices, rather than natural activities which obey some biological laws, and that the care perspective that these activities reflect, and friendship, especially as experienced by women, need to be reflected in discussions of the public sphere. Third, feminists are redefining the concept of the self employed in social science and ethical theory as one of the self-interested individual 'self' who seeks impartiality toward the universal 'all,' to one that also sees as relevant the intermediate stages of family, friends, groups, and neighborhoods, that is, of particular 'others.' The particular others can be actual people in one's neighborhood but, given the mothering and care perspective, can also be children in need in continents far from home, and anticipated children of future generations, rather than the faceless and abstract all. The change in the concept of self also has implications for the concepts of autonomy and private property, changing the view of the self as bounded and excluding the government and the community and autonomy as symbolized by walls around one's property, to notions of self and autonomy in relation to others – both intimate and more distant. The implications for egalitarian and individual rights-based theories of justice discussed earlier are obvious.

In addition to addressing general issues related to reason, mothering and the conception of self, feminist ethicists address the specific question of subjugation of women in society. They discuss the position of women in the political sphere, in the workplace and in the family and the goal of replacing a gender-structured society with a gender-free one, in which basic rights and duties are not assigned on the basis of a person's biological sex. The extent to which such issues can be addressed using traditional theories of ethics and justice, explicitly treating them in terms of the ideal of androgyny, or taking into account masculine and feminine conceptions of self, remains an open question.

## 3.9 Conclusion

This chapter has briefly discussed some major approaches to theories of ethics and justice. It has first distinguished between virtue, deontological, and consequentialist ethics from the perspective of individual actions, and then distinguished between societal ethics in terms of theories of justice which take egalitarian, utilitarian, equity, desert, *and* rights, contractual and communitarian perspectives. We end with two comments.

First, our discussion has many deficiencies. Our coverage of approaches to ethics and justice has by no means been exhaustive. Nor could it be expected to be, given the length of this chapter. We will discuss many of the issues discussed here in more detail in later chapters. Our classification of theories, especially justice theories, can be criticized, both for ignoring such important distinctions, mentioned earlier, between transcendental and comparative theories, or between institution-based and behavior-based (or a combination of the two), and for placing individual multidimensional contributions into a few separate pigeon-holes. Nor have we even attempted to answer the questions we raised about the specific examples mentioned in the introduction to this chapter, which we will come closer to addressing by the end of this book, drawing on the ideas discussed in this chapter and the remaining ones.

Second, despite its deficiencies, our discussion suggests that the theory of ethics implicit in mainstream economics is a very limited and partial one which follows a consequentialism that is related to a particular variant of utilitarianism based on the Pareto principle and the social welfare function. We will discuss these issues in more detail in subsequent chapters.

# Part II

# Ethical Values, Individual Behavior, and Social Interactions

# 4
# Individuals, Norms, and Ethical Values

## Introduction

Why do people behave the way they do? Why do they buy this product or service and not a different one? Why does one person work two jobs, another person one full-time job, another part-time, and yet another not work outside the home? Why does someone buy a huge house with many more bedrooms than family members? Why does someone cheat on his or her taxes, and someone else not do so? Why does a used car dealer sell a car which he or she knows to be a lemon and someone else not do so? Why does one person vote in an election and another person not do so? Why do some people, and not others, volunteer to build houses for the homeless?

Mainstream neoclassical economics has a powerful and simple method of answering these questions – by specifying the preferences of the individual in terms of a utility function or preference ordering, and the constraints (total time, total income, the prices of goods and services, etc.) he or she faces, and by assuming that the person tries to maximize utility or choose the most preferred course of action given the constraints. This approach has been used to understand the behavior of individuals in standard economic activities like buying and selling goods and services, but also, though less frequently, to understand people's actions in social and political arenas, for instance, whether to marry, how many children to have, for whom to vote, and whether or not to join an insurrection. In doing so, it is usually assumed that individuals are self-interested in the sense that their utility depends only on things that happen directly to them, that is, how much they consume and earn, how much they work, what activities they perform, and so on, rather than on what happens to other people. It is also assumed that utility does not depend on what kinds of people they themselves are, or on whether they are guided by principles or ethical values.

These observations raise several questions. First, are people in fact self-interested or do they also care about what happens to others and, in general, do they have ethical values which affect their behavior? This is a question about the nature of people's characters and about what motivates them, but it also raises the methodological question about whether one can meaningfully distinguish between the two kinds of considerations. These issues are addressed in the first and second sections. Section 4.1 reviews what is meant by the optimizing, self-interested agent. Section 4.2 discusses what other motivations drive individuals, and how ethical values, in particular, motivate them. Second, if they do care about others and have ethical values, how – if at all – can that be incorporated into the utility-maximizing approach? This is a question that concerns the extent to which the standard neoclassical approach can be modified to deal with the fact that individuals may have ethics that, at least in part, motivates his or her behavior. Section 4.3 will address this question and critically discuss some ways that have been proposed for incorporating ethics into the optimizing approach. Third, if people follow norms and have ethical values, what is the nature of these norms and values? Section 4.4 addresses this issue by discussing different types of norms and ethical perspectives people have, as well as what individuals think about fairness and justice. Finally, where do ethical values and norms come from, what determines them and how do they change over time if they in fact do so? These questions cannot be fully analyzed at the level of an individual, since norms and values arguably have a social component to them in the sense that values and behavior are affected by what other people believe and do. Section 4.5 will make some preliminary remarks about this issue, which will be further examined in the next two chapters. Section 4.6 concludes.

## 4.1 The optimizing, self-interested agent

Standard neoclassical economic theory assumes that economic agents are "rational." This conception of the economic agent has been appropriated by other social scientists, like political scientists and sociologists, in what is commonly referred to as rational choice theory. The word rationality, however, has various meanings and there is no clear definition of it. For instance, the American Nobel Prize-winning economist, Herbert Simon (1916–2001), distinguishes between *substantive* rationality and *procedural* rationality. Simon (1976, 130–31) defines behavior as substantively rational "when it is appropriate to the achievement of given goals within the limits imposed by given conditions and constraints" and procedurally rational "when it is the outcome of appropriate deliberation." For substantive rationality, rational behavior depends on the agent or actor in only one respect – in terms of his or her goals and preferences – and is otherwise determined completely by the characteristics of the environment in which the decision is made. By contrast, "procedural rationality depends on the process that generated it. When psychologists use the term 'rational,' it is usually procedural rationality that they have in mind... Conversely, behavior tends to be described as 'irrational' in psychology when it represents impulsive response to affective mechanisms without an adequate intervention of thought" (Simon, 1976, 131). Clearly, in the case of procedural rationality, rational behavior depends not only on the goals and preferences of the agent, but also on how he or she deliberates, given his or her knowledge of the environment in which he or she acts.

Let us start with a general conception of what economists mean by rationality which, in Simon's terminology, refers to substantive rationality. Consider the way an individual consumer is often depicted in standard textbooks. The individual is assumed to choose over possible "bundles" of goods, for instance, apples and books, which she can consume.[1] The bundles (like five applies and two books) represent the consumer's *choices*. The individual, of course, cannot consume an unlimited amount of these goods, since it is assumed that he or she has a fixed income and that these goods have fixed prices. The consumer cannot spend more on these two goods than her income, which is an example of a *constraint* faced by the consumer.[2] The consumer can therefore choose among any of the bundles that satisfy the constraints that she faces. In Figure 4.1 these bundles are shown by those in the triangle contained by the line *YY* (which contains bundles exhausting her entire income) and the vertical and horizontal axes which measure quantities of books ($b$) and apples ($a$), respectively.[3]

But which bundle will the consumer choose? To answer that, we will have to know what are his or her preferences and objectives. The consumer is assumed to have *preferences* over the bundles, that is, we assume that he or she can rank bundles according to her preferences. We also assume that these preferences are *rational*, that is, they are *complete* (the consumer can decide, for any two bundles, whether she prefers one or the other, or is indifferent between them) and *transitive* (for any three bundles, $x$, $y$, and $z$, if she prefers $x$ to $y$ and $y$ to $z$, she also prefers $x$ to $z$). With some additional technical conditions (which are not important for

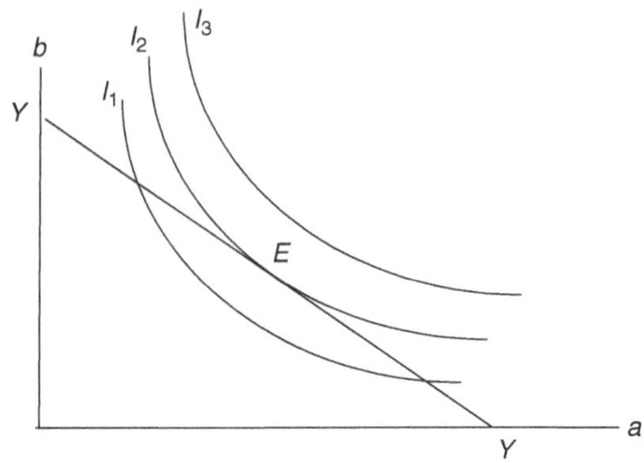


*Figure 4.1* The optimizing consumer

us) we can represent these preferences by what is called the consumer's *utility function*, which can be written as $U(.)$, which states that if a consumer prefers a bundle $x$ to a bundle $y$, then $U(x) > U(y)$, where $U$ is the utility the consumer obtains from consuming the bundle enclosed within the parenthesis. Suppose we can represent the consumer's utility function or preference ordering by the indifference map with three indifferences curves shown by $I_1$, $I_2$, and $I_3$, which represent increasingly higher levels of utility. Note that the map implies completeness (every point is on an indifference curve) and transitivity (which implies that the curves do not intersect), but also some additional properties of the consumer's preferences: that individuals prefer bundles which have more of one good and no less of another compared to another (that is, more is better, which implies that indifference curves further to the right and above represent higher levels of utility), and they prefer "balanced" bundles rather than "extreme" ones (which implies that the indifference curves are convex to the origin).[4] The magnitude of utility levels is meaningless: all that matters is the order, that bundles that are preferred to others have a higher utility level. The consumer is assumed to have the *objective* of maximizing utility, or attaining her highest level of satisfaction. Given these assumptions, the individual will choose the bundle shown by point $E$, that is, the bundle which puts her on the highest indifference curve (or utility level) among all the bundles that she could choose, given the constraints which she faces.

The analysis can obviously be extended to deal with many goods and services, not just two. We can extend it also to make utility depend on how much leisure she has, and her consumption of goods and her leisure at different points in time. The framework can even be extended to deal with quantities of not just private goods, but public goods as well, such as parks, the state of the environment, and so on, although the consumer may not be able to individually decide how much of these goods is available. We can also apply the same ideas to a firm, assuming that the firm chooses to buy inputs and produce goods and services, given technology, the prices of the inputs and outputs, and other possible constraints on production, to maximize profits.[5]

In this general framework we can define individual *rationality* to mean that individuals have rational preferences (that is, they are complete and transitive) and that they choose bundles which provide them with a level of utility or satisfaction which is no less than what is provided by any other bundle that they could have chosen, given their constraints.[6] This general definition does not require any assumptions about the nature of constraints (for instance, we may introduce additional constraints like time constraints), whether more is better, or whether the consumer prefers balanced bundles.

In addition to the assumptions that we have explicitly stated, five other implicit assumptions are worth noting. First, the consumer has full information about all goods and their properties and can evaluate how consuming them will affect her, and in fact has the ability to choose among all of possible bundles. In choosing a car, for instance, she knows everything worth knowing about the car that is relevant for what satisfaction it will provide her, and is able to figure out which car suits her best. Second, there is full certainty about the future in the sense that there is no risk or uncertainty: the consumer knows exactly the future consequences of any of her actions. When she chooses a college to attend, she has full knowledge about what kinds of classes will be offered in the future, how they will fit her schedule, what kinds of friends she will make there, and so on.[7] Third, the consumer's preferences over bundles can be purely subjective, and there does not even have to be any reason for the preferences which she can defend or justify to other people other than saying "I prefer $x$ over $y$." Fourth, the consumer is concerned only about the consequences of what she does, that is, how much and what she consumes, and not what kind of person she is (for instance, is she the kind of person who will consume things which are produced with child labor), or her actions and their motivations (for instance, whether she consumes goods because she is led by envy to consume what others do or whether she really likes them irrespective of what others do), or even how much choice she has (that is, the range of bundles she can choose from). In other words, she is a consequentialist of a particular kind, that is, one that evaluates things according to what and how much is consumed. Finally, it is assumed that the individual is concerned only with what she consumes or what directly affects her, that is, how much of goods she consumes, how much leisure she has, and so on. She is not concerned with what and how much others consume, how her consumption affects others, or more generally with how much utility other people obtain. This assumption, which we may call one of self-interest, when combined with the notion of rationality (of the substantive kind), implies a conception of an individual which has been described as the *homo economicus*. The first three of these assumptions are directly relevant for the definition of rationality, while the last two and the third are directly relevant for ethics. In the rest of this section we will discuss some issues connected with the first three, and turn to further issues concerning the third and the last two in the next three sections.

The first assumption raises questions about whether the notion of substantive rationality is an appropriate one for understanding individual choices in the real world. In the real world, most things that consumers choose from have many characteristics, and it is difficult if not impossible to know everything about these characteristics, and to make well-informed optimal decisions based on this information. The problem arises both from getting the information and about the computational ability to make decisions based on this information. Gathering information is costly, and it is not clear how much information one should collect to maximize one's utility because to know if it is worth getting more information one needs to get that information, which leads to the problem of infinite regress. Our cognitive abilities are also limited, and hence it is not possible to utilize very large amounts of data to make correct decisions. It is for these reasons that Simon argued that it was better to analyze actual decision-making using the notion of procedural rationality rather than substantive rationality which is meaningful only in the simple environments of very stylized frameworks of analysis. In defense of the economists' conception of rationality, it has been pointed out that the notion cannot be criticized because it does not specify what exactly utility depends on and what are the precise constraints to individual choices (see Boland, 1981). However, if we interpret rationality in this way (almost) any kind of behavior can be called rational, and rationality loses its status as the preferred way of analyzing behavior. It holds this place because of its claim that people are in fact rational and that analysis should reflect this fact. The rationality assumption becomes merely an agreed-upon convention that is used for analyzing behavior, and no more.

In any case, it can be questioned whether people are in fact rational optimizers, in the sense of looking at all relevant information and choosing the best option, even in simple situations. Consider two examples which suggest otherwise. One is described by Tversky and Kahneman (1981) in which they survey two groups of roughly equal numbers of people to find out which of two alternative health programs they prefer to cope with the outbreak of an unusual disease that is expected to kill 600 people. One group was asked to choose between two programs, one that will save 200 people and another which will save 600 people with probability 1/3 and save no one with probability 2/3. In response 72 per cent of those surveyed preferred the first program. The other group was asked to choose between a program which will result in the death of 400 people and another one with which no one will die with probability 1/3 and 600 will die with probability 2/3. Here, in response 78 per cent of those surveyed chose the latter. The programs were actually the same, but their effects were stated differently, in terms of deaths or saving lives, and this led people to choose different programs. These preferences do not seem rational in the standard economics sense, but the way the choices were framed affected people's choices. Another example is found on the *Economist* magazine's Web site, which offers three annual subscription choices: online access for $59; print subscription for $125; and print and online subscription for $125. Ariely (2008, 1–6) asked 100 students to choose between these three options, and they were chosen, respectively, by 16, 0, and 84 students. When he asked the same number of students to choose between two options, removing the print-only option, 68 chose the online-only option and 32 chose the print and online option. The student's ranking of the online and print plus online option is reversed simply because of the presence of the decoy print-only option in the first choice. People are being irrational here by allowing an irrelevant option to affect their rankings. They act in this way because in the first choice the presence of the decoy makes the print-cum-online option look very good when compared to it. It is ironic that the *Economist*, which usually takes the position that free markets work well, which requires that individuals choose rationally, is using consumer irrationality to increase its profits!

The second assumption is clearly unrealistic, because many actions have consequences that occur in the future, and the decision-maker does not know with certainty what the future holds. Standard economic theory typically deals with situations in which outcomes of actions are not known with certainty by interpreting decision-makers as choosing among lotteries which have prizes as outcomes. For instance, an individual may choose a bundle which will pay nothing with probability ½,

$10 with probability ¼, and $100 with probability ¼. This extension to situations in which outcomes are not certain may seem straightforward, and one could apply the same notion of rationality to preferences over lotteries as we did to bundles with certain outcomes, that is, for instance, insist on complete and transitive preferences. It turns out, however, that one needs an additional rationality requirement, known as the independence condition or the sure-thing principle, to analyze these cases. This condition implies that if a person is choosing between two lotteries, both paying nothing with probability ½ while the first pays $11 and the second $10 with probability ½, rationality requires preferring the first over the second (under the assumption that more is better). This condition may be violated even if individuals have rational preferences under certainty (for instance, their preferences are complete and transitive). If a person's preferences satisfy all the standard axioms of preferences under certainty and also this condition, it can be represented by a cardinal utility function in which the magnitudes of utility levels, and not just their order, are significant. Under certainty, all that is significant for utility levels is their order, not its magnitude: if bundle A is preferred to bundle B, all that is relevant is that $U(A) > U(B)$; the sign, not the magnitude of $U(A)–U(B)$, matters. In the case of lotteries, however, cardinality is significant. This cardinality allows us to express utilities of lotteries in terms of what is called the expected utility property which states, for instance, that if a person receives an amount *A* with probability ¼ and an amount B with probability ¾, and the utilities for getting *A* and *B* are $U(A)$ and $U(B)$, respectively, the utility that the person receives from the lottery can be expressed as ¼ $U(A)$ + ¾ $U(B)$.[8] The general point is that the requirements of rationality involved here are stronger than they are in the case of certainty, because it involves not just rationality of preference and choice, but also of belief.[9]

These conditions may not always hold under alternative ways of dealing with the absence of certainty. All situations in which outcomes are not known cannot be treated as lotteries with given probabilities attached to outcomes. Following John Maynard Keynes and Frank Knight, we may distinguish between situations of risk and situations of uncertainty. Briefly put, situations of risk involve those in which an event can be repeated many times under similar conditions – the simplest cases being tossing a coin, rolling a die and spinning a roulette wheel – such that objective probabilities of outcomes are available, while situations of uncertainty are those in which an event is repeated in situations that are very different, so that we simply do not know the outcome. Various methods have been used for analyzing situations of uncertainty, and these generally require departures from the axioms of expected utility theory, and it is not obvious what rationality means. The introduction of risk and, especially, uncertainty produces many more examples of behavior which seem not to be rational according to standard economic theory (see, for instance, Hausman and McPherson, 2006, 55–9).

The third assumption highlights the fact that there may be no good reasons for why a person prefers some bundles to others, and all that is required is some kind of consistency of preferences (in particular, transitivity). If a person prefers to play tennis over golf, or prefers to eat Chinese food over pizza, or vice versa, then we may not be too concerned if there are no good reasons behind these personal preferences (although we may pause to think about their health implications). However, if the person prefers to buy lottery tickets rather than food we may begin to wonder. We may even think that the person is not carefully thinking things through if he or she prefers the government to spend on building a brewery rather than building a school. These considerations are, however, irrelevant in judging whether the individual is rational or not, as long as his or her preferences are complete, transitive, and he or she is maximizing utility in deciding consumption bundles.

One may wonder why we have devoted so much space to discussing the economists' notion of rationality and the problems connected with it. What does all of it have to do with ethics? In general, if rationality is not well defined and people are in reality not rational in ways many economists assume, then many other considerations can drive people's choices. These considerations may well include ethical judgments. More specific connections between this discussion and ethical considerations will be examined in later chapters.

## 4.2 Self-interest, altruism, and ethical values

A little bit of introspection suggests that individuals are not just self-interested maximizers. They do not just act to further their own interests in the sense of trying to get as much as possible for themselves. We have emotions, weaknesses of will, habits, sympathy for others, ties to others, group identities, ideas of fairness, moral values, and religious beliefs, and we follow norms and codes of behavior.

Moreover, a great deal of empirical evidence – based on experimental studies, survey evidence, and the examination of actual behavior – has been collected to show that an individual's actions are not just motivated by self-interest, but are driven, at least in part, by other motivations.

For instance, questionnaire evidence suggests that people do, in fact, care about fairness. Kahneman et al. (1986a) asked some questions based on some hypothetical scenarios that they concocted. According to one vignette, there was a snowstorm, and the local hardware store increased the price of snow shovels. The respondents were asked if this was acceptable or unfair. Although standard economics would find this question irrelevant – the rise in demand because of the snowstorm would increase the price of shovels – 82 per cent of the respondents answered that an increase in price from $15 to $25 would be unfair, since they believed that the store was taking advantage of people's bad luck when their actual costs had not increased. Akerlof and Shiller (2009, 21) cite reports on how, after Miami's Hurricane Andrew in 1992, the Home Depot store chain actually absorbed a large part of the increase in the cost of plywood in order to avoid charges of price gouging. Experiments also suggest that people care about fairness (see Akerlof and Shiller, 2009, 22–3). A standard game that is frequently played in experimental laboratories for testing how subjects cooperate and trust each other involves the subjects putting some money into a pot which will be augmented and shared with other members of the group.[10] If all subjects act cooperatively the group as a whole gets the highest return, but individual subjects have an incentive to act selfishly because his or her best outcome is for all others to put money in the pot, but for the individual not to do so. In repeated experiments of this game it is found that subjects initially tend to cooperate, but after learning that other subjects are defectors, they themselves defect, and everyone plays selfishly. Fehr and Gächter (2000) modify this game slightly to allow players, at a cost to themselves, to punish those who act selfishly. They found that people in fact did punish defectors at some cost to themselves, punishment reduced selfish behavior, and many people put money in the pot after many repeated games. The fact that people punished defectors suggests that people care about fairness; in fact, meting out such punishments seems to activate the dorsal striatum area of the brain, which is known to light up in anticipation of many types of rewards and show that people are happy (see De Quervain et al., 2005).

Two kinds of phenomena that seem to contradict the position that people only act in a self-interested manner are that (1) they follow norms and codes of conduct and that (2) they often act in ways that seem to suggest that they care about others. People often follow norms even at some cost to themselves. Norms may be thought of as descriptions of how people think that they and other people should or should not behave. Akerlof and Kranton (2000, 2002) find that people's happiness depends on living up to what they think they should be doing. It is in this sense that they define what is fair. They also get upset if other people think that they are not fair. Moreover, they want other people to be fair, that is, live up to what they think others should be doing, and get upset when they believe that others are not fair. As such, considerations of fairness are a major motivator of many kinds of economic behavior. An example of this is that people tend to get upset when, in an exchange, people do not live up to the social psychological theory of exchange called equity theory, discussed in Chapter 3, which holds that on the two sides of an exchange the input (what they contribute) should be equal to the output (what they receive), not just in the narrow economic view of the market value of these goods, but also subjective evaluations, such as the social status of the parties to a transaction (see Akerlof and Shiller, 2009, 24–5). People also sometimes help others when it does not further their self-interest. For instance, people donate money to others even when they do not know them and can expect nothing in return from them.

Not all norms embody ethical values. For instance, people may follow the norm of driving on the right-hand side of the road in some countries and on the left-hand side in others. There is nothing intrinsically good or bad about following this norm. However, not acting according to norms such as these can sometimes be argued to be unethical, because doing so may endanger other people (but may sometimes benefit the driver by allowing them to get ahead of others, although it may also endanger themselves) and because it may be against the law (in no-passing zones) and it can be argued that non-compliance with laws – except, arguably, unjust ones – is unethical. Compliance with some norms may in fact be difficult to justify as being ethical: for instance, saying "god bless you" after someone sneezes, although it may be considered polite. Some norms may in fact be unethical – such as not sharing meals with people of what is considered to be lower social status or caste. Yet, many norms are indeed ethical, including norms about not cheating, not stealing, not lying, not taking advantage of other people especially when they are in distress, helping those who are in need of help, and not killing.

Likewise, what appears to be altruistic behavior need not necessarily have ethical content. It is possible to help someone with the expectation that that person is likely to reciprocate and further one's self-interest. Helping one's superiors in the workplace can often be done with this kind of strategic motive, and for this reason is often looked down upon by others as "kissing up" or "brown-nosing." Helping one's own family members, kin, and friends is sometimes also motivated by self-interest, not only in the sense of expecting favors in return, but also as extending the conception of "self" as including people one is close to, especially one's children and other family members, while excluding others from similar consideration, and may not be purely altruistic, at least according to some ethical theories. Moreover, such behavior can sometimes be purely instinctive, and, according to social biology, a result of biological evolutionary mechanisms. For instance, behavior which helps one's children or people within small and close-knit communities may have survival advantages which make this kind of nature persist. It is easier to argue that instinctive or unconscious behavior has less ethical worth than behavior based on explicit reasoning, as in Kant's argument, mentioned in Chapter 3. However, consciously adopted ethical behavior may change the individual person's nature in such a way that this behavior becomes unconscious or instinctive, in which case such behavior can justifiably be called ethical.

A question that needs to be raised is whether norms, ethical values, and other such deviations from the more purely self-interested type of behavior can actually be explained solely in terms of self-interested behavior? This question is important because of two considerations. First, it may be argued that there is really no such thing as ethical behavior, since all such acts can be justified in terms of self-interest. Second, on methodological grounds it can and has been argued that one should not extend the standard neoclassical approach, which is argued to have proved itself quite useful, by introducing additional elements such as norms, concerns for fairness, and other ethical values, because doing so could lead to a slippery slope where the theory includes anything and everything anyone wants. These two considerations, while distinct, involve arguments that utilize the same kind of approach that typically proceeds as follows. When we do good things for other people, or take their well-being into account in our actions, we are doing so for our self-interest, because by doing so it is more likely that others will reciprocate, thus furthering our self-interest. We follow norms because if we do not do so we expect others will punish us, or we do so because we perceive that others will reward us in ways that will increase the goods and services available to us. While there seems to be no definitive way of proving or disproving these kinds of arguments, the approach is problematic for a number of reasons. First, many kinds of behavior which are observed in reality would be hard to explain in these self-interested terms. For instance, the fact that individuals sometimes return to their owners lost wallets that they find without any reward and with some cost to themselves is hard to square with pure self-interest.[11] The fact that individuals help complete strangers who they are unlikely to meet again, when no one that they know is at hand to observe this, and they help people who they know are unable to reciprocate, also suggest that self-interest is not always an issue.[12] Second, reducing such behavior to self-interest is likely to result in ignoring alternative explanations for the emergence and persistence of a class of behaviors, since everything is being reduced to individual self-interest. Third, regarding the methodological argument, it is not clear how well neoclassical theory has done in explaining phenomena without introducing non self-interested motives.[13] It may have a good record at explaining some kinds of behavior, such as why people buy more apples when the price falls, but it seems to have a poor record in other things, such as explaining why people vote, why people give blood when they are not paid to do so, and why people consume more and more without significant increases in the life-satisfaction they report as a result of it.

## 4.3 Utility maximization, norms, and ethical values

If altruism, norms, and ethical values are important in reality, how can they be incorporated into the utility maximizing theory of behavior? If we think of the self-interested, optimizing consumer, we can introduce them into the theory either by incorporating them into people's preferences, or introducing them as constraints, while continuing to assume that they are maximizers of utility subject to the constraints they face.

Perhaps the simplest approach is to allow individual utility to depend on these norms and values, in addition to the amounts of material goods and services. An individual's compliance with a moral norm might be seen as generating a sense of satisfaction adding to the agent's welfare, while violating it might be seen as reducing that sense. This approach essentially reduces these values to a status which is comparable to that of goods and services. In essence, each of an individual's ethical norms has a price for which it can be bought: it may be weighted quite heavily among the bundle of preferred commodities, but there can be some finite quantity of other commodities that can lead an optimizer to choose to forgo adherence to the norm. As Goodin (1980, 136–7) argues, individuals who indeed seek to take their principles seriously would object to the failure to differentiate in quality norms from mundane desires.

A second approach to incorporating ethical values into the utility approach is to drop the assumption that individuals have a unique preference or utility function, and replace it by the assumption that they have multiple preferences, and rankings over them, which have been called meta-preferences. This meta-preference approach can incorporate various ideas about possibly conflicting preferences that individuals may have. Examples of this include the modeling of internal conflicts about personal choices concerning overeating and smoking, and conflicts between personal preferences and the preferences of others, and between self-interested preferences and preferences that include ethical considerations (for instance, conflicts between consuming something we enjoy and not consuming it because we think it morally wrong to do so because of the negative effect its production or consumption has on others). While some regard it to be a fruitful way of understanding the choices of morally induced people (see Margolis, 1982; Etzioni, 1987), the multiple-self and meta-preferences approach also raises some problems. Consistent preference rankings over preferences may reduce the approach to a standard utility theory approach, while attempts to allow for different preferences to be relevant in guiding choices in different circumstances introduces excessive mathematical complications and raises questions about what explains and determines the weight attached to the different preferences in these different situations (see Griffith and Goldfarb, 1991, 69n; Hausman and McPherson, 1996, 64).

A third approach treats ethical considerations as constraints rather than incorporating them into preferences. As in a budget constraint, norms would be seen as externally imposing (presumably from the conscience or superego) limits on available choices. Griffith and Goldfarb express concerns with this norms-as-constraints approach (Griffith and Goldfarb, 1991, 65–66). First, the comparison to budget constraints seems strained. While budget constraints may clearly be seen to impose an external limit on choices, normative constraints may in some way be external to the utility function, but they are evidently internalized in some important way. Also, unlike budget and other such purely external constraints, norms may be violated; therefore, the limits they impose are not rigid. Second, attempts to distinguish norms-as-constraints from norms-as-preferences are often a muddy task. On a psychological level, many who comply with norms will assert that doing so makes them feel better about themselves; such evaluations would seem to come dangerously close to the benefits one achieves by satisfying a pleasure. Finally, Griffith and Goldfarb question the analytical and predictive advantages of utilizing this framework. There is no mechanism described that might explain the why and how these constraints would emerge and what form they would take.

All of these methods of incorporating ethical values into the standard utility maximizing theory of the agent have been attempted and they all have some problematic features. Nevertheless, ethical behavior can be inserted into the approach. Moreover, there is nothing sacrosanct about the utility maximizing approach. One can examine individual behavior in terms of people using rules of thumb and other regular, but not unchanging, patterns of behavior which are actually observed, and which embody all kinds of norms, including ethical ones.

## 4.4 The nature of norms, ethical values, and individual conceptions of justice

If individuals are motivated by ethical values concerning fairness among other things, one can ask which notions of fairness and justice do they subscribe to. In the previous chapter we discussed alternative theories of justice. There have recently been several attempts to learn, using surveys and experiments, what people's views and behavior imply about which theories of justice they subscribe to. As reviewed by Konow (2003), several theories receive some support, but the evidence suggests that all of the approaches may have some relevance for actual behavior and, moreover, the notions of justice which affect behavior may be context-dependent.[14]

Regarding egalitarian and need-based theories, the support is mixed. In vignette studies of what is called micro-justice (fairness toward and among individuals), people often tend to support unequal outcomes; equal ones are preferred in special cases, for instance, when factors that are considered relevant for fairness are equal across people. Survey studies of macro-justice (that is, distributional justice at the societal level) frequently reveal strong opposition to complete or near equality of income. Evidence from ultimatum game experiments, however, seems to suggest that equality and need are considered important components of justice. In an ultimatum game, a proposer offers a share of a total amount of money (available to two players) to a responder, who can choose to accept, in which case the total is divided as proposed, or to reject in which no one gets anything at all. Experiments with these games show that players usually end up sharing the total roughly equally, although it would seem that optimizing, self-interested proposers would take a very high share and responders would agree to take the small share rather than get nothing at all. Moreover, experiments suggest that responders are more likely to accept low shares offered to them by proposers (who, unknown to them, are fictitious) who appeal to their own need. But surveys of macro-justice suggest that only 13 per cent of 1500 US respondents agree that a person's income should be based on family needs rather than skills. But the same study shows that a large minority (41 per cent) believes that it is fairer to pay people based on their living needs rather than on the kind of work they do.

Laboratory experiments involving university students who are introduced to different distributive rules (including maximum expected value of income and Rawls's difference principle) find scant support for the difference principle, and strongest support for a mixed rule which maximizes expected value subject to a constraint on the minimum income.

Regarding utilitarian approaches, the evidence is also mixed. Survey questionnaires suggest that although a large minority thinks it fairest to allocate goods according to the pleasure people derive from them, the majority thinks it best to split the goods equally. However, questionnaire respondents do seem to take into account how goods affect people in deciding on allocation, and not just dividing the goods equally. For instance, those surveyed chose an allocation with unequal quantities of food to people in order to equalize the total derived health benefit to them, and they also favored the equalization of people's psychic satisfaction rather than equalization of actual outcomes (in terms of goods). The focus on equalizing outcomes in terms of each individual's psychic utility seems to favor equality, rather than the utilitarian approach which would require equalizing marginal utility in order to maximize total utility. However, there seems to be a fair amount of support for efficiency in the Paretian sense. In experiments involving dictator games with anonymous counterparts, "dictators" must select between two allocations, one giving the two people the same and the other favoring unequal outcomes usually slightly greater for the other person, but having a total payoff to the two larger than the one with the equal division. Under these conditions people choose allocations that maximize the total surplus even at a small loss to themselves.[15] In terms of macro-justice, survey evidence suggests that a majority of Americans surveyed believe that in a fair economic system people with more ability would earn higher incomes, and that giving everyone the same income irrespective of the type of work they do would affect effort adversely, and therefore reduce efficiency.

Regarding equity and desert theories, again, the empirical support is mixed. Robert Nozick's principle of justice in transfer, discussed in the previous chapter, can be illustrated with his well-known example about the American basketball player Wilt Chamberlain. Nozick asks the reader to suppose an initial distribution which fully satisfies the reader's notion of justice, and then allows fans to voluntarily drop a separate admission price into a box for Chamberlain which results in his receiving a much higher level of income than at the initial distribution. Nozick then challenges the reader to find the new distribution unjust, since people moved to it with voluntary transfers. Updating the vignette with a current player, Konow asks US respondents whether the distribution after a voluntary transfer is fair. The majority found it unfair if the distribution follows the basketball season, and a still larger majority found it unfair if it preceded the season. Regarding desert, experiments and survey results imply that people think that it is fair to reward performance and effort, but for a given level of effort, rewards for good luck and inherited characteristics do not seem to be favored. In terms of choices, a survey of professionally active men suggests that professions requiring greater training or education deserve higher income, although the distribution thought desirable is less unequal than the actual distribution. Thus, experiments and surveys suggest that people support inequality based on people's responsibility for their contribution, but not for those factors outside his or her control.

In addition to notions of fairness based on theories of justice which refer to general principles, empirical work suggests that views of fairness are context-dependent. Kahneman et al. (1986a) develop a theory of fair transactions between firms (such as merchants, landlords, and employers) who are price setters and transactors (customers, tenants, and employees) who are price takers, which takes into consideration the history of the terms of transactions and what they call framing effects. Based on the past history, there are reference transactions characterized by a reference price and a reference profit (for the firm), to which transactors and firms, respectively, feel entitled. Transactors resist infringements on their reference price by the firm trying arbitrarily to increase their profits, but if firms' profits are threatened, they may be allowed to set new prices to protect their profits. Vignettes and questionnaires from telephone surveys in the United States suggest that firms are allowed to receive a positive profit, but not change the terms of the transaction arbitrarily, or even due to changes in opportunity costs and demand shifts, unless there is a change in their actual money costs. These context-dependent ideas of fairness imply that people psychologically adapt to a stable state of affairs, although what is stable may not always be considered what is fair, for instance if it emerges under conditions of limited competition in which one party has a disproportionate amount of power to influence the outcome. Nevertheless, in many cases reference prices and wages may have an influence on what is considered fair, for instance, regarding the level of the wage, or the relative wages for different occupations.[16]

This discussion of empirical results about theories of justice suggest that notions of what is fair is governed by many considerations, and no justice theory irrespective of context fits peoples' values best. Definitive conclusions on this issue cannot be drawn, not least because it is necessary to be cautious about extrapolating the results of surveys and experiments to how people actually behave in the real world. Views about what is fair are context-dependent, and the extent of adherence to a particular theory of justice within a pluralistic theory which gives some weight to all of them, is also affected by the context. However it is worth emphasizing that this kind of evidence does not tell us which of the alternative theories of justice is better in some sense and ought to be followed, but only which kind of theories is more consistent with people's actual beliefs and behavior. People's beliefs and behavior, as we have noted, are influenced by many factors, including the norms prevalent in a society, which do not necessarily have any legitimacy in normative terms.

## 4.5 Where norms and ethical values come from and why they change

Individuals acquire ethical values in a number of ways and the persistence of these values may be explained in a variety of ways. Extreme views include those that argue that people are inherently ethical, and those that argue that people are fundamentally self-interested and devoid of ethics, and agree to be ethical only for the sake of survival (a position consistent with that of Hobbes), and ethical values require no further explanation. Less extreme views include the following. Ethical norms may be the result of biological evolution: some kinds of behavior or people endowed with some characteristics which are ethical may have higher genetic survival chances and are therefore likely to persist. They may be ingrained by one's upbringing and may become matters of habit. They may be a matter of conscious choices based on abstract reasoning about right and wrong, which may or may not become completely internalized. They may be the result of seeking approval or avoiding condemnation and even retaliation by others and avoiding shame, although in this case it is easier to explain ethical acts which are observable by others rather than ethical traits which are not directly observable. They may also be driven by internal feelings of guilt. They may follow from one's religious faith. Religious traditions are almost universal in valuing ethics, not only in terms of proscriptions against bad actions, but also in terms of urging charity toward others, respect for nature, and even heroic selflessness and acts of self-sacrifice. These different motivations may also be interdependent: for instance, condemnation by others or feelings of guilt may be reinforced by religious beliefs, and religious beliefs may be the result of deliberate choices or one's upbringing and environment.

However, ethical values also change over time and they are also not universally applicable. For instance, some behaviors – such as marriage as opposed to cohabitation, or taking care of one's parents – may lose their ethical content over time, and the frequency of what continues to be seen as ethical behavior – such as lying or cheating – may change over time and over space. Some of the explanations and mechanisms discussed above are better able to explain these variations than others. Changes in the social environment may explain why some traits and behavior that once had survival value may not continue to do so, and therefore may disappear. For instance, if cooperative behavior within groups was once necessary for survival, the provision of social safety nets by the state may reduce the survival value of such behavior. Changes in the influence of religion in people's lives may explain why some ethical behaviors may emerge or disappear. Less interaction between people may result in people not being constrained by what others think of them, or feeling less guilty about doing things which potentially hurt people with whom one has little interaction. The number of people who follow some norms may also influence how likely it is that others will follow them. If there are many violators, the cost in terms of possible condemnation and retaliation by others will fall both because there are fewer people to sanction violations and because the chances of being noticed as a violator will be smaller (as the examples of taking bribes and cheating in examinations suggests). In some cases if most people violate some norms, there is a danger of incurring large costs by not following them. For instance, if most people cheat in examinations, by not cheating one may receive a low grade, whereas if few do so, it may not matter much. All of these cases explain why more people follow a norm when the number of followers of that norm is higher. It is also possible that in some cases not following an ethical norm may be more attractive if most people are following it: if most government officials are not corrupt, the potential return to becoming corrupt will be much higher because the supply of the "favor" will be small; and if the degree of adherence to ethical norms is high, the benefits from being recognized by others as a special person who is ethical is likely to be low. Economists are especially interested in how ethical behavior depends on the level of economic development, say as measured by the average per capita income. It is possible that at low levels of income people may be more likely to act unethically if by doing so it allows them to avoid extreme material deprivation or allows them to significantly increase their incomes (consider policemen with low salaries), especially if low-income countries do not have well-funded law enforcement systems. However, if relative income considerations are important, such behavior can also be expected to occur at much higher levels of income.

These examples suggest that there are multiple motivations people may have for following and not following ethical norms and being and not being ethical, and that the degree of adherence to ethical behavior may also change over time and vary across space, depending on a variety of factors. We will return to these issues when we discuss the social implications of ethical behavior in subsequent chapters.

## 4.6 Conclusion

This chapter has argued that the standard economists' conception of the individual as self-interested and rational in the sense of being optimizers is problematic. It is not at all clear that individuals are rational in the economists' sense, or that they even can be. Moreover, there is a great deal of evidence that suggests that people follow norms and care about others, and many of this reflects ethical values and behavior. Such behavior can be incorporated into the utility maximizing approach, but one would have to go beyond the idea of the purely self-interested individual. Studies of individual behavior show not only that people have ethical values and beliefs, but also that they have certain kinds of ethical values and ideas of fairness and justice depending on the particular context. Moreover, these values may change over time and space in more or less predictable ways. The main point is that people are not just self-interested, optimizing agents, but embody ethical values. The next two chapters will examine the implications of individual behavior which is influenced by ethics when individuals interact with others in society.

# 5
# Social Interactions and Ethical Values

## Introduction

We argued in the previous chapter that individuals have ethical values which influence how they behave. This chapter examines the implications of that behavior for societal outcomes. The outcomes, obviously, depend on how individuals interact with each other. Therefore the main task of this chapter is to examine how the interaction between individuals results in social outcomes, and what role ethical values have in the nature of these outcomes.

Even if we confine ourselves to economic issues, narrowly defined, such as consumption, production, and trade, there are many ways in which individuals interact. Thus, they may interact by sharing things with each other in a family, by making agreements with each other at meetings of firms and workers, by working with each other within a firm, and by buying and selling with each other in markets. Economists mostly focus on interactions in markets, but they also examine interactions in nonmarket spheres, such as in firms, groups, and families.

A technique that has been especially useful for economists in analyzing interactions in general – market and nonmarket ones – is game theory. In fact, game theory has been applied to a variety of contexts, including discussions of war and conflict (such as arms races, and interactions between governments and terrorists), political strategy, and social interactions. In this chapter we will use simple game theory to understand how individuals interact, what outcomes are produced by such interaction, and how ethical values affect these outcomes.

Section 5.1 discusses some general examples of how economic interactions may be affected by ethical norms and ethical behavior. Section 5.2

briefly describes games and the prisoners' dilemma and how games involving this dilemma lead to undesirable outcomes. Section 5.3 examines how ethical values and other considerations can overcome such undesirable outcomes. Section 5.4 discusses some issues connected with the emergence and dynamics of norms using game theory. Section 5.5 makes some concluding observations.

## 5.1 Interactions and ethical values

We begin our discussion with some examples of interactions and the role ethical values can play in affecting their outcomes.

First, consider interactions between two individuals (or two or more groups of individuals) who can cooperate with each other to produce something together and then divide what they produce among themselves. Examples of such possible cooperation may include a range of activities from actually producing goods and services together with a business partnership, a family through marriage, or a political or military coalition. Assume that individuals can devote their time to productive activity – which increases their joint production – or to activity which increases their likely share of the total output they produce. Thus individuals may spend more time on producing, or, for example, they may spend more time acquiring armaments or doing exercises to become stronger. The individuals cooperate to produce more together than the sum of what each could produce individually. If each individual is interested in the share of the output they get, they are both likely to spend some time producing and some time in ensuring that they get a decent share of the product. If they spend most of their time on getting a large share, instead of producing, the total pie will be too small. If they spend most of their time in production, they may be deprived of their share by a partner who becomes very powerful. They therefore end up getting less than what they would if they spent all their time on joint production. In this situation, if they trusted each other, or if they cared not just for what they obtained, but also what their partner obtained, at least to some extent, they would both end up getting more.

Second, consider interactions through markets, where goods are exchanged at prices determined in the market. Because of the large number of issues raised by examining market interactions explicitly, we will discuss them in the next chapter.

Third, we turn to the interaction between individuals within a firm. Consider a firm which employs workers and produces for the market. We will return to this case when we consider markets, since the employer–employee relation is in part a market relation. However, this relationship is not just a simple market relation. Unlike many markets in which the two parties enter into a transaction and that is the end of their relationship, the relationship here is very likely to be a relatively long-term one – even if it is for a month, but it is often for a year – and one in which the firm is not hiring a certain amount of labor services, but a certain number of explicit or implicit hours of labor. When the labor contract is made the employee knows his or her wage, but has not yet provided the labor services. The employer may not be able to monitor exactly how hard the employee works, especially in more complex jobs, even with supervisors, and the employee has a great deal of leeway about how much effort he or she will put into the job. The degree of effort, in turn, will depend on how the employee believes he or she is being treated by the firm. A symbol of this treatment is the wage paid to him or her, although other conditions of work also count. Akerlof (1982) likens this to a gift exchange: if employees believe that they are being well treated and well paid, they will in return be loyal to the employer and buy into the employer's goals. The main point is that if they believe they are unfairly treated, they will not be loyal and feel no sense of duty to get the job done; they will shirk and only work the least amount that they can get away with, and may even sabotage the production process. If, however, they feel that they are treated more than fairly, they will feel satisfied with their job and proud of working for the employer, and therefore put in a great deal of effort. The result will be that if employers believe that this is the way their employees will respond, they will pay a fair wage and will try to provide a good working environment. Productivity and wages would be higher than if they did not pay a fair wage and provide for good working conditions. Moreover, there are likely to be fewer labor–firm disputes, which will have a positive effect on efficiency.

Issues about fairness and trust are important not only in the relationship between the employer and the employees in a firm, but also in the relationships among employees. If there is an absence of trust between employees within a firm, overall labor productivity may be adversely affected. In some cases, especially, when there are different ethnic groups represented in the work force, there may be a low level of trust among workers in a firm. Firms may try to take advantage of the lack of trust among employees to keep wages low, by discriminating between workers from different ethnic groups in terms of wages paid. Although firms may be able to set employees against each other, and thereby even to raise productivity by threatening favored workers with lower wages and providing the incentive to low-paid workers to raise their wages, the resulting climate may be one which is considered unfair, and which may reduce productivity for the firm overall.

Fourth, consider nonmarket relations between firms which are located in one region and which can potentially share technological knowledge. It has been found that firms in a particular industrial area – sometimes called an industrial district – can benefit by drawing on each other's technical knowledge based on what each learns through experience. This is more likely to happen if there develops trust between firms which allows them to exchange knowledge. Using the concept of social capital, Putnam has argued that participation and trust are mutually dependent: "The theory of social capital presumes that, generally speaking, the more we connect with other people, the more we trust them, and vice versa" (Putnam, 1995, 665). As firms trust each other, they can draw on each other's technological knowledge and speed up technological change. This process has been used as an explanation of the success of industrial districts in Italy (see Pyke, et al., 1992) and elsewhere. The process can be explained in terms of simple game theoretic analysis (see below) in which individuals care about each other. However, in business and other relationships, problems may arise because firms are engaged in competition in some spheres (for instance, in competing for markets and skilled workers), and individuals and firms who form associations can harm society by adversely affecting third parties, as in the case of organizations like the Ku Klux Klan and business cartels.

As a final example, consider the issue of managing common property resources. In the widely discussed problem called the tragedy of the commons, it is argued that if there is open access to resources, individuals will overuse them, and the result will be that all individuals will be worse off. A standard solution to this problem that is often recommended is the privatization of common property resources. Some would consider privatization to be inequitable. But is it always efficient? Many common property resources are what are called local common property resources – such as fish stocks, forests, and grazing lands to which relatively few people, who live in an area, have access – rather than global common property resources, such as the global environment, which is relevant for the global warming problem. Many economists recommend that for the efficient use of these local common property resources, these resources should also be privatized and be owned by individuals. What this overlooks is the fact that, as discussed by Ostrom (1991) and others, in several parts of the less-developed world communities have established informal systems of cooperation which overcome the commons problem through the development of trust relationships. Introducing private property into these communities can destroy these trust networks and impose costs which can lead to inefficient outcomes, for instance, by increasing costs of guarding individual private property. Game theoretic models and other analyses have been developed to illustrate these issues (see, for instance, Seabright, 1993, 2004).

## 5.2 Games and the prisoner's dilemma

Game theory is concerned with the analysis of situations in which, usually, individuals interact with other individuals and it addresses how individuals behave and what the outcome of such behavior is for all individuals.[1] A game is defined by its *players*, the *actions* open to each player, and the outcomes of each action (by each of the players) for each player, called the player's *payoffs*. Games can be expressed in two forms: strategic or normal form games and extensive games. The latter examine moves made by the players, sequentially and one at a time, and are depicted using tree diagrams which show the payoffs for the players after each move by a player. For our purposes it is more useful to examine normal form games which are depicted by tables showing the payoffs for the players for each action by each player. Games are of two basic types – cooperative and noncooperative games. The former applies to situations in which binding agreements between the players can be made and are fully enforceable. The latter applies to situations when these assumptions cannot be made. Here we will only examine noncooperative games.[2]

A simple game with two players with two actions each is shown in Table 5.1. The two players are the row player and the column player (so called here because the strategies of the two are shown in the rows and

*Table 5.1* A simple game

| | | Column | Player |
|---|---|---|---|
| | | Cooperate | Defect |
| Row | Cooperate | 3, 3 | 0, 4 |
| Player | Defect | 4, 0 | 1, 1 |

columns, respectively). Each player has two possible actions, cooperate or defect, which refer to whether they decide to abide by an informal agreement they made to cooperate or they decide not to. The payoffs are shown with the numbers in the four cells. By convention, the first number shows the payoff to the row player and the second to the column player. Thus, if the row player cooperates and the column player defects, the row payer gets a payoff of 0 and the column payer gets a payoff of 4. The payoffs may be amounts of money or goods, or may refer to the utility (utils) each player obtains.

This simple game may be "played" only once, in which case it is called a one-shot game, or it may be repeated, in which case it is called a repeated game.[3] If it is repeated forever, the game is called an infinitely repeated game. In repeated games the sequence of actions for a player can be represented as a *strategy*, which gives a complete characterization of the actions of the player in each move. Examples of strategies include: always cooperate; always defect; toss a coin before every move and cooperate if you get heads and defect if you get tails; and start by cooperating and continuing to cooperate if the other player cooperates, but if the other player defects in any move, defect and continue defecting forever, or until the end of the game (a strategy that is called tit for tat). In the case of repeated games the overall payoff to a player is usually obtained by adding up the payoffs for all moves after converting them to their present value using a time discount factor which reduces the value of future payoffs.[4]

One can look for a solution to a game in several ways. One is to look for equilibrium solutions, the most well-known of which is the Nash equilibrium, named after John Nash (b. 1928), the American Nobel Prize-winning economist and mathematician. The Nash equilibrium is an array of strategies, one for each player, such that no player has an incentive to deviate from that strategy since he or she cannot increase his or her payoff by adopting a different strategy, given the strategy adopted by the others.[5] Notice that this concept of equilibrium involves a notion of rationality since players try to do the best for themselves by maximizing their payoff given what others do. But it is not specific about what the payoffs represent: are they amounts of goods and services, are they levels of utility, and do they involve self-interested behavior in the sense that the players only care about themselves (since their payoffs may reflect what other players receive, a point to which we will return below). This notion of rationality will imply that the players will actually choose the strategies associated with the Nash equilibrium. Sometimes there may be multiple Nash equilibria, in which case additional considerations need to be introduced to attempt to find a unique equilibrium.

In the one-shot game shown in Table 4.1 the Nash equilibrium occurs where both players defect and receive payoffs of 1. Neither player will have an incentive to change his or her strategy given what the other player is doing, since by so doing (moving to cooperate) they will obtain a payoff of 0. Note that the players both receive a payoff of 3 if they both cooperate, and both are better off cooperating than they are by defecting. However, the outcome in which both players cooperate is not a Nash equilibrium, since both players will have an incentive to defect and try to increase their payoff to 5. None of the other two possible outcomes, in which one player cooperates and the other player defects, is a Nash equilibrium. For instance, in the outcome in which the row player defects and the column player cooperates, the column player can gain by defecting, since his/her payoff by defecting, that is, 1, is higher than his/her payoff by cooperating, that is, 0, when the row player defects.

What makes this simple game very interesting is that the unique Nash equilibrium, in which they both defect, will be the outcome when both players choose their "rational" strategy, but it leaves them both worse off than they would be if both cooperated. If we evaluate what is socially optimal in terms of Pareto optimality, the Nash equilibrium is not a Pareto optimal state, while the Pareto optimal state (where both cooperate and both players are better off than at the Nash equilibrium) is not a Nash equilibrium. This type of game, in which the individual optimization of "rational" agents leads to an undesirable social outcome (which is not Pareto optimal) is called a Prisoner's dilemma game.[6]

Not all games are Prisoner's dilemma games. For some, the Nash equilibrium may also be a Pareto optimal outcome. But situations analogous to the Prisoner's dilemma game may be quite common in the real world. Cooperation may be good for both players if they both cooperate and therefore they may agree to cooperate. But if one player does cooperate and the other player, who has the temptation to break the agreement, does so, the first player becomes a "sucker" and loses a great deal. If agreements are not enforceable, then both players may try to play it safe and break the agreement, to avoid being a sucker. Suppose we interpret the payoffs as amounts of goods and services or money each player obtains, or their utility level which depends positively on what they get. Then having the objective of maximizing their payoff amounts is what we called self-interest. Why, in general, does self-interest not lead to the socially optimal outcome which is Pareto optimal as it does under certain conditions for the perfectly competitive market outcome?

This happens because each player in the game knows that what they do will affect the other player, and vice versa, and will therefore take this into account in making their decisions about what they do. In other words, the two players interact strategically. In perfectly competitive markets each player is so "small" that they assume that what they do will not affect anyone else, and can therefore ignore the reactions to their actions when they decide what to do. Thus, problems arising from strategic interactions do not arise.[7]

## 5.3 How ethics and other factor affect outcomes in games

Let us suppose that the prisoner's dilemma problem arises in many cases of economic (and other) interactions between people. If individuals are self-interested, socially suboptimal results may well occur. Under what conditions can we avoid such undesirable outcomes? Economists and other game theorists have discussed a variety of possibilities.

One possibility is that we find a third party which can enforce agreements and contracts. The obvious third party is the government and the legal system. The very existence of such an enforcement mechanism may be able to overcome the problem of breaking agreements, and if they are still broken, the player who has been wronged can sue. While this is clearly a possibility in many cases, for various kinds of interactions the payoffs may be relatively small in comparison to the costs of litigation (and the uncertainty of the outcome of the lawsuit) to make this solution practicable. Moreover, this solution may be inequitable if the chances of winning a lawsuit depend positively on how much money is at the disposal of the litigants.

Another possibility which has received a great deal of attention is that cooperation is more likely to occur if there are repeated interactions in which a prisoner's dilemma-type game is played infinitely many times and if people do not discount future payoffs too heavily. The reason why two players are more likely to cooperate in this case is that each self-interested player will take into account the fact that the other player may punish him or her if they defect and make them into suckers by refusing to cooperate in the future. This refusal will make their payoffs in the future lower than they would be if both parties cooperate. If the discount factor is not high (that is, players do not discount future payoffs too heavily because they are impatient), there will be little temptation to make a killing now by breaking an agreement. The psychologist Robert Axelrod has found, using strategies that were sent to him by contestants in response to his announcement, that the strategy that provides the highest payoffs in repeated interactions in a round robin in which every contestant plays every other contestant (in a computer simulation), that the tit-for-tat strategy does best in terms of total payoffs. Axelrod's argument is open to some technical criticisms which need not detain us here. But it is a powerful argument that suggests repeated interactions may sustain behavior which can promote cooperation from self-interested people who do not have any values or norms which induce them to cooperate in a way that is against their self-interest. It also leads to some practical suggestions on how to encourage this form of cooperation, for instance, by encouraging repeated and frequent interactions between people. However, there are problems that may arise with this form of interaction in the real world. If players interact with each other only a few times, or only once, because they are likely to interact with many others in an increasingly globalized world, then the assumption of an infinitely repeated game will not hold. Moreover, if someone is made a sucker and destroyed economically or even physically, then the game will not be repeated with the same payoffs. Further, sometimes a player may interpret a move by the other player as defection, but actually the move was unavoidable, because external circumstances prevented the player from delivering on his or her promise, resulting in a series of retaliatory defections. There are ways around some of these problems, for instance the problem of not having repeated interaction can be addressed through concern for one's reputation by word of mouth and ratings published on the internet, but these need not always result in more cooperation if reputations and ratings can be falsified or are unfair.

A third possibility is that we address the issue that strategic interaction is one of the sources of the problem and change the situation from one in which there are two (or a few) players to one with many players. In this case each individual player becomes too small relative to the entire playing field to have any effect on the other players and hence elicit a response. This change can be achieved by breaking down barriers to entry and by encouraging entry by other buyers and sellers. An example would be to allow more competition from foreign sellers. While this may work in some cases in removing suboptimal equilibria, it will not always do so, as when there are positive feedbacks in the form of externalities. In such cases, society as a whole may end up with socially nonoptimal outcomes even with people pursuing their self-interest. For instance, if people find it beneficial for them to use QWERTY keyboards on their computers (over an alternative, the DVORAK keyboard) and if the number of people already using it is large (which means that they are more familiar with them and that there are many stores which will repair them), everyone may end up using QWERTY keyboards and the DVORAK keyboard will die out, even if the latter allows people to type more quickly, and society would be better off if everyone used it (see David, 1985).

Although these three solutions, and others, may increase cooperation, ethical values also can improve social outcomes. We discuss three possibilities. First, suppose individuals are ethical in the sense that they decide not to tell a lie (not even in response to someone else lying to them). Then, if they say that they will cooperate, they will cooperate. Thus, even without repeated interactions and without government enforcement, the prisoner's dilemma situation will result in people choosing the cooperative solution. This solution will actually be beneficial for both parties even from their self-interested point of view, even if they get no additional utils from keeping their promises and not lying – something that they constrain themselves never to do. Players here do not tell lies not because they want the socially optimal outcome but because they intrinsically value not telling lies. And the result of not telling lies is instrumentally good by making the society more efficient.

Second, suppose that people care about other people, so that their payoffs reflect not only their self-interest, but also what others get. Suppose they value what others get just like they value what they get, then the game of Table 5.1 will be converted from a prisoner's dilemma game to one in which the Nash equilibrium is socially optimal, as shown in Table 5.2. In this game we add the payoff received by the two players for each pair of actions in Table 5.1 and give them to each. For instance, if both players cooperate, and both players are virtuous in the sense discussed here, both will receive payoffs of 6, that is, 3 from what they get and 3 from what the other does. Clearly, cooperation by both becomes

*Table 5.2* A game with altruistic individuals

| | | Column Player | |
|---|---|---|---|
| | | Cooperate | Defect |
| Row | Cooperate | 6, 6 | 4, 4 |
| Player | Defect | 4, 4 | 2, 2 |

the Nash equilibrium. It is also socially optimal if we use the payoffs shown in this table, and we get it even if one views social optimality in terms of self-interested utilities. Note that "full" altruism in the sense that we care about others as much as we care about ourselves is not necessary to get this result.

In fact, suppose we weigh other people's self-interested payoff only half as much as we weigh our own, we get the payoffs shown in Table 5.3, and again the Nash equilibrium will be socially optimal in both senses. What if the extent of people's altruism in this sense is different? Suppose that the row player is fully altruistic in our sense, but the column player weighs the row player's self-interested payoff only half as much as his/her own. In that case the payoffs will be as shown in Table 5.4. For instance, if both players cooperate, they both receive self-interested utils of 3, which implies that the row players utility level will be $6 = 3 + 3$ and the column players, $4.5 = 3 + (1/2)3$. But even in this case we can see that the unique Nash equilibrium will involve both players cooperating, and both getting their highest levels of self-interested utility.

*Table 5.3* A game with partially altruistic individuals

| | | Column | Player |
|---|---|---|---|
| | | Cooperate | Defect |
| Row | Cooperate | 4.5, 4.5 | 2, 4 |
| Player | Defect | 4, 2 | 1.5, 1.5 |

*Table 5.4* A game with individuals with different levels of altruism

| | | Column | Player |
|---|---|---|---|
| | | Cooperate | Defect |
| Row | Cooperate | 6, 4.5 | 4, 4 |
| Player | Defect | 4, 2 | 2, 1.5 |

Third, consider the ethical value that one should not be envious. Sometimes prisoner's dilemma situations arise not because of the absolute amounts people receive, but because their payoffs reflect envy in the sense that they care about what they get relative to what others get. Tables 5.5 and 5.6 illustrate this situation. Table 5.5 shows the self-interested utility levels that the two obtain from their actions. It can be seen that the unique Nash equilibrium involves both people cooperating, with each player obtaining a level of self-interested utility of 7; we can think of these as amounts of income. Now suppose that the two players are also interested not just in their income, but also what they receive relative to what the other player receives. Suppose, more specifically, that each player's utility is their own income plus four times their income relative to that of the other player. In other words, we have

$$U_i = Y_i + 4(Y_i/Y_j), \quad \text{for} \quad i \neq j$$

where $U_i$ denotes the utility level of player $i$, $Y_i$ the income level of player $i$, and player $j$ is the other player. The amended game with the

*Table 5.5* A game without envy

| | | Column | Player |
|---|---|---|---|
| | | Cooperate | Defect |
| Row | Cooperate | 7, 7 | 3, 6 |
| Player | Defect | 6, 3 | 2, 2 |

*Table 5.6* A game with envy

| | | Column | Player |
|---|---|---|---|
| | | Cooperate | Defect |
| Row | Cooperate | 11, 11 | 5, 14 |
| Player | Defect | 14, 5 | 6, 6 |

payoffs embodying this form of envy or relative concerns is shown in Table 5.6. For instance, when the row player cooperates and the column player defects, the row player receives an income of 3 and the column player gets 6. The row player's utility level is then $3 + 4(3/6) = 5$, and the column player's is $6 + 4(6/3) = 14$.[8] It is easy to see that in this case the unique Nash equilibrium is one in which both players defect. Neither player will wish to move to "cooperate" because their level of utility will fall from 6 to 5. However, the Pareto optimal outcome in which both players are better off than at the Nash equilibrium – in which both cooperate – is not a Nash equilibrium because both player will have an incentive to defect and increase their utility from 11 to 14. The modified game is therefore a prisoner's dilemma game. This example shows that if one introduces concern for relative income into a game one can convert it from one which does not exhibit the prisoner's dilemma problem to one that does. It follows that if people are not envious in the sense discussed here, they may both be better off in terms of income and utility (even if this utility includes concern for relative income in the evaluation of the outcome, but not in terms of influencing how people act) even if they obtain no additional utility by being good in the sense of not being envious.

## 5.4 Games and the emergence of norms and ethical values

Game theory can also be, and has been, used to understand issues concerning the emergence and persistence of norms and ethical values. We commented on some general considerations concerning this in Section 4.5 of the previous chapter. In this section we make some brief comments about how what are called evolutionary games can shed light on the evolution of norms and ethical values.

An evolutionary game is a game in which there are several types of players, for instance, in prisoner's dilemma games, those who always cooperate, those who always defect, or in other games, those who are always hawks (who initiate aggressive behavior and not stop it till they get injured or the other backs down) or always doves (retreat whenever an opponent attacks). These players are therefore not optimizers, but follow fixed strategies. The game is played many times, but it is not a repeated game in the usual sense, because the number of players of each type can change over different iterations of the game. The evolutionary feature of this game is that the number of players of each type changes over time according to the payoffs they receive in a particular round. In a particular round the players are assumed to interact with each other following some rules of interaction – such as those involving random pairings of individuals. Players who follow a strategy with a higher return increase in number while those who do less well find their numbers diminish. In natural evolution this type of dynamics occurs because of fitness to the environment and the transmission of genes through biological reproduction. In economic and social phenomena the dynamic may be the result not only of reproduction through habit formation and family upbringing, but also of conscious choices by individuals who change their strategies to emulate more successful ones.

The outcomes of such models have been explored in two main ways. The first method is by finding evolutionary stable strategies, where a strategy is defined as evolutionarily stable if players using it do better against itself than does any other strategy. More formally, we start with a situation in which a particular strategy is played by all players and then a small number of "mutant" players enter the game playing a different strategy. The initial situation is evolutionarily stable if these other strategies do not do better against the first and thereby progressively reduce the number of players using the initial strategy. A second method is by specifying explicitly the dynamics of population shares to see where the dynamic system leads to. The dynamics of population shares of player types may follow different patterns, with one type of player dominating, or with different types of players coexisting, or with cycles in which the share of one type of player increases and then falls, and the process continues in this way.

Axelrod (1984) has shown that if people adopt strategies which, on average, yield higher payoffs in infinitely repeated interactions in one round, more and more people will adopt the tit-for-tat strategy in subsequent rounds, which will result in everyone cooperating (since, according to this strategy, everyone cooperates till someone else does not) although their strategy is not, in fact, always to cooperate. Moreover, an "invasion" by a small number of players who follow a different strategy would not dislodge this equilibrium, making it stable in the limited sense in which the strategy does no worse when played against itself as it does when played against some other strategy. Axelrod uses this to argue that the tit-for-tat strategy will drive out other strategies like "always defect." In fact, everyone will always cooperate, although they will not actually be playing the strategy "always cooperate" but rather the tit-for-tat strategy. People will not be following the golden rule but rather use a rule of retaliating if others do, but everyone will actually be living by the golden rule.[9] This model seeks to explain how cooperation may evolve in a system with prisoners dilemma games which are infinitely repeated and when people do not discount the future too much, even when they are purely self-interested.

Another example which shows how ethical norms can emerge can be found in an evolutionary game in which people compete for shares in a good which can be divided among them. Assume that there is competition between two players in each round and that if their claims are compatible (that is, their claimed shares add up to a number less than or equal to unity) they get what they claim, and if they are not (their shares exceed unity) they wind up fighting and getting nothing.[10] Suppose players of a particular type follow the strategy of asking for a particular share of the good. To make the model simple, assume further that there are only four types of players who ask for, respectively, 1, $\frac{2}{3}$, $\frac{1}{2}$, and $\frac{1}{3}$, of the good. Then assume that different types of players meet randomly and play the game against each other. At one step of the game, the entire population of players comprises the four fixed types, and their interactions lead to some payoffs. For instance, if one who wants $\frac{2}{3}$ meets one who wants $\frac{1}{2}$, no one gets anything, and if one who wants $\frac{1}{2}$ meets a player of the same type, both will get payoffs of $\frac{1}{2}$, and if one who wants $\frac{1}{2}$ meets one who wants $\frac{1}{3}$, they will each take what they want and the remaining $\frac{1}{6}$ will go to waste. Suppose the number of people who follow a strategy which does better in terms of their payoffs increases in each subsequent step of the game. Depending on the details of the dynamics, it can be shown that the dynamics of the system will evolve to one in which everyone wants $\frac{1}{2}$, and that this equilibrium is also evolutionarily stable. Thus, while fairness in division can be justified on abstract theoretical grounds, it can also be shown to evolve using this type of evolutionary game-theoretic model.

## 5.5 Conclusion

Our discussion of how ethical values can affect outcomes has a number of implications. First, the presence of ethical values, which relate to virtues – such as not being envious and caring for others – and to actions – such as not telling lies – may be able to transform social outcomes which are ethically bad to ones that are ethically good. Second, these ethical values may be virtue-related or deontological at the level of the individual, but the good that occurs for society as a whole may be ethical in a consequentialist sense or even utilitarian sense of bringing about the highest level of utility for the highest number. This illustrates the problem that we encountered in Chapter 3 when we tried to classify ethical and justice theories neatly into separate groups. Third, there is no guarantee that good people and good acts will necessarily improve social outcomes in this sense. For instance, if some people are virtuous or do good acts, while others are not and do not, it is not clear that everyone will be better off in the sense of obtaining higher levels of utility. Moreover, if some people do good by helping others, and that reduces the incentives for the latter to help themselves (something that the former did not foresee), it is possible that everyone will get lower payoffs. But that does not detract from the goodness of these acts or these virtues in a nonconsequentialist sense. Trying to obtain high levels of self-interested utility is not the motivation for being good or doing good in the virtue or deontological sense: if it were, these people would be consequentialist and in fact be a member of the *homo economicus*.

Finally, regarding game theory, the models often used in that approach can be argued to be both too narrow and too general. The games that have been discussed in this section and the previous one are very narrow in terms of the assumptions made about the environment in which the individuals interact. For instance, individuals have a given number of actions, the actions have certain outcomes in terms of payoffs, the payoffs are known to both individuals and known to be known by them, individuals do not have outside options, and the notion of rationality used is open to question. The games are also too general and nonspecific because they do not specify clearly the actual behavior of individuals in actual institutional settings. While some of the assumptions of simple games can be modified in games with more complicated structures, and game theoretical models can be applied to more specific settings, it is an open question to what extent a particular game captures the essence of situations of strategic interaction between individuals in actual economies and societies. There may be no absolute answer to this question, but there is no doubt that game theory models can formalize many kinds of interactions between individuals and show how norms and ethical values can affect outcomes, sometimes making them better in a precise sense, and therefore provide a powerful tool to analyze the role of ethics in individual interactions. However, there are deeper debates about solution concepts used in games, which may limit the applicability of various game theory models, an issue which is too complex to discuss here.

# 6
# Markets and Ethical Values

## Introduction

Chapter 4 examined the idea that individuals are not simply self-interested, optimizing agents, but may have emotions, feelings, and in fact have ethical values. It also briefly discussed where individuals' ethical values come from, and why they possibly change. Chapter 5 examined the relevance of ethical values for interactions between individuals, but did so in fairly general terms, to a large extent using the tools of game theory. This chapter continues with the examination of the relevance of ethics for interactions between individuals, but in the specific context of interactions in markets, arguably the most important institution of modern economies. We will explore how the fact that individuals have ethical values affects markets in which these individuals participate. It will also examine how participation in markets affects the ethical values that individuals hold.

These issues are complicated ones, not least because it is not at all obvious what a market is, how it functions, and how a market affects people. Much of standard mainstream economics takes a view of markets in which ethical values have no role to play. But even a little reflection suggests that the market is actually a very complex institution in terms of what it is, how it operates, and how it affects people.

We will start, in Section 6.1, with a brief discussion of markets, beginning with the orthodox view in which ethics do not enter, and then introducing ways in which ethical values may matter to the study of markets. This discussion of markets will allow us to explore, in Section 6.2, how markets are affected by the existence of ethical values, and in Section 6.3 how, in turn, participation in markets affects people's ethical values. We will find that these effects are highly controversial.

Some argue that the presence of ethical values is required for markets to operate properly, and others to argue that the values interfere with the smooth working of markets. Some argue that markets strengthen morals while others argue that they are often destructive of ethical values. These different views, in fact, lead some analysts to question the goodness of the market, and others to extol its virtues. This overall evaluation of markets, however, will be postponed till the next chapter. Section 6.4 will offer some conclusions.

## 6.1 Markets

The standard view of markets which is to be found in most introductory textbooks in economics, and even in scholarly research, is that they are collections of buyers and sellers who interact with each other to trade in goods and services and money at market prices. The individual buyers and sellers may be households and firms or individual people and, as mentioned earlier, the standard view is that of the *homo economicus*, the self-interested, optimizing buyer and seller. In each market individuals trade in a single good or service (and in a few applications, in closely related goods or services which vary in quality), and the number of buyers and sellers can range from one of each to many of each. Usually, the operation of the market establishes a single price of the good or service (though in a few cases multiple prices may coexist). Individuals buy and sell these goods and services voluntarily, given their resources, their preferences, and their technologies. If markets are perfectly competitive, and are free markets, they (at least under certain conditions) result in efficient outcomes, in the sense that no one in the market can be made better off without making someone else worse off.

This description of the market does not involve use of the word ethics or values. Indeed, self-interested optimizing individuals do not have any ethical values. It is self-interest that makes people better off. Nor is there any need to discuss ethical values in this depiction of markets, since markets seem to work smoothly and achieve good results for society, without people having any ethical values.

There are at least four ways that this view, in which ethical values are absent, is problematic. First, if people do have ethical values, it does not make much sense to examine how markets operate by assuming that market participants are driven only by self-interested calculations and are not affected by ethical values. Real-world markets could operate very differently from markets in which individuals have no ethical values. Second, removing ethical values from the analysis may be inconsistent with the rest of the theory of markets, which requires ethical values to exist so as to prevent stealing, cheating, and breaking contracts. To the extent this is true, these values need to be taken into consideration in analyzing markets. Third, ignoring ethical values may provide us with an incomplete picture of society, leading us to ignore some destructive features of society as a whole (of which markets are a part). Under certain conditions which have prevailed in the past and which still exist in many parts of the world today, markets produce terrible conditions for some people who participate in them. For instance, if firms are driven only by the profit motive, they will try to produce as cheaply as possible, and make workers labor under extremely unsafe and unsanitary conditions, make children work as well, and in fact make people work almost as slaves. Employers may be able to do such things because laborers have very few employment opportunities, and because a few firms may band together to create monopsony power for their advantage. The fact that employers do not always do such things may be the result of their personal ethical values, ethical values embedded in the culture, and laws and regulations imposed by government. Markets have been regulated by governments to prevent such excesses from occurring, and these regulations have been a response to social and political movements which result from the ethical values of people. Finally, if we do introduce ethical values into the analysis of markets, we need to ask if and how these values are affected in turn by people's participation in markets.

If the standard economics depiction of the market is incomplete, how should one reconceptualize it to take ethical values into account? The virtue of the standard approach is its simplicity, but perhaps this simplicity is not an advantage if it involves oversimplification and leaves out essential features of markets. Is it possible to develop a more complex conceptualization of markets which allows us to introduce ethical values into the discussion of markets without making the analysis too complicated? A useful way of characterizing markets is suggested by Anderson (1990a, 184) in terms of five (to some extent related) characteristics of the market. First, market relations are impersonal ones. In other words, buyers and sellers are strangers and have no obligations to each other apart from fulfilling the terms of their sales contract, their only involvement being the exchange of monetary equivalents. Second, the market is understood to be a sphere in which one is free, within the bounds of the law, to pursue one's personal advantage unrestrained by any consideration of the advantage of others. Third, the goods traded on the market are exclusive and rivals in consumption. People can be excluded from having or using them if they do not pay for them, and more than one person cannot use the good at the same time. Fourth, the market is purely want-regarding: from its standpoint all matters of value are simply matters of personal taste of people with purchasing power, and not affected by the intensity of need. Finally, dissatisfaction with a commodity or market relation is expressed primarily by "exit," not "voice."[1]

Not all markets, of course, satisfy all these properties. Thus, in some markets, impersonal or arms–length relationships may be replaced by more personal ones, especially in the case of long-term buyer–seller arrangements. Also, markets can exist for goods which are not "naturally" excludable, for instance by government-enforced legal means, such as in the case of cable television, patents, and copyrights. However, these properties can be argued to correspond to an ideal type of market, both in the sense of Max Weber's ideal type which stresses elements common to most markets, and in the sense that some people argue that it produces the ideal outcome in the sense of an efficient outcome.

The exercise of individual freedom in the context of the market (as characterized by these five features) provides the valuation of commodities as what Anderson (1990a) calls "use," which she contrasts with three other modes of valuation. First, in the market commodities are used to further one's own ends (to obtain higher levels of utility for individuals) rather than given a higher form of regard, such as respect, which refers to the intrinsic value a good or service may have. This is analogous to Kant's distinction between using people as means and respecting them as ends. In fact, the market values people only to the extent they further other people's ends, that is, the maximization of their profit and utility. Second, use is an impersonal mode of valuation, rather than one which values something for personal, sentimental, or symbolic reasons, such as heirlooms, wedding rings, and gifts from special friends. In the market commodities are interchangeable and equivalent, while in personal valuation they are unique and irreplaceable. Third, use values resulting from private acts of use can be contrasted with shared values, in which one values things according to how others enjoy them, and which requires a shared public understanding of the meaning of the goods. While in the next chapter we will return to these issues to examine some specific applications of Anderson's approach to different types of exchange, in this chapter we will refer to it to discuss the effects of markets on values.

## 6.2 How ethical values affect markets

The discussion of how ethical values affect markets usually takes one of two perspectives. One perspective starts from the premise that markets run into problems if people do not have ethical values and focuses on how the presence of ethical values can overcome these problems. The other perspective questions the theory of the market without ethical values to argue that it portrays actual markets in an excessively favorable light, and argues that the presence of ethical values results in problems with the smooth operation of the market. Let us consider each in turn.

The first perspective can be clearly understood by asking why, if people are in fact self-interested agents, they stop at making the sales and purchases most advantageous to themselves: why do they not steal from other people, and cheat them when they interact, to further their own interests? Of course people do cheat and steal in the real world, but most do not. One can argue that this is because there are laws and government enforcement which prevent more of such activities. However, people can and do break laws, bribe government officials, and do all kinds of things to get their own way, and there are many gray areas in law. If cheating, robbery, and stealing and making use of the gray areas are rampant, markets will break down, because consumers will not buy things which others will steal from them, producers will not store inputs and products because they will get stolen, and buyers and sellers will not wish to trade if everyone cheats everyone else. Perhaps they do not cheat and steal because they have ethical values which induce them to be virtuous and to not commit ethically "bad" acts?

The appropriation by some people of the property of others may directly interfere with markets because people's economic incentives to produce, trade, and purchase goods will be reduced. Also, reneging on contracts or outright cheating and lying in trade can prevent markets from developing. Although many economists tend to think of markets as natural and take them for granted, noneconomists, including historians and sociologists, have recognized the importance of developing institutions and trust for the emergence and continuation of trade, especially for long-distance trade. Sociologists have emphasized the social embeddedness of markets (Granovetter, 1985). Economic historians have focused on how long-distance trade required the development of trust and institutions: Greif (1997), for instance, has examined the role of these factors in early long-distance trade.

To the extent that economists have dealt with some of these issues, they have often incorporated them into the catchall concept of transaction cost which, while sometimes emphasizing important problems and issues, has relegated important considerations into a tautological black box. More interesting specific ideas have emerged from the notion of asymmetric information. This concept has been used to analyze why, when buyers and sellers have access to different types of information, markets may disappear altogether. Akerlof (1970) considers the case of "lemons" in markets for used cars. Suppose that there is a market for used cars in which sellers know the quality of the car they are selling, but buyers do not. Suppose that buyers know only the average quality of the cars being sold in the market, and therefore they will be willing to pay only for the average quality car. Sellers who have high-quality cars to sell know this and will refuse to sell their cars, and instead, leave the market and hold on to their cars. As the sellers of good quality cars leave the market, buyers will know that the average quality of cars in the market deteriorates, and offer still lower prices, and this process may continue till no cars remain in the market and the market disappears. The very fact that this process will be expected to occur may prevent the market from appearing in the first place.

There may be ways in which this problem of missing markets may be overcome by individual actions or by government intervention, for instance, by sellers providing guarantees, buyers getting cars inspected, or with lemons laws. These fixes, while they may reduce the problem, may not completely eliminate it because guarantees are usually not unconditional and litigation may be expensive. Ethical values can clearly play a role in allowing markets to exist, to the benefit of both sellers and buyers.

The fact that ethical values are needed for the smooth operation of markets, and sometimes to have them operate at all, does not imply that the appropriate ethical values that overcome these problems are actually held by people. However, the fact that markets do exist and seem to function, and have done so from antiquity, suggests that people who operate in markets do have ethical values and bring them to the market, so to speak. Those ethical values can be reinforced by adding social mechanisms to reinforce them, such as professional codes and associations for handling buyer complaints.

The awareness of asymmetric information that exists between buyer and seller results in market failures that could be remedied if benevolence could be brought into the picture. If used-car salespersons possessed a justified history of honest and straightforward dealings, the distortions resulting from buyers' fears of being sold a "lemon" might be mitigated. Indeed, Hirschman (1977, 300), following Arrow (1972), points to professional codes of ethics, such as that of surgeons not to perform unnecessary operations, as manifestations of institutionalized benevolence. The professional code seeks to dissuade the surgeons from exploiting their informational advantage in the pursuit of self-interest.

This is not to say that surgeons never perform unnecessary operations but that there would be even more if these codes did not exist. Should these codes become eliminated or ineffective, the additional costs of independent oversight would be substantial. That such codes do not exist among used-car salespersons only exacerbates many customers' fears that they are purchasing a possible lemon.

It can be argued that successful market economies are precisely those that have in place the social institutions and legal structures to keep in check the destructive excesses of self-interested dealings. The transactions-cost literature can be seen as evidence of business enterprises' recognition and attempt to mitigate the effects of opportunism in trade. The emergence of the modern corporate firm transforms open-market relationships into ones handled within a hierarchical structure of governance and authority. Citing Williamson's (1985) work, Platteau (1994, 554–5) argues that one of the prime motives spurring the creation of the modern firm is the entrepreneurs' quest "for attenuating opportunism through the establishment of authority relations."

Adam Smith, widely recognized as the father of economics, had a clear understanding of many of these ideas, though he is rarely credited for this understanding. Indeed, the Smith that is known to most modern economists is a caricature of the real Adam Smith. The popular image of Smith represents him as arguing that the so-called invisible hand of the free market and the pursuit of self interest by individuals drive the economy to achieve the social good. This view is captured in the oft-quoted lines from Book IV Chapter II of the *Wealth of Nations*:

> As every individual... endeavours as much as he can, both to employ his capital in the support of domestick industry, and so to direct that industry that its produce maybe of the greatest value; every individual necessarily labours to render the annual revenue of the society as great as he can. He generally, indeed, neither intends to promote the publick interest, nor knows how much he is promoting it... [B]y directing that industry in such a manner as its produce may be of the greatest value, he intends only his own gain; and he is in this, as in many other cases, led by an invisible hand to promote an end which was no part of his intention. (Smith, 1776, 456)

However, a more careful reading of Smith's writings, especially his *Theory of Moral Sentiments* suggests that he had a much more nuanced understanding of human beings than the one which assumes that individuals are driven solely by self-interest (see Sen, 1986). Although he argued that self-interest has a strong influence on people's behavior, he had a pluralist view of human nature, in which sympathy – the ability to perceive things from another person's perspective – has an important role. He also emphasized that "rules of conduct" influence people's behavior in a positive manner:

> Those general rules of conduct, when they have been fixed in our mind by habitual reflection, are of great use in correcting misrepresentations of self-love concerning what is fit and proper to be done in our particular situation. (Smith, 1759, 160)

Moreover, his views on the role of self-interest leading to the common good are not so clear cut either. For Smith, the way that the connecting principles of the economy, through the invisible hand, gives rise to order reflects the planning and handiwork of the Deity as designer (see Evensky, 1993). He thought that "humanity, justice, generosity, and public spirit, are the qualities most useful to others" (Smith, 1759, 190), and seems to have believed while self-interest is useful in certain situations, these other virtues are useful in others. Especially toward the end of his life he began to have doubts about the role of the invisible hand and self-interest in yielding the common good. In the "Additions and Corrections" (which is the only major revision of the text) to the *Wealth of Nations*, published in 1784, he discussed how the mercantile system was distorting commercial society. In his revision of the *Theory of Moral Sentiments* in 1789 (a book which had seen no earlier revisions), he added "a compleat new sixth part containing a practical system of Morality, under the title of the Character of Virtue" (Smith, 1776, 1976, 319–20). In this revision he argues that society is comprised of a layered web of communities with divergent interests, and that these can result in the creation of destructive factions. He appeals to all people to place the well-being of society as a whole above that of their own factions, and stresses especially the role of statesmen in constructing such a moral society through their actions and by setting examples for others (see Evensky, 1993, 2005). Indeed, for Smith virtue serves as "the fine polish to the wheels of society" while vice is "like the vile rust, which makes them jar and grate upon one another" (Smith, 1759, 1976, 244). Clearly, Smith sought to distance his thesis from that of Mandeville and the implication that individual greed could be the basis for social good. As Evensky argues, for Smith "ethics is the hero – not self-interest or greed – for it is ethics that defend the social intercourse from the Hobbesian chaos" (Evensky, 1993, 204).

The second perspective can be understood using some examples of how ethical beliefs of people and groups can make the market operate quite differently from how it does in standard perfectly competitive markets with self-interested, optimizing agents. In labor markets, ethical values such as fairness can explain why there is involuntary unemployment. For standard perfectly competitive labor markets, in which firms and workers are price and wage takers, and they maximize profits and utility in a self-interested manner, neoclassical theory proceeds by using labor demand curves and labor supply curves. Assuming diminishing returns to labor, firms demand labor up to the level of employment at which the marginal product of labor is equal to the real wage; this provides us with a negatively sloped demand curve for labor which shows that at a higher real wage firms want to hire fewer workers. Workers maximize utility, which depends on their income and leisure, and this produces a supply curve of labor which is usually drawn to be positively sloped. Suppose, now, that the real wage is at a level at which the supply of labor exceeds the demand for labor so that some people who want to work at that wage are involuntarily unemployed. According to this theory, with the price level given, the money wage will fall due to competition among workers who will want to find employment and offer to work at lower wages. When the real wage falls firms will want to hire more workers and, possibly, some people who were willing to work at higher wages will not want jobs any more, and therefore there will be a lower amount of labor supplied. As the money, and hence the real, wage falls, employment will increase, and eventually we will have full employment in the sense that everyone who wants to work finds a job. This kind of labor market equilibrium is shown in Figure 6.1, where $W$ is the money wage, $P$ the price level of the good (we assume, for simplicity that there is only one good produced in this economy), $W/P$ is the real wage, and $N$ the level of employment. The labor supply and demand curves are market $N_S$ and $N_d$, and labor market equilibrium occurs at the real wage $(W/P)_1$.

While this demand–supply story may work for some goods and services, as noted in Section 5.1 of the previous chapter, the labor market is unlikely to function in this way. As many economists have noted, firms and workers agree on a wage and the hours worked, but typically not on how much work each worker will perform. Economists distinguish between labor employment and efficiency units of labor. Given that the worker has some leeway in deciding on how much effort he or she will exert, it is likely that firms will try to gain the trust and cooperation of workers by giving them a fair wage above the minimum at which they

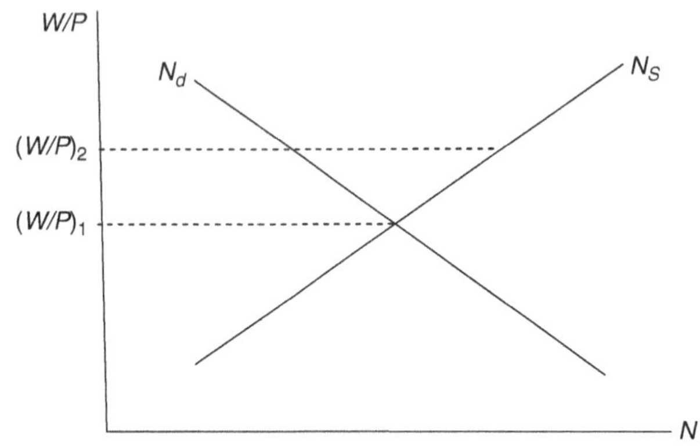


*Figure 6.1* Supply and demand in the labor market

would be willing to work. By doing so, as Akerlof (1982) argues, they will be giving a gift to their employees, in return for which the employees will gift the firm their loyalty. Thus, firms, not wishing to lose this loyalty and work effort, will have an incentive not to cut wages even when there are unemployed workers. The result is that the equilibrium will be at a wage higher than the market-clearing wage, so that unemployment will result. In terms of Figure 6.1 the equilibrium wage will be a wage such as $(W/P)_2$.

Akerlof's story has some similarities with the standard efficiency wage theory. According to this theory employers pay workers a wage higher than the lowest needed to obtain workers. They do so in order to reduce shirking. At this higher wage workers would not like to get caught shirking and lose their jobs (something that they would not mind so much if they were paid the lower wage, since they could obtain another job at that same wage).[2] In the efficiency wage model, there is unemployment in equilibrium because the wage is at a level higher than the labor market-clearing level, and because firms have no incentive to reduce the wage since their profits will be adversely affected by lower productivity due to increased shirking. Unemployment and the higher real wage provide a stick and a carrot to workers which make them provide greater effort because of the fear of getting fired and becoming unemployed. However, the gift exchange story is different because it explicitly brings in the issue of fairness. People react well when treated fairly, and not well when they feel unfairly treated. The story involving fairness is not only more realistic than the one that only involves shirking and the fear of losing one's job, but is also better able to withstand criticism as an explanation of high wages. Shirking can be avoided by giving workers the incentive of seniority rights without paying higher wages to all workers, and workers may fear being fired and losing their reputation as good workers and thus exert a high level of effort without being paid high wages (see Akerlof and Shiller, 2009). Moreover, in work which requires group effort and where the individual's contribution is hard to measure, workers may free ride on the efforts of their colleagues while getting paid higher wages. The fairness argument is able to withstand all these objections.

Considerations of fairness concerning the relative wages of different workers in the economy can also be used to explain money wage rigidity. Suppose, as discussed in Section 4.4, that workers have ideas about fairness of wage differentials between different sectors of the economy. If, as Keynes (1936) argued, wage bargains occur at different times in different sectors of the economy, workers in a particular sector who are negotiating their wages during a recession with substantial unemployment will resist – and be able to prevent – a wage reduction because they feel that they are being unfairly treated in comparison to workers in other sectors. As a result, money wages will not fall overall even though there is unemployed labor.

These considerations imply not only that the labor market will operate in a manner which is different from what is shown using the simple demand–supply model of the labor market, but also that macroeconomic analysis as a whole will be different. Macroeconomists of various shades accept that fluctuations in aggregate demand result in fluctuations in output around what is considered to be the "full employment" level of income or, according to some, the level of income corresponding to the natural rate of unemployment or the nonaccelerating inflation rate of unemployment (NAIRU). Many agree that these fluctuations result in variations in involuntary unemployment as well.[3] But there seems to be a consensus among many macroeconomists that these effects are only of a short-run nature. In the longer run, it is argued, the economy returns to full employment, or to the natural rate of unemployment or NAIRU, and corresponding levels of output. This is because money wages are flexible in the longer run and because people's price expectations are corrected over the longer run. A simple illustration of this is that as wages are fully adjusted and so are expectations, the economy will be at the point shown by the intersection of the supply and demand curves in Figure 6.1, which is determined solely by factors that affect the supply and demand curves for labor (factors which are independent of what affects aggregate demand, such as the expectations of consumers and business firms about their future incomes and sales). Thus, government policies that affect aggregate demand can only have short-term effects on output (and possibly unemployment), but no effect in the longer run.[4] The government can do little, with fiscal or monetary expansion, to reduce unemployment below its natural rate. All that changes in the longer run is the inflation rate (and not real magnitudes such as output and unemployment), and everyone sees through the veil of money, having no "irrational" money illusion.

There are many reasons to doubt that the long-run rate of unemployment and output cannot be affected by aggregate demand. For instance, it is possible that long bouts of unemployment in the short run can result in people losing their job skills and employment habits, and may effectively become unemployable, so that the natural rate of unemployment can increase. However, as Akerlof and Shiller (2009) argue, fairness issues which make the money wage rigid due to the presence of money illusion can also result in a negatively sloped Phillips curve in the longer run. For instance, suppose that workers believe that they are being unfairly treated when there is a money wage cut even when the price level falls, because they attribute changes in the money wage to direct actions of their employers (and a discontinuation of the terms of their gift exchange) and they attribute changes in the price level to extraneous factors. Or suppose that they think that they are being unfairly treated if their money wage falls in comparison to those of workers in other sectors. These considerations, discussed earlier, imply that people may have money illusion after all, and the effects of inflation on output and employment may persist in the longer run. A drop in aggregate demand will reduce the price level but not the money wage, even in the long run, and this will reduce output and employment, as can be seen from Figure 6.1 (as the economy moves further up from the real wage $(W/P)_2$ along the demand curve for labor). If this is the case, by not conducting expansionary policies, the government may be keeping the unemployment rate higher in the longer run than they could, leading to considerable and avoidable human misery and suffering.

## 6.3 How markets affect ethical values

To the extent that ethical values are shaped by the environment in which individuals live and act, and since markets are an important part of their environment, it may be expected that markets will affect the individuals' ethical values. In fact, economists, other social scientists and philosophers have debated the effects that markets and the market economy have on individual ethics.[5] These debates have examined the effects of markets narrowly defined as an institution through which people buy and sell, but also more broadly as a system which motivates production, consumption, and other activities, that is, capitalism itself. Since capitalism means different things to different people, we will not discuss the effect of capitalism on ethics and morality, but rather focus on the effects of markets – though the boundaries of the market may sometimes be difficult to precisely demarcate.[6]

Many of those who emphasize the effects of markets on ethical values stress the corrosive effects of markets and the market economy. First, involvement in markets for the purpose of buying and selling makes people more self-interested because they become more focused in maximizing their utility and profits, and this behavior also influences their behavior in nonmarket spheres. Competitive pressures in markets, it is argued, make it necessary to be self-interested maximizers in order to survive in the market: for instance, those sellers who do not act in their self-interest will find themselves losing out to their competitors and, sooner or later, have to exit the market. As self-interested maximizers, they are likely not to care much, if at all, about other people, take advantage of them whenever it is to their advantage to do so, and even break laws to pursue their self-interest. They are more likely to hide information from trading partners to further their own interests. They are more likely to terminate personal relationships when they find that they stand to gain by doing so, leaving family to obtain more lucrative jobs in other locations, and leaving colleagues, friends, and family for other people who are likely to benefit them more. As competitors they are more likely to see themselves as competing for gains rather than cooperating, so that even when trade is mutually beneficial, the parties to a trade compete by seeking a disproportionate share of the gains for themselves. Participants in markets are more likely to treat other individuals as the means to making more money, rather than as ends, thereby violating Kant's practical imperative mentioned in Chapter 3, Section 3.1. Second, the impersonal nature of the market obscures the social nature of exchange. Marx (1867) describes alienation and commodity fetishism under capitalist market relations as making what are relations between people seem like relations between things. Since people may be moral and things are not, morals are adversely affected by markets. When participants in markets suffer hardships, in the absence of an identifiable villain, there is no one to blame, and therefore little reason to feel responsible for ones actions in markets (Wilber, 1984).

Third, greater involvement in markets as buyers and sellers make people devote more time and effort to trading, consuming, and producing, and leave them with less time for family, friends, and community relationships. They are more likely to work more and spend more time consuming and making more money to consume private goods, and therefore more likely to spend less quality time with family and friends, and more likely to go "bowling alone" rather than participate in bowling leagues and other community organizations (see Putnam, 2000). All of this weakens the role of these influences in teaching and sustaining virtues and ethical behavior norms. Fourth, involvement in markets can have an adverse effect on social virtues. For example, a number of studies show that market policies can crowd out the intrinsic motivation to contribute to the social good. Frey and Oberholzer-Gee tested the "base motives driving out noble ones" hypothesis by analyzing the preparedness of citizens to accept a nuclear waste repository in their hometown (Frey and Oberholzer-Gee, 1997). They found that if citizens were offered financial compensation, the acceptance rate declined from 51 per cent to 25 per cent. Detailed statistical analyses showed that civic-mindedness and care for the broader social costs had a significant positive impact on the willingness to accept the waste repository. When compensation was offered, the positive impact of these social factors on the willingness to accept the repository disappeared. Frey and Oberholzer conclude that where public spirit prevails, the use of price incentives tends to crowd out civic duty and therefore needs to be reconsidered as an instrument of social policy. Fehr and Gächter (2002) present an experiment in which an increase in monitoring of workers and the imposition of fines in case of verified shirking significantly reduce workers' efforts. This indicates that explicit incentives may destroy embodied ethical motivations.

There are also numerous claims in the literature that markets actually strengthen ethical values and develop virtues. First, since markets imply that people trade with each other, they are more likely to maintain their relationships by cooperating with each other, rather than, for example, engaging in violent competition. Hirschman (1977) provides an illuminating discussion of how markets (and capitalism) developed and were deliberately promoted to strengthen values and divert the passion of competition from self-destructive violence to competition in markets. This argument has been extended to trade between countries with the Lockean claim that if countries trade with each other and therefore are more dependent on each other, they are less likely to go to war against each other because doing so would deprive themselves of the economic benefits of trade. Second, it is argued that market interactions transform individuals by building communities and developing solidarity that would otherwise not exist or would be weak. It is also likely to be the case that if people interact with each other, they are likely to have a better understanding of each other, and – especially with long-term relationships – develop a sense of fellow feeling, and behave more ethically toward each other. Third, it can be argued that markets allow individuals to become more virtuous by allowing them to flourish and prosper spiritually. The fact that markets expand choices has been related to the idea that the expansion of choices leads to people being able to achieve their fullest potential. In a more religious vein, it is argued that markets allow people to become producers not just for mundane survival, but to live in a way that makes them creators and model themselves after the creator God (see McGurn's essays in Blank and McGurn, 2004, 76–8).

The discussion on moral habits and virtue is particularly interesting. Novak (1993, 225) asserts that "when a country moves from being a traditionalist society to becoming a market society, the moral habits of its people generally show improvement – at least in certain specific ways." He argues that markets encourage people to be "law abiding, cooperative and courteous even to strangers (such as customers)" (Novak, 1993, 227). Although Novak is aware that markets cannot solve all the problems, McCloskey (2006) is far more optimistic. She provides a detailed analysis of how markets are likely to promote virtues in individuals by discussing the effects of markets on all seven virtues, that is, the cardinal virtues and the theological or Christian virtues.[7] Wisdom or prudence is promoted at the individual level by engaging in business, developing the knowledge of buying cheap and selling dear and calculating the consequences of business decisions, and at the level of countries by engaging in trade rather than war. Restraint, moderation or temperance is promoted by the need to do hard work and to save for business expansion. Markets can be argued to promote courage and fortitude, by inducing producers to engage in new ways of doing business and overcoming the fear of change. Justice is promoted because markets and business activity induce individuals "to insist on private property honestly acquired... [,] to pay willingly for good work, to honor labor, to break down privilege, to value people for what they can do rather than for who they are, to value success without envy." Markets promote faith "to honor one's community of business... to build monuments to the glorious past, to sustain the traditions of commerce, of learning, of religion." The market gives hope "to imagine a better machine... to see the future as something other than stagnation or eternal recurrence, to infuse the day's work with a purpose, seeing one's labor as a glorious calling." It promotes love and charity, not only to take care of one's own, but also to take care of employees, partners, colleagues, customers, and fellow citizens. Business firms also engage in a fair amount of philanthropy, and some of them pursue goals explicitly designed to benefit society at large.

Although the two sides of the debate make some compelling arguments, they are arguably excessively polemical. In some cases they ignore obvious counterarguments. For instance, arguments about the corrosive role of markets ignore the fact that there are other influences, such as families, secular community organizations, and religious organizations, which are argued to promote virtues have sometimes been known to promote parochialism, exclusivity, and even violence instead. On the other side, faith in one's community of business may be in conflict with faith in a religious sense. The conflicts between faith in God and mammon are too well known to require much discussion, and one example – regarding the difference in views of the environment as an instrument for economic gain or as intrinsically important as a gift of God – will suffice. The narrow notion of justice and wisdom that seems to be promoted by markets, at least in McCloskey's discussion, leaves it unclear whether markets promote these virtues in other broader senses. Moreover, it is ignored that markets may promote vices such as greed (making more money for oneself), gluttony (because markets make consumers want to consume more and more), envy (for others who are doing better for themselves financially or by consuming more), and pride (for succeeding in business), and even lust (because of its relationship to power and because of the existence of markets that promote sexual fantasies and activity).

The problems with some of these arguments can be examined in more detail by considering how market relations affect values, since this effect is stressed in both sides of the debate. Rather than simply arguing that market relations positively or negatively affect values, it is useful to distinguish between the objectives behind, and the nature, scope, and timing of these relationships. It is also worthwhile comparing market relationships to other kinds of relations, such as personal and civic ones.

It stands to reason that the objectives behind relationships matter in how they affect values. Some relationships, such as personal and civic relationships may be other-regarding, while others, like market relationships, may be self-regarding, and therefore, are likely to promote different types of experiences and influences on a person's character. This distinction seems to make it more likely that the market critics are correct, because virtues like love and charity are more likely to be harmed by market relations than personal and civic relations. If people have a plurality of motives, involvement in market relations rather than these other relations are likely to increase the importance people attach to self-interest, rather than sympathy or civic-mindedness. However, even if people's objectives become increasingly one-dimensional and self-interested, it is not always the case that they will necessarily destroy virtues. Self-interested market participants may do certain things – like be courteous toward others, be more honest, be fair in their dealings, to make charitable donations – to pursue their self-interest. Repeated actions of these types may, over time, change how people are, and make them more virtuous. But this is an empirical matter which may or may not be true, and cannot simply be taken for granted. The view of market proponents has some validity, and market relations may rule out many types of obvious and easily discovered egregious ethical transgressions, especially when there are well-informed consumer groups and institutions spreading information about such acts. However, it may only prevent unethical behavior which is likely to be detected, rather than transform people and firms into becoming virtuous. They may even become less virtuous to the extent that they become more secretive about their unethical behavior, and may spend more time and effort on cover-up operations which are also unethical.

Regarding the nature of the market relationship, several dimensions can be distinguished, including what can be called their distance, duration, and symmetry. Distance refers to whether the relationships involve people meeting each other or whether it is of a long-distance nature with very little contact. It can be argued that close market relationships are more likely to develop sympathy and fellow-feeling than more distant ones, and impersonal relationships develop very little if they occur through email messages and videoconferencing, rather than by talking and exchanging pleasantries and shaking hands. In an increasingly globalized world, it can be argued that more distant relationships become the norm, so that market relationships may be, overall, weakening virtues. Duration refers to how many times two parties to an exchange interact with each other: long-lasting relationships are more likely to develop meaningful relationships than one-shot transactions. If increasing globalization implies more one-off transactions – which it need not – then virtues may be weakened by markets. Symmetry refers to relative bargaining power of the two parties to the market transaction (which in turn may be affected by how much information they have on what is being traded, and what alternative opportunities the two parties have for trade) which has an effect on the outcome in the sense of how they divide the gains from trade. Greater symmetry is more likely to result in fellow-feeling and less symmetry likely to result in distrust and feelings of being unfairly treated. For instance, if unemployment levels are high, it is possible that workers may be paid less than otherwise, and therefore feel that they are being taken advantage of. Lack of symmetry may imply that the person on one side of the relationship does not find his or her choices expanding and therefore makes no progress in achieving his or her full potential. A more careful analysis of the qualities of market relationships is required before we can decide on whether markets corrode or develop ethical values.

The scope and timing of market relationship are not properties of a given market relation, but of how broad is the scope of market relationships which could possibly develop virtues, and at what stage of a person's life they occur. Concerning scope, under certain conditions, sellers may be courteous to their customers, but it is not clear that they will have any compulsion to be courteous to their competitors, and workers who compete with each for the same job (especially if they are from different ethnic backgrounds) may also not develop such civility in their dealings with each other (Yuengert, 1996). Concerning timing, the moral development of people is likely to be strongest in a person's formative years, when they are children, and when they typically do not engage in market transactions for themselves, as workers and/or sellers (see Maital, 1982). Nevertheless, markets do affect them, through advertisements and through the influence of their peers, and by whether they spend time with family or in front of the television. The limited scope and the timing at which they have an influence seem to tilt the balance toward the market critics.

Comparing market relations with other relationships (other than in terms of their objectives, which we have already discussed), if markets possess the characteristics enumerated by Anderson (1990a) discussed in Section 6.1, they are more likely to be those which are impersonal in nature and do not involve loyalties outside the market relationship, tend to emphasize consumption and use as rivalrous rather than complementary, and which promote exit as a mechanism of change rather than the exercise of voice, and therefore more likely to weaken the quality of relationships. Moreover, because markets stress tastes rather than reasons for wanting and needing, they are more likely to take the focus away from helping others who are in need. However, it is necessary to keep in mind that the nature of these personal and political relationships is also important. Thus, if people are subject to exploitation by more powerful people in personal relations, or if people feel that they are forced to do things by government officials or other people in positions of authority, it is more likely that a switch to market transactions that do not involve such exploitation and coercion may develop virtues.

## 6.4 Conclusion

This chapter has argued that market interactions will be affected by norms and people's ethical values, while these ethical values and norms may in turn be affected by market interactions. The effects on both sides may be positive or negative or zero, as shown in Table 6.1. The standard view of mainstream economists is that there is no interaction, so that we can expunge ethical values from economic analysis. However, as this chapter has argued, it is possible for market interactions to have a negative effect on ethical values (in the sense of weakening them), or a positive effect, and it is also possible for ethical values to have a positive effect on the performance of markets by improving relationships and reducing self-interested behavior, or a negative impact.

The interaction of these effects may have an overall negative or positive effect on society as a whole, which is typically not examined in standard theories because they seldom incorporate the role of ethical values. On the one hand, it is possible that the expansion of market activity may weaken ethical values and produce unfavorable market outcomes which in turn may make people try to engage even more in market transactions to reduce their losses, which will lead to a negative spiral. Increasing market engagement can result from the weakening

*Table 6.1* Relation between markets and ethical values

| **Effects of** | **No effect** | **Positive** | **Negative** |
|---|---|---|---|
| Markets on ethical values | Standard neoclassical view | Increasing and improving relationships, encouraging altruism, and strengthening virtues | Weakening relationships Strengthening self-interest. Weakening virtues and strengthening vices |
| Ethical values on the performance of markets | Standard neoclassical view | Effects of strengthening cooperation, and honesty | Fairness causing unemployment |

of communities and ties of friendship which makes people less happy and which induces them to obtain more happiness by increasing their incomes and the possession of more goods. On the other hand, it is possible for market expansion to improve ethical values and therefore improve the functioning of markets, and thereby have an overall positive effect on both market outcomes and ethical values. Of course, these outcomes are not the only possibilities, because the operation of markets does not just depend on ethical values and the development of ethical values does not just depend on market activities. For instance, if ethical values and norms lead to inefficient market outcomes because of the problem of unemployment, governments can try to improve matters by combating the problem of unemployment through macroeconomic policy, or ethical values can be developed through the more concerted efforts of families and religious organizations even when markets have a major – but perhaps circumscribed – role in the economy.

The main implication of this chapter is not that the incorporation of ethical values into the discussion of markets will lead us to the view that markets overall have positive or negative effects on society, but rather that no serious analysis of market interaction can be conducted without incorporating the role of ethical values into the analysis.

# Part III

# Ethical Issues for Evaluating Economies and Economic Policy Analysis

# 7
# The Morality of Markets and Government Intervention

## Introduction

The previous chapter examined how markets are affected by the fact that individuals have ethical values, and how participation in markets affects the ethical values people hold. This chapter turns to a related question: what is the moral standing of the market from the perspective of society as a whole. Is the market system good? Is it good to have markets wherever possible? Or are there some limits and objections to goods and services being allocated through markets?

At one level these questions may seem odd. Markets allow people to exchange goods and services. Imagine a world in which people are not allowed to trade with each other. They would have to produce for themselves everything that they need or want, from every kind of food, clothing, and housing, to services like medical care, education, and security against crime! The world would indeed be a rude place where we would be able to do very little other than produce for our consumption and life would be difficult. But markets are not the only institutions which allow us to obtain goods and services we do not ourselves produce. We can gift things to each other. We can form cooperatives where we share what we produce. The government can organize production and supply things to us and we in turn can produce for the government. There may also be combinations of these methods: for instance, markets may exist but be regulated by the government. So the issue is not so much one of having markets or not having them, but of having free markets and understanding their moral limits; those limits may require replacing markets with some other method of allocating goods and services.

The rest of this chapter proceeds as follows. First, Section 7.1 examines whether the market system as a whole is moral or ethically good, and we will do this by analyzing the market system in terms of different conceptions of what is good, including consequentialist, egalitarian, desert, and rights-based perspectives that were discussed in Chapter 3. Next, Section 7.2 distinguishes between different types of possible markets and examines whether they differ in their degree of goodness and examines different moral limits to the use of markets. Section 7.3 will then examine some examples of goods and services which are controversial in terms of whether markets in them should be established or abolished, that is, markets in human blood, surrogate motherhood, and human organs. Section 7.4 will then briefly discuss the moral standing of another institution which plays a major role in modern economies, the government. Section 7.5 will make some concluding comments.

## 7.1 The morality of the market

Is the market system a good one? The answer to the question obviously depends on what we mean by "good." In this section we will explore several alternative notions of the good society, or theories of justice, and examine what they imply about the goodness of markets. It also depends on what the market system is being compared to. We will not be specific about the alternatives, but implicitly take it to be some form of government intervention. Our analysis will therefore be necessarily incomplete without explicitly considering the goodness of possible alternative arrangements.

### 7.1.1 Rights

One argument for the morality of markets is rights-based. Participation in markets can be seen as a part of the exercise of some fundamental "rights." In this view markets are defended not in terms of what markets achieve, in terms of consequences such as efficiency or fairness, but in terms of antecedent rights, as in Nozick's approach discussed in Chapter 3. It follows that the argument is not contingent on some properties of the real world. However, one may ask, as Sen (1985) does, whether the rights of ownership and exchange, which allow markets to exist, should have this kind of "foundational" status irrespective of their consequences. Sen (1981) has argued that many major famines, leading to the death of millions of people, resulted from large decreases in the amount of food to which people had access due to significant increases in the price of food or losses in employment and wages. This result was consistent with the exercise of legal rights of people in markets, rather than being caused by acts of nature which reduced the overall availability of food. For instance, a major famine in South Asia occurred during World War II mainly because the war effort increased the demand for food for soldiers, raised the price of food, and food was exported from food growing regions, leaving many locals to starve. Sen states that it is "not easy to understand why rules of ownership, transfer, etc. should have such absolute priority over the life and death of millions of people" (Sen, 1985 [1993], 97). Nozick himself leaves open the question whether "catastrophic moral horrors" can justify the violation of some rights, but Sen argues that doing so undermines the rights approach by opening up the possibility that less central rights may be violated because of less disastrous consequences. For instance, even if there is no dramatic disastrous event like a famine, but steady and continuing problems such as poverty and malnutrition, could one justify the abrogation or at least limitations on the right to buy and sell at free market prices?

It should be noted that in the libertarian rights-based view, markets are usually defended on the ground that markets involve voluntary exchange and free choice, since participants can choose not to participate in markets. In some other methods of allocation – such as government provision through taxation – this is not the case. The issue of the extent to which voluntary choice implies freedom in a more fundamental sense is not clear, however. Consider a person who is being robbed at gunpoint, and is given the choice of being shot or handing over his or her valuables to the robber. The person may choose the option of acquiescing to the robber, but it is obvious that the choice is not a free one. It follows that not all market exchanges are truly voluntary and some may contain an element of *coercion*. When people buy and sell things under conditions of severe inequality or out of extreme economic necessity, calling it voluntary seems to be off the mark. Rather, there is more than a little coercion involved and is thus unjust. A poor person may agree to sell his/her kidney or cornea in order to feed his/her starving family, but his/her agreement is not truly voluntary. He/she is coerced, in effect, by the necessities of the situation.[1]

### 7.1.2 Increasing choices

A second argument in favor of markets is that they give people the freedom of choice and increase the number of choices for them. This argument for markets has been made, among others, by the American Nobel Prize-winning economist Milton Friedman (1912–2006) in his popular coauthored book, *Free to Choose* (Friedman and Friedman, 1990). This argument states that markets expand choices open to people and that if the government controls the market people's choices are restricted, something that is undesirable. It should be noted that restrictions on freedom are considered to be bad according to this argument even if they are not binding, that is, if what is removed from the choices is not something we would, in fact, choose.[2] Thus the argument is not the same as the standard economist's argument which states that markets make people better off because they allow us to consume or produce more. Note also that this argument is not the same as the right-based argument for markets which requires no other justification. Thus, it is possible to argue against this argument on empirical grounds. First, it is not necessarily the case that markets always expand choices for people. For instance, if markets imply that some people do not find employment which allows them to earn income, their choices can be severely restricted. Also, if markets result in very high prices for some goods, many people may not have the choice of buying them. Second, it is possible that having more choices need not necessarily make people better off. For instance, having a bewildering variety of choices may make it very difficult and time-consuming for people to choose. Moreover, having a plethora of choices could result in people making choices that they later regret, sometimes with good reason, because they did not have all the necessary information when they made their choice.

### 7.1.3 Desert

A third argument is that markets are fair and result in people getting their just deserts. Personal connections or allocation by the state may result in people being treated unfairly because they do not know the "right" people. The argument states that the impersonal forces of the market avoid such unfairness and provide income to individuals based on what they produce and contribute to society. Peter Bauer (1981), for instance, argues that "economic differences are largely the result of people's varied capacities and motivations" (p. 19). "Incomes, including those of the relatively prosperous or the owners of property, are not taken from other people. Normally they are produced by their recipients and the resources they own" (p. 12). For Bauer, therefore, "it is by no means obvious why it should be unjust that those who produce more should enjoy higher income" (p. 17). A more precise statement of this argument uses the marginal productivity theory of distribution. This theory states that in free perfectly competitive markets, the economy (given certain other conditions) arrives at an equilibrium in which every factor of production is paid its marginal product. This result follows from the assumption that firms maximize profits. For instance, when firms maximize profits they hire labor up to the level at which the value of the marginal product of the last unit of labor they hire (their marginal benefit from hiring labor) equals the wage (their marginal cost of hiring labor), which implies that the physical marginal product of labor is equal to the wage divided by the price of the product (or the real wage). It follows, it is argued, that the worker gets paid what he or she contributes.

There are many problems with this argument, however. The conditions under which the marginal productivity theory holds may not prevail in the real world. Thus, if prefect competition does not hold, such as when there is one firm which hires workers in a particular area (a situation described in economics as a monopsony), the wage will fall below the marginal product of the worker because the firm will not hire up to where the wage equals marginal product (due to the fact that hiring more workers is likely to increase the wage, which increases the marginal cost of the firm above the wage). More fundamentally, even if the marginal productivity theory holds as a theory of distribution, it is incorrect to argue that people get paid what they contribute by equating the marginal product with what people contribute. In cases of production by individuals unaided by other people or other resources, it is possible to attribute to one person what he or she produces.[3] However, when production is the result of the joint use of a number of resources, it is not possible, in general, to ascertain what resource produces what part of the total production. The use of the concept of the marginal product does not allow us to do so, since it only measures the additional output which results from one additional unit of a resource, holding the amounts of all other resources constant. In general, adding up marginal products and quantities of inputs does not add up to total output (except under special conditions in which the so-called adding-up theorem holds, such as constant returns to scale). Even if the adding-up theorem holds, marginal products in equilibrium measure the additional contribution to output of the last unit of that resource used, and not of the contribution each resource makes to total output. The problems are compounded by the fact that there are different kinds of output, which have to be weighted, making the attribution of total output even more arbitrary: valuing outputs of different goods at market prices raises many kinds of questions, including their "worth" to society. Further, this approach takes the view that owners of resources such as land and capital actually produce the contribution that these resources make to output, which leaves open the question of how they obtained these resources – through their own effort, through luck, or even through illegal means.

The upshot of all this is that even though what Sen (1985) calls the "personal production view" has some appeal and can lead to a case for inequality based on people's effort and production, it is difficult to sustain in terms of the distributional outcomes even in perfectly competitive economies, let alone in those in which various "distortions" exist. Moreover, it has to compete with other claims based on other consideration such as need: should people who do not produce (perhaps because they cannot do so) have to starve to death?

### 7.1.4 Efficiency and growth

The argument in favor of markets that is most common among economists is the one based on efficiency. The argument uses the fundamental theorem of welfare economics, which states that under certain conditions (such as perfect information, the absence of externalities, etc.), a perfectly competitive outcome is efficient in the sense of being Pareto optimal. In other words, the result of free markets under these conditions is that the economy will be in a situation in which no one can be made better off without making other people worse off in terms of their utility, which typically depends on the amount of goods they consume.

This argument is open to many objections. First, the conditions under which the fundamental theorem holds may not exist in reality; many argue that in fact they do not. The economy may be characterized by numerous departures from the conditions which ensure perfectly competitive equilibrium due to the existence of large corporations, imperfect and asymmetric information, and externalities. In the presence of these features, as is well known, market failures occur and the welfare theorem does not hold. Second, the argument says nothing about the issue of distributional justice or fairness. If some people get most of the goods and others get very little or hardly any at all, the situation can be Pareto optimal, but yet judged to be unjust and therefore undesirable. It may be preferable to have a fairer outcome in terms of distribution and some amount of inefficiency. The efficiency argument, however, can be rescued by what is called the second or converse theorem of welfare economics, which states that under certain conditions (somewhat more stringent than those required for the fundamental or direct theorem), any Pareto optimal outcome can be attained by a competitive outcome with some initial distribution of resource endowments among people. What this means is that if we can change the initial distribution of resources that people own, the free market can produce the most desirable position of the economy, one that is not only efficient in the sense of being Pareto optimal, but also distributionally fair. The problem with this argument is, however, that it is not clear how to actually make the distribution of ownership equitable, in the sense that the outcome will be fair, in a free market capitalist economy. Will it be politically feasible, and how will the enormous amount of information required for the appropriate type of redistribution be obtained? Moreover, it overlooks the fact that such interventions can weaken people's incentives, and result in inefficiency. Third, the argument overlooks entirely other important claims to the good society, including rights, personal virtues, and personal and civic relationships. Fourth, the standard argument for markets in terms of allocative efficiency overlooks some other aspects of the efficiency argument, such as production efficiency and informational issues. The standard neoclassical theory assumes that firms are always on their production function, producing efficiently in the sense of producing as much as possible with given inputs. However, as emphasized in theories of X-inefficiency, firms may not always produce efficiently.[4] It is possible that more competition increases production efficiency, but that is not an argument which is part of the neoclassical theory of market efficiency.

A popular argument interprets efficiency not in the standard sense of Pareto optimality, but in the sense of increasing output and income, and the rate of economic growth. Economic growth is usually measured in real and per capita terms to abstract from the effects of absolute price changes and of larger output because of larger population. The claim made for markets is that they are better at increasing the rate of real per capita income growth of a country by increasing its efficiency at a point in time, and by allowing it to save and invest more, and experience a higher rate of technological change, than in alternative systems using state intervention, through state ownership of enterprises, regulation of the economy, and diverting resources from productive investment to redistribution. This claim is backed up by empirical evidence which is marshaled to show that a greater use of markets speeds up economic growth. It has been argued that economic miracles in South Korea, Taiwan, Singapore, and Hong Kong since the 1970s, and the later economic rise of China and India, were the result of economic liberalization and the promotion of market-based economies. These are, of course, empirical issues, and not directly ethical ones, although one may ask whether in fact higher growth represents greater efficiency or whether economic efficiency is a desirable goal. The empirical issues are not clear, moreover. Careful studies of the East Asian miracles suggest that they were the product not of free markets, but of a fair degree of state intervention, especially in the allocation of finance and the promotion of exports (see Wade, 1990; Amsden, 1991). It can be argued that what distinguishes successful from less successful growth strategies is not so much whether markets have been relatively free or restricted and controlled by the government, but whether government intervention has been successful in giving rewards based on economic performance, as in South Korea and Taiwan, or whether government intervention has been ineffective, because of the inability or unwillingness of the government to enforce performance standards on firms.

### 7.1.5 Equality and morality

So far the arguments that we have discussed have started as arguments in favor of markets. We now turn to two arguments that are usually made against the moral standing of the market. The first is that it is unfair in the sense of violating egalitarian principles, and the second is that it makes people less virtuous and encourages bad actions.

The egalitarian argument states that the market may, and often does, result in outcomes that are inequitable. Markets may be efficient under certain conditions but, as mentioned earlier, the free market outcome does not prevent someone from getting all the goods and some people getting very little or even nothing. Thus, the market may be unable to provide people with things they need even for basic biological subsistence, while others may get more goods than they can ever use. Some people may have no homes while others may have so many homes that they do not know how many they have! The egalitarian argument may be questioned, however. First, it is possible to defend the market from this criticism with the reverse welfare theorem mentioned earlier, by first redistributing resources appropriately and then allowing the market system to operate. However, as noted earlier, there are problems with this argument. Second, it can be argued that the concern against inequality may be misguided because it ignores issues about rights, incentives, desert, and so on. These issues have already been addressed, and need not be repeated.

A final argument states that markets corrupt individuals, inducing them to commit bad acts and become less virtuous. Thus, for instance, it can make people more self-centered and self-interested, making them less altruistic, compassionate, and civic minded. Against this argument, some have claimed that market involvement makes people more virtuous. We have discussed some of these issues in the last chapter and will return to them in the next section.

## 7.2 Are there moral limits to markets?

The issues examined in the previous section relate to the goodness of the market system as a whole. While this question has been hotly debated in history, most people who are not dogmatically wedded to free markets or socialism in the form of state ownership of all production activity argue that it may be best for society to have a mixture of markets and government control, and to rely on their synergy. A more practical question is: what are the limits of markets, the government, and of other institutions. This section examines the moral limit of markets by (1) examining different types of goods and services to analyze for which the market may be more or less good and why and (2) outlining several objections to extending the reach of market valuation and exchange.

One reason for limiting the market is that some goods and services are considered so important for human beings that to the extent possible, no individual – including those who cannot or will not pay for them – should be denied access to them. Economists sometimes refer to these goods as merit goods. One justification for a good being a merit good is that society as a whole thinks that everyone has a right to have them. If these goods and services are supplied in markets, people who cannot pay for them will not have access to them, so that their right to them will be violated. The public provision of such goods and services may also be defended on egalitarian grounds, because inequality in the distribution of these goods and services can be causally related to inequality in other spheres. For instance, inequality in access to education can lead to inequality in wages. Goods and services which may be considered a part of such rights could include food for basic nutrition and for children, education, and health care. Note that while libertarians usually conceive of rights and promoting freedom in a negative sense – of protecting people from having some basic rights, like private property or freedom of speech, being taken away by other people or by the state, this conception of rights can be thought of as promoting positive freedoms. The distinction, however, may be a semantic one in some cases, because the protection of these rights prevents people from being denied the right of living healthy lives, and so on.

Another problem is that for some goods and services markets will either not be able to provide them at all, or provide them in amounts that are not "efficient" for society as a whole. Public goods, as discussed in Chapter 1, are nonexcludable and complementary in consumption and, therefore, will not be provided at all in markets, although governments can "marketize" them to some extent by contracting and paying private producers. Goods and services that create strong externalities, positive or negative, may or may not be candidates to be marketized by government. For instance, if health care creates positive externalities (because healthy people reduce the need for others to seek health care for infectious and contagious diseases), market outcomes will be less than what is socially optimal, since suppliers will only supply to the point to which their marginal cost equals the marginal benefits of people who pay them, not for those who are positively affected through the externality. If drugs result in negative externalities because addictions create adverse effects on family members and others (due to traffic accidents and criminal activity, say), there may be a case for not allowing markets to exist in distributing drugs, although the issue is complicated by the fact that banning the purchase and sale of drugs can create other problems of law enforcement by raising the price of illegal drugs.

A third way of examining the limits of markets – although some of the issues are closely related to the two arguments already mentioned – is based on the relationship of some goods to the concepts *duty* and *virtue* and the impact of markets on the evolution of human values, preferences, and character. It examines different values which are ideally upheld or promoted by different kinds of relationships involving the exchange of different goods and services. This makes particular goods and services especially suitable for allocation through these relationships because of the values they uphold. The implication is that if the goods most suited for one type of exchange relationship are assigned to a different exchange relation, inappropriate values are upheld and promoted, so that society is worse off as a consequence. Following Anderson (1990a, 1993) we may distinguish between three kinds of values or ideals, use value, personal value, and political value. "Use" value refers to the use of goods or services for one's own personal ends, without regard to its intrinsic value or personally or socially shared values, that is, what Anderson calls economic values.[5] These values are promoted in market relations, which – as mentioned in the previous chapter – are impersonal, in which people are free to pursue their personal advantage, in which goods traded are exclusive and rivalrous (rather than enjoyed by more than one person), which are want-regarding (rather than need-oriented), and where dissatisfaction is expressed by exit (rather than voice). Exchanges of many kinds of consumer goods for personal use – which Anderson calls economic goods – can be appropriately conducted in these market relations. A second type of value is related to personal relationships in which exchange is based on intimacy (that is, "sharing private concerns and cherished emotions attuned to the other's personal characteristics") and commitment (that is, "dedicating oneself to permanently living a shared life with another person ... [T]he other partner also enjoys this life, ... each partner realizes this, ... and she knows that the other knows it").[6] Examples of these relationships are marriages, other family relationships, and friendships between two people or small groups. Goods exchanged in these take the form of gifts which are different from market exchanges because they tie the donor and recipient together and are therefore shared, they do not involve strict reciprocity in terms of a single act of exchange but only informal reciprocity in the long run, and the goods and services exchanged are of a personal nature rather than important for what individual wants they satisfy. A third type of value is political, reflecting a shared understanding of commitment between members of society as a whole, and involving the concepts of fraternity and democratic freedom. Individuals have fraternal relationships with each other when they agree not to lay claim for certain goods for themselves at the expense of those who are less well off, and they consider the provision of these goods to the latter as being a part of their own good. These relationships are based on democratic freedom in which individuals come together as equals and through democratic deliberation. Unlike market relationships, the ideals of the distribution of goods are expressed through the use of voice rather than exit, according to the shared principles (through public discussion) regarding what is needed by all rather than unexamined wants and desires, and by making goods accessible to all and not just who have the ability to pay for them.[7]

When goods that uphold personal or political values are allocated through markets, society is worse off because of the distortion of values that this entails. Prostitution, which involves the buying and selling of sexual services through the market, debases a personal relationship which is ideally exchanged as a gift of a shared good, where a couple enjoys their sharing and not simply their separate physical gratification. Anderson (1993, 154–6) argues that market exchange in sexual services results in a failure to realize a good, but also the degradation of the prostitute, the value of whose actions are reduced to the services to a customer and equated to the amount of money paid. It may be noted that this argument is different from the objection to prostitution based on the argument that poverty may coerce someone into it.[8] Anderson

(1990a) further argues that other values are also undermined if one party to an exchange offers something as a gift and the other responds not in kind but in the spirit of a commercial exchange, as can occur when firms attempt to establish a paternalistic relationship with their workers, engendering feelings of gratitude and loyalty on the part of the latter, resulting in a exploitative relationship.

Problems also result when political goods are exchanged in markets. One set of examples is that of the commons, such as streets and parks which, aside from congestion problems,[9] are capable of being enjoyed by all and no one is excluded for the nonpayment of fees. In some cases, which economists call public goods – like national defense – exclusion for nonpayment is not possible and there are no congestion problems – so that exchange through markets is not possible in the usual way (although privatization and market exchange are sometimes possible with the government contracting out some services to private firms). But for other goods and services for which people can be excluded if they do not pay, privatization and market exchange is possible; markets are recommended and sometimes introduced. This results in inefficiency if the additional cost of supplying the good or service to one more is negligible and individuals can benefit from having it without reducing the ability of others of enjoying it (since a Pareto improving change is possible under these conditions). However, it is sometimes argued by libertarians that dividing these commons into privately owned plots or "parcels" increases freedom because people aren't forced into paying taxes for their public upkeep. A problem with this view is that although people do own their own parcel, they become subjects of the owners of, and lose rights over, parcels that others own. There is, moreover a loss in terms of public spaces – like parks – in which people can engage in fraternal relations on equal terms for public discussion and other kinds of spontaneous interactions (Anderson, 1993, 159–61). Similar issues, moreover, arise in cases where the goods involved are not necessarily public goods or goods with negligible marginal costs (which raise efficiency problems when allocated through markets), such as the provision of free food, education, and health care by the government, as opposed to cash vouchers.[10] Economists often prefer giving cash vouchers because people who receive them enjoy more freedom to spend what they have according to their own wants and desires, and also obtain higher levels of utility than if they are constrained to consume some in-kind goods provided to them. One problem with such vouchers is that while they give people the ability to exit, they do not result in a shared commitment to guarantee everyone in society the fraternal right to receive certain goods whether they choose to pay for it or not, goods which satisfy needs (rather than individual wants and desires) which – through public deliberation – society accepts as needs. Note also that this argument is related to the argument about well-being being reflected in people's functionings, rather than just their incomes (see Chapters 3 and 9).

We should end with the caveat that there may be situations where we may agree that the sale of a good or service through markets is morally objectionable and yet the practice should not be legally banned for practical reasons. For example, the outlawing of the sale of alcohol in the US in the 1920s led to a rapid growth of organized crime and many economists think that the outlawing of recreational drugs is the source of much crime and violence at the present time. And there may be other, better ways of discouraging it. For example, a tax on cigarettes or a reduction in the public places that smoking is legal instead of outright banning. The moral status of a good or service should count as one consideration among others in determining its legal permissibility.

## 7.3 Some examples and controversies

This section examines whether it is ethical to allow markets for some goods and services for which sale and purchase in markets are highly controversial. Aside from the fact that the controversies make these examples interesting in themselves, they illustrate some of the general issues that have been raised about the morality of markets for specific goods and services, and may be instructive for examining the ethical status of other markets.

### 7.3.1 Human blood

First, we consider the market for human blood, for which markets do exist. Titmuss (1971) examined alternative systems of human blood collection for transfusions. He focused on the systems in the United Kingdom, based entirely on voluntary donations, and the United States, where some blood is donated and some purchased. He found that blood shortages were greater, the incidence of blood-borne diseases such as hepatitis higher, and the monetary costs of the system were much higher, for the United States than in the United Kingdom. He also found that in Japan the system was voluntary before World War II, but became commercial after it, and blood donations dropped sharply and the consequences changed from being more like the United Kingdom to being more like the United States. From these finding, Titmuss concluded that the problems were caused by the existence of the market for human blood.

Titmuss's conclusion is clearly at odds with standard neoclassical economic theory. The introduction of a market for human blood, in which people get paid for supplying blood, can be expected to increase the supply of blood because it increases the return to doing so. The introduction of the market can also be expected to increase efficiency, reducing the inefficiency due to the missing market. However, in this case, the introduction of the market did precisely the opposite. Blood donations fell and the shortage of blood increased, and efficiency, in terms of standard indicators which relate to the quantity and quality of the good or service and the cost of producing it, declined.

Titmuss explained his main findings by arguing that "the commercialization of blood and donor relationships represses the expression of altruism, erodes the sense of community." The Nobel Prize-winning American economist, Kenneth Arrow (b. 1921) criticizes Titmuss's argument that the willingness to donate blood would fall as a result of a market being established, because "it does not explain why this willingness should be affected by the fact that other individuals receive money for these services, especially when the others include those whose need for financial reward is much greater" (Arrow, 1972, 351). However, this criticism seems to miss the point that when blood can be purchased for a price, donors may reasonably feel that instead of giving the gift of blood, which is priceless, they are simply giving the equivalent of an amount of money. Creating the market for blood therefore may reduce the number of altruistic donors and increase the propensity of the poor and the sick to donate blood, thereby possibly worsening the quality of blood. We may also invoke Anderson's (1990a, 1993) concept of political goods, in which individuals feel that they have a civic duty to donate blood for the common good, and the political values which give rise to these ideas may be eroded by introducing payments to blood donors, which treats blood like an economic good (in Anderson's terminology). These arguments may be correct or not in the case of the market for blood, but it seems impossible to understand the issues involved without taking into account ethical concerns.[11]

Thus, the supply of blood provides a clear illustration of the role of ethics in economics. A person is not born with a set of ready-made values; rather the individual's values are socially constructed through his or her being a part of a family, a religious organization, a school, and a particular society. If these groups expect and urge people to give their blood as an obligation of being members of the group that obligation becomes internalized as a moral value. Blood drives held in schools, churches, and in Red Cross facilities reinforce that sense of obligation. As commercial blood increases, the need for blood drives declines. Thus, the traditional reinforcement of that sense of obligation declines with the result that the embodied moral value atrophies. There is also an information problem. As blood drives decline it is rational for an individual to assume that there is no need for donated blood. The final outcome is that a typical person must overcome imperfect information and a lack of social approbation to be able to choose to donate blood.

This suggests that the type of policy recommended will have implications for the type of society that will develop. Inherent in the type of policy suggested is a preference as to the motivational attitudes that are appropriate and should be encouraged. Such attitudes, in turn, will influence the effects of policy changes.

### 7.3.2 Surrogate motherhood

Consider next the market for surrogate motherhood, in which a surrogate mother sells the service of conceiving and giving birth to a child by agreeing to be artificially impregnated with the sperm of an intended father, and transferring the child to an intended father who pays a certain sum of money to a broker, who then pays part of this to the surrogate mother.[12] After the child is born, the surrogate mother is required to terminate her parental rights to allow the intended father and his partner to raise the child exclusively as their own. Arguments in favor of markets in surrogate motherhood have been made on a number of grounds.[13] First, it allows people (who are well-informed and free to make their own decisions) to exert their fundamental rights of contract and of procreation as long as children are not harmed. Second, it may represent the only avenue of some people – who cannot otherwise have children despite their desire to do so – to raise families, given the shortage of children available for adoption and the problems of qualifying as adoptive parents. Third, surrogacy is an act of altruism, which should be encouraged for the development of virtues. Finally, its ethical implications are no different from those of other accepted social practices related to parenting, such as adoption, artificial insemination by donors, and day care, making it inconsistent not to extend markets to surrogacy.

Anderson (1990b, 1993, chapter 8) argues that surrogate motherhood treats children and women's labor as mothers as if they were commodities (to be bought and sold), and is harmful and degrading for both children and women. Treating children as commodities contradicts the fundamental obligations of parents to their children to love them, to not use them or manipulate them for personal gain, and to treat their parental rights as trusts which must be exercised in the interests of the children. The surrogate mother's renunciation of her parental responsibilities is for her personal advantage or in the interests of the intended parents (if the motive is altruistic), and not in the interests of the child, whose interests are not represented in the exchange. Also, the norms of parental love dictate that the parents love their child unconditionally, and not on the basis of any particular characteristics of the child. The parents who acquire the child from a surrogate mother violate this norm, because they choose the mother based partly on IQ and other characteristics, so as to ensure the "quality of the product." Finally, like the surrogate mother, the surrogacy agency acts solely in the interests of the couple who pay the fee, for example, by doing everything in its power to pry the child free from the birth mother. All of these violations of parental norms amount to treating the child as a commodity, which is degrading to the child. It is easy to dismiss such effects as merely symbolic, but children in general may be hurt by the degradation, and there is anecdotal evidence that such transactions can increase insecurity among other children of the surrogate mother (who fear the prospect of being abandoned) or even among the children who are being "sold" (who may fear being "resold").

Treating women's labor as a commodity, it is argued, also violates the respect and consideration due to women; that is, protecting her autonomy and being sensitive to her emotional relationships. Anderson (1993, 175–7) argues that the "pregnancy contract denies mothers autonomy over their bodies and their feelings. Their bodies and their health are subordinated to the independent interests of the contracting parents, who through the threat of lawsuits, exercise potentially unlimited control over the gestating mother's activities ... The surrogate industry dominates the birth mother's feelings in ways that deny her autonomy in interpreting her own perspective on her evolving relationship with her child." Surrogate mothers are not always altruistic about their actions, but make decisions for financial reasons and the emotional needs of giving birth, needs which can be manipulated by brokers. Finally there are significant differences between surrogate motherhood and other social practices which may seem similar to it. Thus, for instance, adoption involves the placing of children in families only when the birth parents cannot or will not discharge their parental responsibilities, and artificial insemination does not involve the sale of fully formed human beings. Indeed, there are restrictions on selling human beings: a person cannot even sell himself or herself into slavery or into indentured servitude. Based on these arguments Anderson recommends either the prohibition of surrogacy contracts or, at least, not allowing these contracts to be enforced by courts.

Since surrogate motherhood services are also internationally traded (especially couples from rich countries renting wombs of women in poor countries), there are additional possibilities of abuse. The surrogate mother's health may be of no concern to buyers or their agents (especially because the period for which women can be ideal surrogates is rather short), women may be forced into surrogacy by economic necessity due to poverty, or even by direct coercion, and there may be no control on what is done with the children born in this way – since they could be used for human organs or trafficking. Thus, at a minimum, there is a strong case for government regulation of this market in these countries.

### 7.3.3 Human organs

As a final example, consider the case of the market for human organs. In the period 2000–07 doctors in the United States annually performed 25,000 lifesaving organ transplants. But for every person who received a transplant, two others were added to a waiting list that in the United States now averages more than 80,000 people. In 2002 alone over 6000 died in the United States while waiting for organs. Because of the shortage of human organs, some have suggested that markets for human organs should be legalized. Currently, in many parts of the world laws specifically ban the sale of organs. US law, for instance, prohibits any "valuable consideration" resulting from an organ donation and imposes hefty fines and 5-year jail terms for illegal purchasers. There are no international laws that regulate human organ trade. Presently Pakistan and Iran are the only countries that have legalized the purchasing of organs. Other countries such as India, Brazil, Turkey, China, Russia, South Africa, and Iraq all seem to allow these transactions to take place even without legal sanction. For example, consider the case of kidneys for which there is a large demand in rich countries like the United States, and for which there is a large supply, especially in less-developed or transitional regions of the world. In areas such as South America, the Philippines, Singapore, China, Turkey, Romania, South Africa, Brazil, India, and Pakistan – where the price paid for kidneys from living people (who do not face significant health problems if they sell one of their kidneys, at least if the other one does not fail) is anywhere between $800 and

$10,000 dollars – this can significantly improve the sellers' financial situation (Naim, 2005). Brokers arrange for such international transactions, often arranging international travel and quality medical care for the purchasers.

One argument for legalizing the market for kidneys is the consequentialist one that it will increase the number of people who can receive transplants while receiving high-quality medical care. Moreover, it will make it easier for sellers to receive payments for their kidneys, reducing brokerage fees, thereby helping those who would otherwise not have the economic opportunities to enjoy a better life for themselves and their families. It can also be defended on egalitarian lines, since it will provide opportunities for the poor to augment their income. Yet another argument is the right-based one, which states that people have full ownership rights over their persons and should be allowed to sell their organs if they so choose, even if one cannot sell oneself (which would lead to the loss of autonomy for the person). Like surrogate motherhood, the argument can also be made that people should be encouraged to become altruistic, helping others with the gift of life.

However, the legalization of the market for kidneys also can be criticized from the egalitarian perspective. First, kidney transplants save lives, but only for the rich, who can afford to pay the large fees. If the ultimate aspect of people's functioning and capability – that of life itself – is to be protected, should it be protected based on one's income and wealth? Once markets are legalized, it is very likely that the availability of kidneys for transplant for those who cannot pay high prices will shrink drastically. This is because people would be unwilling to donate their kidneys except to help close family members or friends. It is likely that even some people who sign up to be organ donors (allowing their organs to be removed when they die) will refuse to become donors altogether, or opt to sell their organs. The poor cannot benefit from this market if they need kidney transplants, but can only benefit as donors, from the money they receive. Second, as far as the poor are concerned, it can be argued that they lose their personhood and become reduced to being a supplier of spare parts for the rich, and a source from which you can harvest a product. When the market is legalized in rich countries, the (effective) demand for kidney transplants will increase, and more people from poor countries will be reduced to this status. In addition, the increase in demand is more likely to increase the abuses of the system which already exist, since regulation will remain weak in poor countries. Current abuses are reflected in the close association of trade in kidneys with the trade in people, with unscrupulous brokers selling vendors (who are within their power) once they have harvested their kidney (Naim, 2005). They are also reflected in the theft of kidneys and in improper medical care given to vendors. The money actually received by the vendors is small in comparison to what purchases pay to the brokers, and given the highly elastic supply of potential kidney vendors because of the existence of a large number of poor people in the world, broker margins are likely to remain high. The other arguments for legalizing markets – based on rights and altruism – do not seem to be convincing, since it is difficult to argue that people who are in desperate financial conditions are voluntarily giving up their organs, or acting out of altruistic motives. Clearly, a poor person selling an organ such as a kidney out of desperation is being coerced and not exercising free choice.

Does this imply that the status quo should be preserved? Should people be dying while waiting for kidney transplants? Our point is not that people should be allowed to die, but that the market solution creates all kinds of problems which should be carefully evaluated before a decision about marketization can be made. Moreover, there may be alternative ways of increasing the supply of kidneys. Measures can be taken to increase the supply of kidneys by encouraging more people to sign up as organ donors on their driving licenses in rich countries. The proportion of people who sign up as organ donors in European countries is higher than in the United States, and it has been suggested that this may be due to the fact that in the United States people have to opt into becoming organ donors if they want to be donors while in Europe that have to opt out of being one if they choose not to be donors, since people reveal a bias in favor of choosing the status quo, and frequently do not like to opt out of things when they do not have a strong opinion on whether or not to opt out. Thus, it is possible that changing the nature of the question people are asked may increase the supply of organ donors.

## 7.4 Morals, the government, and government intervention

In the previous chapter and in this one so far we have been concerned with ethical issues related to markets, arguably the major institution examined by economists. But the market is by no means the only institution economists study. The market is often contrasted to the state or the government. In this section we turn to the issue of the moral standing of the government and examine how moral is government intervention. Since the market and the government are often viewed as alternative institutions, it is not surprising that markets and governments are often evaluated using similar criteria. It is convenient to discuss government policies using conceptions of moral worth which were used in Section 6.2 when discussing the morality of markets. There will inevitably be some overlap between the arguments made in that section and those made here, but we will be emphasizing different aspects of the same issues and not repeating arguments made there. For instance, we will not argue again that government intervention can reduce or increase choices.

Starting with rights, we saw that markets have been championed as guaranteeing some fundamental rights, such as the rights to hold property and to transfer them. These rights have often been seen from the view of protecting people from infringement of these rights by the state. However, it is not sufficiently recognized that the government may be required to ensure that rights are not violated. First, even for the rights of such things as property and transfer, it is not merely the case that people have rights against state intervention, but that government ensures that people do not have these rights violated by it and by other people. If people have the right to private property and transfer, what will ensure that their property is not seized by other people, and that they are not defrauded when they attempt to trade? By supplying law and order governments protect the rights to private property and transfer. Sometimes, in fact, in the presence of imperfect information, markets may cease to exist, thus preventing people from exercising their right to trade. George Akerlof, who was mentioned in the previous chapter, has analyzed the market for "lemons" – markets for used cars – one in which buyers do not know the quality of used cars which sellers do know, thus leading them to offer prices which are so low that eventually the market disappears. Second, we may value as fundamental rights other than property rights and the right to trade. For instance, we may take the view that every individual has a right not be discriminated against on account of their race, religion, gender or sexual preference, or to a job if they want it, or they have a right to at least basic food and health care sufficient for them to live. If society does wish to provide people with such rights, it is not enough to simply declare them as rights by common consent, but also that these rights are in fact protected. As mentioned earlier in Section 7.2 in the discussion of limits of the market, the state is the obvious institution that can protect these rights.

An argument against the state is that it can result in unfair allocations in the sense that people do not receive what they contribute. Government officials may distribute favors according to personal or kinship ties, or to gain political support. Those who can manipulate the bureaucratic system better, by ingratiating themselves to people in high positions, or those who spend a lot of time in attaining these positions, rather than by contributing to society as a whole, will be favored. While there are certainly cases in which these bad consequences do occur, it is not clear how widespread and ubiquitous they are, and how the government compares with other institutions which allocate goods and services. Such abuses can be checked through greater transparency in the activities of government officials, and greater public oversight. Moreover, the market may not allocate goods according to any standard equity principle. Furthermore, other institutions, such as large corporations, can experience various kinds of nepotism with respect to salaries and promotions. It is an empirical question as to whether the government results in more or less unfairness in the sense of desert in a specific context than other institutions like markets and firms.

An argument in favor of government intervention in the economy is that it can promote efficiency by removing or reducing market failures. For instance, it can introduce effluent fees to reduce the amount of pollution due to externalities. It can enact and enforce lemon laws (which require sellers to allow buyers to return defective products) to allow markets to operate efficiently when information about the nature of the product is imperfect. While these arguments are often made, and government intervention often justified on the basis of this argument, they are open to objections. First, how widespread are such market failures: are they widespread enough to warrant widespread government intervention? Some people argue that the empirical importance of such imperfections is exaggerated, and what seems like an imperfection merely reflects behavior which makes markets more efficient.[14] Second, it is argued that even if the market does fail to produce efficiency, the government will not be able to correct them. For instance, even well-meaning governments may not have information on how their intervention might affect people. Aren't people more informed about their situation than the government can ever be? While this may be true for some kinds of information that affect people, it is unlikely to be the case for other kinds of information of a more global or systemic nature, for instance, information about the future of the economy as a whole. Moreover, sometimes market failures are not corrected simply with information, but by overcoming coordination failures – for instance, unless a large number of firms expand to create markets for the products each one produces (as inputs or as goods and services that workers in the firms will buy), none of the firms may be profitable and therefore not exist, resulting in an inefficient outcome. Third, "correcting" some market failures need not make the economy more efficient because of the problem of the second best. Correcting some market failures while others cannot be corrected may make the situation worse in terms of efficiency (at least according to standard theory). Finally, government intervention can interfere with incentives, making people exert less effort and become less productive. For instance, high taxes may dissuade people from working and producing. Aside from the empirical issues about whether specific government interventions have these adverse effects on things like income, production, hours worked, and saving, one may well ask why these are necessarily bad (they can lead to overwork and bad health, etc.); in some cases government intervention may be aimed at reducing incentives for precisely those activities which create inefficiencies – such as production which causes excessive pollution.

Government intervention is often advocated on distributional grounds. It is claimed that the free operation of the market leads to high levels of inequality, based on inequalities in the distribution of endowments and other things, and governments need to reduce the inequality in the distribution of income with redistributive taxation and government expenditure policies, by supporting institutions which help to equalize opportunities, and by even redistributing assets. Against this argument, however, it is claimed that governments, even if well-intentioned, may fail to bring about reduced inequality. For instance, by trying to enforce minimum wages it can create more unemployment and worsen the position of the poor. Moreover, governments do not always represent the interests of the poor, and are often instruments of the rich and powerful, because the latter are overrepresented in government, or because politicians are dependent on the rich for financial support, and actually support policies that make the distribution of income and wealth worse.

It is sometimes claimed that government intervention in fact leads to the deterioration of moral values in society. Government rules and regulations encourage among people what some economists call directly unproductive activities by favoring them with special privileges, such as access to credit and tariff protection, and to outright illegal activity, such as bribery. Corruption breeds further corruption, and this leads to a general decay in ethical values in society. Corrupt politicians and government officials, who stand to gain most when governments intervene to a greater extent in the economy, also erode morality directly, and indirectly, by setting bad examples for people outside government. Rather than encouraging honest productive effort, government intervention encourages dishonest and unproductive efforts by people who attempt to capture larger shares of a shrinking pie. However, it needs to be kept in mind that while excessive government intervention in the form of countless rules and regulations may breed corruption in some societies, corruption can also result from the necessary activities of the government in maintaining law and order and enforcing contracts. For instance, politicians and other government officials may help out some parties in legal proceedings in return for bribes, and their tendency to do this may increase when other avenues of money-making are denied to them!

Moreover, many mainstream economists who take the view that ordinary human beings only act in their interests and do not have ethical values, extend this notion of *homo economicus* to individuals in government, whose objective is usually taken to be the maximization of their private income. In reality, politicians and other government officials may be self-interested, but also have other motives, such as remaining in power, representing their class or ethnic group, helping others and being public spirited, and following their ethical values in general. Studies of how governments and its constituents actually function suggest that while some states are predatory, others actually operate to successfully promote development and others are prevented from doing so by the constraints they face in their relations with civil society (see Evans, 1989). It is surely simpleminded and unrealistic to conceive of politicians and bureaucrats as only being self-interested individuals trying to maximize their income.

## 7.5 Conclusion

This chapter has examined the moral standing of markets and the government in the economy. It has examined the overall case for the market system and of government intervention, and also examined the ethical issues concerning these two institutions in specific parts of the economy. It has found that the market and the government can be evaluated in terms of a variety of criteria which relate to their consequences in terms of efficiency and inequality, in terms of the values they promote, in terms of their ability to expand freedom and individual rights, and in terms of communities they create. No definitive and unqualified argument in favor of either the market system or government intervention can be sustained on ethical grounds, and we have found that the ethical worth of each depends on a variety of factors, including context, an assessment of consequences within a given context, and the weights one wishes to apply to the various criteria. In terms of specific spheres of the economy, also, various complex issues arise, but there may be more agreement about the ethical standing of markets and government intervention – in terms of prohibition of markets, government regulation of markets, or government provision – in particular markets than about entire economic systems.

The market and the state can be seen as two of the major institutions of modern economies. This raises the question of what are institutions. The term institution has many meanings in economics, especially if one extends the meaning of economics to encompass nonorthodox approaches to the subject. One meaning of institutions is the "rules of the game" according to which economic (and other kinds of) activity takes place, including laws and regulations, norms of behavior, and even patterns of habitual behavior. Another meaning refers to specific organizations of individuals which operate in the economy, whether formal organizations such as the government and its various branches, firms, clubs and societies, religious bodies, and non-governmental organizations (NGOs), or informal organizations such as families (nuclear or extended), and informal groups of individuals, such as neighborhoods or a circle of friends. The two different meanings of institutions are also related, because "organizations" may – and often do – create or enforce "rules of the game." Markets can refer to both meanings, because they have certain rules, and may have specific organizing groups (like boards of trade or stock exchanges), or may be regulated "spontaneously" by market participants, or by the state, and the government can be both a group and a creator and enforcer of laws and other rules. Our examples suggest, however, that they are not the only institutions in actual economies. The morality of other institutions may also be examined. Indeed, Jeremy Bentham used utilitarianism to evaluate the legal system and specific laws can be evaluated from other ethical perspectives. In Chapter 11 we will briefly examine the ethics of two other institutions as organizations, that is, business firms (particularly financial ones) and labor unions.

# 8
# Individual Preferences, Efficiency, and Cost-Benefit Analysis

## Introduction

Individual preferences have a central role in mainstream economic theory not only because they can be used to *explain* and *predict* individual and group behavior, but also because they can be used to *evaluate* the aggregate outcomes of such behavior. Thus, they are employed to examine whether a particular outcome is good or bad, and also to evaluate if a change that occurs is good or not. More specifically, they are utilized for evaluating the desirability of particular economic policies and to examine whether this or that policy change should be undertaken. For instance, should the government cut taxes on rich households? Or they can be used to answer whether a policy change which has been undertaken has been successful or not. For instance, is the increase in the tax rate on cigarette sales to be considered a success? Even more specifically, they are used to evaluate specific projects: Should the city government build a sports stadium? This chapter will examine to what extent such evaluations based on individual preferences are justified.

The way that individual preferences are used for evaluative purposes is as follows. Individual preferences are assumed to be depicted by utility functions (which order their preferences) relating their consumption of particular goods or more generally, the state of the world (which could include how much leisure time they have, or how clean the environment is), to their level of satisfaction or utility. Typically it is assumed that an individual's level of utility increases with the amount of goods and services they consume and decreases with the amount of time they work. Individual preferences in this sense are used for the overall or social evaluation of states of the world. If individuals are all better off by their own reckoning, that is, in terms of their utility functions, then we can say that society is also better off. This approach is appealing because social outcomes are evaluated in terms of how individuals in society evaluate them, rather than in terms of how some group of people, or even a dictator, evaluates them. It is also closely related to the idea that the consumer is sovereign in the marketplace (the concept of consumer sovereignty).

There are two immediate issues that arise when one uses individual preferences to evaluate social outcomes in these ways. First, at least in the way individual preferences have been interpreted here (which is the way they are usually interpreted in standard economic theory), good and bad are interpreted in exclusively consequentialist terms. According to this approach, policies are considered to be good because they result in good consequences, in the sense that individuals obtain higher levels of utility because, for instance, the consumption bundles they are able to obtain are preferable compared to what they obtain without the policy change. By implication, policies are not evaluated according to other criteria, such as whether they provide individuals with more freedom or more opportunities in some sense. Second, changes in the state of the world, for instance, due to changes in government policy, do not always – or even usually – lead to changes in the level of utility of all individuals in the same direction; some people may be better off, and some may be worse off. Thus, trade liberalization may make some people better off (because they obtain goods more cheaply or because they receive higher income as a result), but may make others worse off (because they lose their jobs or receive lower income). If a change occurs which makes some persons better off and no one worse off – what is called a Pareto improvement – one can say that society is better off. In general, when changes do not result in Pareto improvements, it is not possible to judge whether the state of the world is good in some sense, or a change leads to an improvement, unless we can somehow decide how the gains and losses for different individuals affect social welfare as a whole, that is, employ some externally imposed aggregation rule. Arrow (1951) showed that it is impossible to derive a social ordering or voting rule from individual orderings (in situations involving more than two choices) satisfying some desirable axioms, including unrestricted domain, nondictatorship, Pareto efficiency, and independence of irrelevant alternatives.

In this chapter we will sidestep the issue that good or bad may be defined in nonconsequentialist terms until the concluding section. Before then we will concentrate on how individual preferences can be used for evaluating well-being using some standard rules of aggregation.

We start in Section 8.1 with the simple case of a single market with given demand and supply curves, in which well-being is often judged according to the total surplus accruing to buyers and sellers. Then we examine, in Section 8.2, the more general case of many interconnected markets and discuss the notions of efficiency, Pareto optimality and the social welfare function. In the next three sections – Sections 8.3 through 8.5 – we examine three kinds of reasons why the use of individual preferences to evaluate social outcomes is problematic – the case of the endogeneity of preferences, the case of future time periods and generations, and the case of imperfect information. In Section 8.6 we examine whether the standard assumption that more (of goods and services) is better for individuals is a valid assumption to make. Section 8.7 briefly discusses the method of cost-benefit analysis. Finally, Section 8.8 draws some general conclusions.

## 8.1 Consumer and producer surplus

The simplest way in which economists employ standard economic theory to analyze the desirability of states of the economy or of the effects of policy changes is by using the ubiquitous demand–supply framework for a single market and the concepts of consumer surplus, producer surplus, and total surplus. Assuming, as usual, that the market price rises when there is an excess demand for goods, falls when there is excess supply, and remains unchanged when the quantities demanded and supplied are equal, equilibrium price is shown at *E* in Figure 8.1. To examine

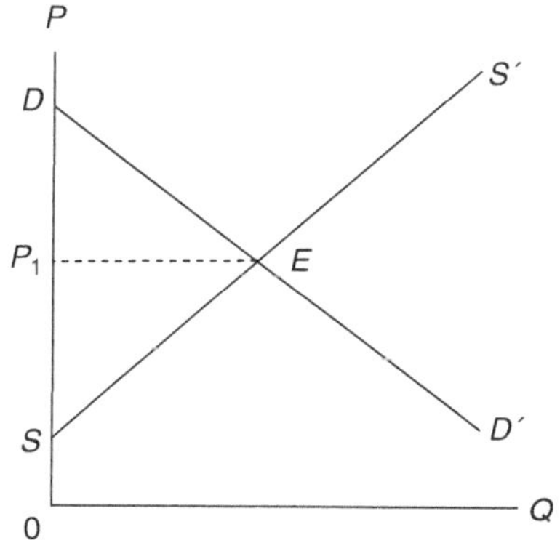


*Figure 8.1* Supply and demand

the desirability of this equilibrium, we note that the consumer surplus at this equilibrium – the area below the demand curve *DD′* and above the price line, showing the difference between the maximum amount consumers wish to pay for a unit of the good and the amount they actually pay – is shown as the area $DEP_1$, and the producer surplus – the area below the price line and above the supply curve *SS′*, showing the difference between the price actually received per unit and the minimum amount for which the sellers would wish to sell – is shown by the area $SP_1E$. Hence, the total surplus – the sum of the consumer and producer surpluses – is *DES*. This is a measure of the net benefit to society at the equilibrium: the maximum additional amounts people are willing to pay is a measure of the additional or marginal benefit people receive from the additional quantity, and the minimum additional price at which firms are willing to supply an additional unit of output represents the additional or marginal cost. It is easy to see that price at which the total surplus is highest is the equilibrium price $P_1$. For instance, if a price floor is set at price $P_2$ in Figure 8.2, equilibrium quantity would be given at $Q_2$, and despite the excess supply, price would not fall, given the price floor. The consumer surplus is then $DFP_2$ and the producer surplus is $P_2FGS$, so that the total surplus is given by *DFGS*, which is less than *DES* by the amount *FEG*, which is usually called the deadweight loss. Where the surplus is maximized (at *E*) changes in price, quantities, who buys and who sells, all have the effect of reducing the surplus. Take for instance, replacing a buyer who is buying by one who is not. This means that we are replacing someone to whom the good is worth more (since he or she is willing to pay more for it) by someone to whom the good is worth less.

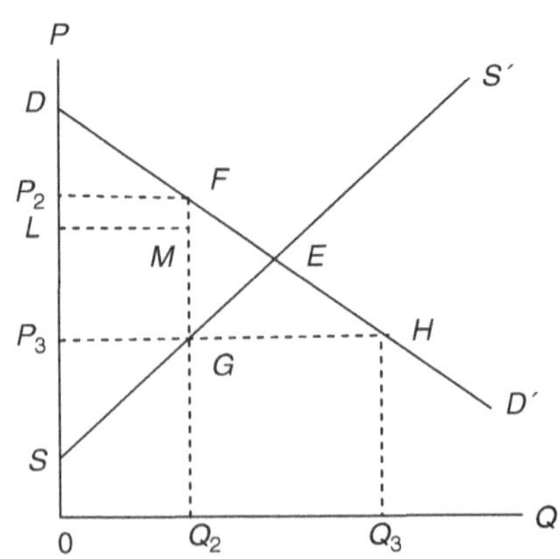


*Figure 8.2* Supply and demand with price ceiling

Governments often try to influence the market by introducing price and quantity controls like the price floor just discussed. Another such intervention is a price ceiling, at price $P_3$, as shown in Figure 8.2. An example is rent control, a policy pursued by governments in many cities in the world. At price $P_3$ there will be an excess demand of $GH$, and not all consumers who want to rent at that price will be able to find a rental. Renters whose quantity demanded is shown all along the entire line $0Q_3$, including some of those who wish to pay less than price $P_2$, rather than only those (who are willing to pay more than or equal to price $P_2$) on the line $0Q_2$ will be renters. If we assume that those who are able to rent are randomly selected from all those who want to rent (independently of the maximum amount they want to pay), the average maximum amount is given by $0L$ (where $L$ bisects line $DP_3$). Since $OQ_2$ renters wish to pay on average a maximum of $OL$ each, the consumer surplus is given by $LP_3GM$ and the total surplus is $LSGM$, less than the surplus without rent control, $DES$. Thus rent control is clearly undesirable. But now suppose that people who are willing to pay more do so not because they have a more intense liking – or even need – for apartments, but because they have the resources to pay the rent, and those who are willing to pay less do so because they have fewer resources and not because they need them less. For instance, suppose someone who is very rich wants to rent an apartment because they want to visit the city to attend an occasional play, and someone who is rather poor wants to rent the apartment for his or her family, since the only work he or she has is in the city and it is prohibitively expensive to move to a different job. Then, can we be sure that society is still better off without rent control? The problem with the surplus view is that it involves adding together the benefits received by different people in terms of the maximum they are willing to pay, without making any distinction between who wants it and why. If we feel that the society as a whole is better off if the apartment is rented by the more needy family rather than by the person who leaves it vacant for most of the year and uses it only occasionally, the surplus approach will not be adequate. The surplus approach does not take income distributional issues, or the nature of needs, into account, and merely adds up money values of maximum amounts people are willing and able to pay.

## 8.2 Efficiency and Pareto optimality

The concepts of consumer and producer surplus provide a simple method for evaluating welfare, but have the problem of simply adding up the marginal benefits of different people and marginal costs of different firms. Adding up the benefits accruing to different people implies disregarding issues of distribution and equality. Moreover, the basic model used is a simple partial equilibrium one.

When economists examine economies with many interacting markets, they typically use a different notion of what is good for society. They invoke the concept of efficiency or what is called Pareto optimality. An outcome is defined as being Pareto optimal if, given people's preferences and resources and technology available for the economy, it is not possible to make anyone better off in the sense of obtaining higher utility without making others worse off in the sense of having lower levels of utility. In other words, all possible ways of increasing any one person's utility, by utilizing resources previously unutilized, by shifting resources and workers between different producers and, and by redistributing goods and services between different consumers, have already been exploited.

Figure 8.3 shows the utility possibility frontier for an economy with two people, 1 and 2, the levels of utility for whom are shown by $U_1$ and $U_2$, as the negatively sloped heavier line. It shows the maximum utility that can be obtained by one individual given the utility level of the other person. All points on the frontier are efficient in the sense of being Pareto optimal. It can be seen that point B is not efficient because, starting from it, both people can be made better off (as implied by a move from B to C).

The so-called fundamental theorem of welfare economics states that under certain conditions a perfectly competitive general equilibrium in which all markets clear, in which all individuals maximize utility

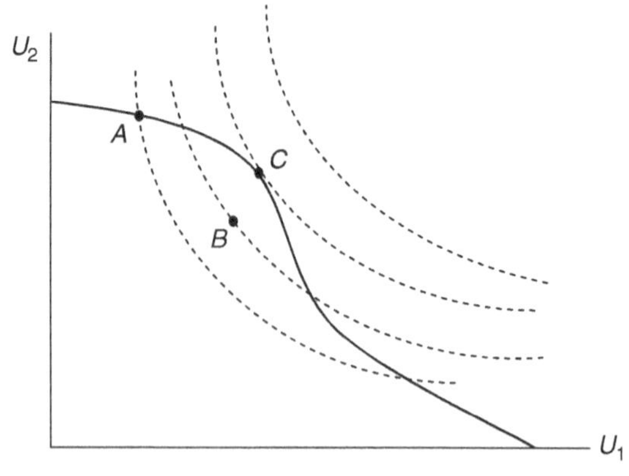


*Figure 8.3* Utility possibility frontier and social welfare function

and in which all firms maximize profits, is also a Pareto optimal or efficient outcome. This is roughly analogous to the result in the partial equilibrium model which states that the competitive equilibrium at the intersection of the supply and demand curves is also efficient in the sense of maximizing the value of the surplus. These results are interpreted as showing that the free-market economy produces good outcomes. However, economists have examined conditions which, when violated, imply that the first welfare theorem does not hold, that is, the market equilibrium fails to produce an efficient outcome, so that markets "fail." Market failures occur, for instance, when there are externalities, public goods, situations of imperfect information, and, of course, departures from perfect competition – such as monopolies and oligopolies.

The analysis of desirable outcomes has, so far, been made only on the basis of efficiency using the notions of Pareto improvements and Pareto optimality. Since many changes in the economy involve utility gains for some and utility losses for others (such as a move from *A* to *B* or from *A* to *C* in Figure 8.3), these changes cannot be evaluated. Moreover, a situation in which one person achieves a very high level of utility while others obtain very little may be Pareto optimal (a point like *A* in the Figure 8.3), but may not be considered a good outcome on grounds of fairness. To evaluate and rank such situations economists sometimes use a social welfare function which shows the relationship between social welfare, $W$, and individual levels of utility, $U_i$, where it is assumed that $W$ increases with each person's utility.[1] Iso-welfare contours, each of which show a given level of social welfare, illustrating the social welfare function, are shown by the dashed downward-sloping lines in Figure 8.3. Iso-welfare curves further to the northeast show higher levels of social welfare. According to this social welfare function, social welfare at *C* exceeds that at *B* which exceeds that at *A*. Such a ranking of states according to a social welfare function implies that it is possible for a move from a Pareto-optimal state to a state which is inefficient (like a move from *A* to *B*) to result in an improvement in social welfare. However, to achieve the state with the highest level of social welfare, that state has also to be Pareto optimal, as is the case with point *C* in the figure. What the social welfare function does is to combine the notion of efficiency with that of fairness.[2]

Even if we do not consider the issue of fairness – which we will consider in Chapter 10 – and rely only on efficiency criteria (say the notion of Pareto improvements) to rank social states, we may run into several problems. In the next three sections we discuss three such problems which arise from the facts that: first, preferences, as represented by utility functions, may change with changes in the state of the world; second, future states of the world have to take into account the utilities of people who will be born in the future; and third, people's knowledge about states of the world may be imperfect.

## 8.3 The endogeneity of preferences

Individual preferences may depend on the state of the world in which individuals find themselves, and when the state of the world changes, their preferences may change. When such changes occur it is not in general possible to rank states of the world according to individual preferences, since this measuring rod itself changes.

There are numerous reasons why individual preferences may change with the state of the world. In some cases individuals may learn to like some things (like classical music or literary works) only after they have had some experience consuming them. In other cases, individuals may become addicted to some things (like cigarettes and television viewing) when they consume them, and therefore continue to consume them, even if they do not experience high levels of utility as a result of doing so. In other cases, individuals who are used to a particular lifestyle may be satisfied or yearn for a different one. If changes in the state of the world induce changes in the lifestyle they are used to, individuals' preferences may change. Perhaps they will come to prefer the new state that they have achieved because they have developed new identities or they need to reduce cognitive dissonance[3] or, nostalgically, they will prefer the one they left behind.

In these cases it is possible that the status quo may be Pareto optimal given people's current preferences, but a policy-induced change in the state of the world, may make some people better off and no one worse off according to their new preferences. An example of this concerns the subsidization of classical music, which people may not like given their initial preferences, but which may make them better off given their new preferences. Another relates to policies which promote industrialization in a country at the expense of agricultural development, which may be unwelcome initially if people prefer their pastoral lifestyle, but then they come to enjoy the benefits of city life.

The endogeneity of preferences implies that it is not possible to argue that some states of the world are better than other states only by appealing to individual preferences, since these preferences can change with the state of the world. There have been some suggestions by which the individual preferences yardstick may still be usable. One suggestion is that one can evaluate two states of the world, *A* and *B*, and say that *A* is socially preferred to *B* if individuals prefer *A* to *B* in terms of both their old and new preferences. There are many problems with this method. First, it can produce too many cases in which rankings are simply not possible because the ordering is reversed when one uses the two sets of preferences. Second, it may be in general impossible to forecast how an individual's preferences may change when the state of the world changes without actually implementing the policy change, and thus impossible to rank states according to future unknown preferences. Third, in some cases where a particular state may be preferred to another state, it may be the result of cognitive dissonance, and it is not obvious that this form of endogeneity can yield individual preferences which should be used for evaluating states of the world and enacting policy changes. Another suggestion that has been made concerns the use of metapreferences, or the use of a production function approach to preference formation (see Stigler and Becker, 1977). Thus, individual utility from consumption is determined by a given, unchanging utility function, but depends not only on the quantities of goods, and so on, consumed, but also on their stock of what we can call consumption capital. As people consume more of certain goods, their consumption capital increases, and this will make them enjoy more the consumption of certain goods. For instance, as people listen to classical music their consumption capital which allows them to enjoy classical music more increases, so that they enjoy classical music more than before. Here, people's preferences have not changed, only the amount of their consumption capital which determines how much enjoyment is 'produced' by listening to classical music, which affects their utility level. If individuals know the relevant metapreferences or how consumption affects consumption capital and how that in turn affects what consumption contributes to utility, then the endogeneity of preferences is not a problem either for what people choose or for how they evaluate these choices, since the metapreferences are unchanged. However, it is not at all clear that even for simple things like classical music consumption people know all the relevant functional relationships and are able to take them into account in making optimal decisions. The solution also does not work for certain kinds of preference changes which relate to the weakness of will or conflicts between multiple selves within an individual. An example of weakness of will is the person who places the alarm clock across the room from the bed. This requires a person to get up and cross the room to turn off the alarm. By that time the person is awake enough that they can overcome their weak will and not go back to bed. The two selves theory assumes that individuals have two utility functions. There is conflict between the two utility functions with one representing the farsighted self and the other the shortsighted self. Sometimes the shortsighted self is in control so the rationality of the farsighted self is constrained by the not-always-rational shortsighted self's utility function. In fact, the alarm clock example can be analyzed as a two utility function case as well as one of weakness of will. All of this implies that individuals may not be able to choose among alternatives taking into account their metapreferences and their changing stocks of consumption capital. The solution also does not work for situations in which the preference change depends not only on what people consume, but also on what other people consume, something that people are not able to control or predict.

## 8.4 Future generations

Many policy changes involve outcomes which occur in the future, where the world is populated by people who have not yet been born, or are not currently expressing their preferences in the ballot box or the marketplace. Consider three examples. First, should the level of government spending be increased by allowing the government to increase its level of borrowing from the public? This question has implications for future generations because increases in government borrowing will increase the level of government debt and thereby increase the debt burden that has to be borne by future generations, and also because the increase in government spending may have consequences for growth and for the general state of the economy future generations will experience (for instance, if the additional spending goes to developing public infrastructure or to research and development which improves technology, it may increase the level of production and income for future generations). Second, should social security benefits and taxes be left unchanged even if this implies lower benefits and higher taxes in the future to keep the social security system of a country in a solvent state? Third, should we reduce our level of consumption now in order to reduce the extent of damage we cause to the natural environment, say by exacerbating the problem of global warming? In all these examples we cannot know whether the situations are efficient, or whether changes are preferable, simply because we do not know how future generations will be affected by what we do now.

There are a number of problems which arise regarding the preferences of people not yet born. First, what we do now may determine whether or not some people will be born in the future. It is well known that the birth rate of an economy (the number of people born per thousand people) responds to economic conditions prevailing in a country: for instance, countries in which people are richer, or where women tend to work outside the home more, have lower birth rates. Since what we do now will affect future conditions, our current actions can determine how many people will be born in the future. Second, our actions now will very likely affect the preferences of those who are born later, because it will affect the kind of people that they are. These are very difficult issues to come to terms with, and economists often assume these problems away by assuming that there is a constant rate of growth of population and that the preferences of all individuals – those who exist now and those who will be born later – are the same. These assumptions, for instance, are made in models of economic growth which deal with environmental and resource issues. Assuming that all people have identical preferences, by the way, implies that many fairness issues that afflict welfare economics are removed, if we also assume that everybody (at least those living now) has the same income, every individual (who is living now) becomes identical.

The question still remains: should the weight we attach to the preferences and utility levels of people today in determining social welfare be the same as the weight we attach to people in future generations? It would be difficult to justify that because we are alive today and we are making decisions today, we should give less weight to the preferences and utility levels of future generations. However, people who are alive now may attach a smaller weight to their own future utility levels, because of what economists call the rate of time preference which arises from the fact that people are impatient, and they therefore give more weight to utility from current consumption than to that from future consumption. If we do this, we would be valuing the utility we get in 30 years' time the same as those who will be born in 10 years' time when they will turn 20. Many economists argue that people make decisions which suggest that they give less weight to their own future utility from consumption and therefore this should be taken into account in estimating the social rate of discount. But, it can be argued, the fact that people are often impatient – or as some argue, that they are myopic with defective telescopic faculties – does not imply that society should take this into account in valuing the utility of future generations. Is there an ethical case for having a positive rate of social time preference? While economists tend to use it, there seems to be no clear case for it. The argument is sometimes given that in future people will be richer, and therefore there should be less weight given to their consumption. But this does not apply to utility levels, which already take into account diminishing marginal utility – what is being added is not consumption levels but utility. Some argue for it based on uncertainty about the future – since we are less certain about what will happen in the future, we should weigh future utility less. However, for the case of future catastrophic events which could occur, this would call for trying to reduce the chances of such events occurring, by using low, declining or even no rates of discount (which would make us value the future highly and therefore take appropriate actions now, for instance, to reduce the damage we do to the environment).

## 8.5 Imperfect information

The preferences of individuals over states of the world may not be based on what economists call perfect information. In some cases people may not be fully aware of the well-established facts regarding the consequences of certain choices: for instance, they may not be aware of the risks of cancer from asbestos insulation. In cases such as these, should individual preferences be used to make a judgment about what is best for society? Should people who feel that they are better off if they use asbestos insulation based on imperfect information, or who buy snake oil thinking that it will cure some deadly disease (when in fact there is no evidence that it does), be left free to do these things for the social good? One may try to increase the amount and quality of information available to people to allow them to have less imperfect information, but it is not at all clear whether people can obtain all the necessary information and process it properly. There is a considerable amount of evidence that, especially in situations of uncertainty, individuals reveal biases in decision-making (see Kahneman et al., 1982). It has been found, in fact, that individuals are in some ways predictably irrational in making certain kinds of decisions in situations in which rational decisions may be possible. For instance, people tend to have a preference for the status quo, they tend to misestimate events with small probabilities, and they often use information to make decisions about unrelated issues, just because that information is available to them.

It has been suggested by some that we try to correct for these problems by considering the preferences of people – what Cowen (1993) calls cleansed preferences – which they would have if they were fully informed. In other words, we can try to find what people would want if, hypothetically, they had perfect knowledge and beliefs. However, there are many problems with this approach. For instance, if we had perfect knowledge, we would give up the joys of being surprised, or we would be constantly reminded of extremely unpleasant things. Moreover, in some cases the scientific evidence is not very clear, and the outcomes of some events are truly uncertain, so that no one knows what perfect information means. Finally, even if some remedy which does not actually work gives some solace and false hope to a person who will inevitably die of some disease, is it right to deny that person that opportunity?

## 8.6 Decision utility versus experiential utility

Preferences relate to two things which economists often conflate. One relates to the role of preferences as guiding their behavior, and can be called decision utility. This is what is relevant for analyzing decisions people make about, for instance, what and how much they consume. The other relates to how people evaluate what they experience after they have made their choices, and can be called experienced utility. This seems to be what is relevant for evaluating states of the world. The implication of this distinction is that just because people make some choices and decisions, we should not automatically infer that they are actually better off by making them.

An important example of this relates to how consumption and income affect utility. There is a great deal of evidence that suggests that people often make decisions which increase their consumption and income. They often decide to change jobs if they can increase their income by so doing, and they tend to consume large amounts of many things when they are able to (and sometimes when they are not able to do so from their own resources, by borrowing). Economists therefore assume that utility depends positively on consumption and income of a person. In recent years there has been a large amount of empirical work that suggests that increases in income and consumption do not always make people feel better off by their own reckoning, at least after a certain level of income and consumption. These are issues we will discuss in the next chapter.

What we need to note here is that we cannot evaluate outcomes based on what people choose, without finding out how people feel after they have made their decisions and experienced the outcomes. Yet this is precisely what is done by many economists in evaluating states of the world. For instance, it is the approach adopted in the surplus approach to demonstrating the efficiency of the perfectly competitive equilibrium discussed in Section 8.1 and in the fundamental theorem of welfare economics discussed in Section 8.2. These approaches infer what people experience merely from the choices they make.

## 8.7 Cost-benefit analysis

Cost-benefit analysis is a form of applied welfare economic analysis which is often used for evaluating whether or not a particular project should be undertaken, usually by a government agency which is interested in increasing social welfare rather than maximizing monetary returns. Sometimes international institutions and other donors insist that the government of a country conduct cost-benefit analysis of a project planned for that country, or the donor may have independent consultants do a cost-benefit analysis, or do their own before funding the project. It is also used for analyzing the effects of projects after they have been completed, which actually requires less analysis about complex effects of projects, although it may still be difficult to isolate the effects of a particular project from those of other extraneous changes. We will discuss examples of planned projects.

The basic idea of cost-benefit analysis is simple enough. Any project will have certain benefits and costs which accrue to society. Benefits may include an increase in output levels, increases in productivity and income in related activities, improvements in health conditions, or improvements in literacy. Costs include the expense of resources required for the project, but the way economists seek to measure it is in terms of opportunity costs or, the cost of not having the next best alternative use of the resources. If the benefits and costs accrue over several years, to obtain total benefits and costs some appropriate rate of discount is used to add up amounts from different periods of time. After the total benefits and costs of the project are quantified, the net benefit of the project can be calculated, and the project is deemed to be worth doing if its net benefit is positive.

It is useful to compare the method by which the net benefit to a project is calculated to the way it is done for a private money-making project. The private producer's benefit from a project is the revenue it generates to the firm, which depends on the amount it can produce and sell and the price of each unit produced. Its costs refer to the cost of the resources the firm uses, which depends on the amount of different resources used (including the opportunity costs of its own resources).

A public project of the type for which cost-benefit analysis is typically done differs in several respects from a private project. First, since the benefits and costs of a private project mostly reflect market transactions (apart from the opportunity costs of the firms owner's labor and capital, for instance) the money values are easily quantifiable. For public projects the costs and benefits often do not reflect market transactions, so that we have to assume that they are quantifiable and estimate actual numbers for them. For instance, if a project is undertaken to save rain forests, we have to value the forest in some way, or if a project improves health and reduces mortality, we have to put some value on the lives and improved health. One way to do that is by finding out what people would be willing to pay for these benefits. But this also raises problems. How do we make people truthfully reveal what they would actually pay for these benefits, when they may try to hide this information if they feel that revealing it would make them pay for it? Economists try to devise clever methods which can elicit such information. Second, the costs and benefits that are incurred in social projects do not refer to private costs and benefits as in a private project. We are interested in knowing not only how much the project costs in terms of actual outlays, but also its opportunity cost to society as a whole. Suppose a project results in hiring some people for road construction. Should we value this cost at the amount the workers are actually paid? Or should we value it according to what the society loses in terms of what they could be producing elsewhere? To take an extreme case, if there are many unemployed people in the economy who do not add to output anywhere, the social cost of hiring these workers is zero, although the money cost is positive. In general, economists try to figure out appropriate "shadow" prices for resources used in production and for valuing output produced. There are many methods employed for these purposes, some more complicated than others, but all involving a great deal of guesswork. Basically the difference between market prices and shadow prices are caused by things like distortions (like government tariffs and minimum wage laws) and externalities (which would make the shadow price of the output of the project higher than the imputed market price if there are positive externalities, that is, the social benefit exceeds the private benefit). These social effects may also be very complex, and it would, in general be an extremely complicated matter to accurately predict all possible relevant consequences, let alone derive shadow prices for the relevant goods and bads. Third, the benefits of the project may accrue to different individuals, for instance, to the rich and the poor – some could lose (have a negative benefit) and some could gain. The private firm cares only about the bottom line, and not about how different people are affected. But in terms of social welfare, we may have to weigh the benefits to different people differently. For instance, the amount the rich are willing to pay for a project may be considerably greater than what the poor are willing to pay not because it benefits them more, but because they have more resources with which to pay. This problem is very similar to the problem of adding up individual consumer surpluses. The solution proposed has usually been to give more weight to the benefits to the poor than to the rich.

This discussion suggests that cost-benefit analysis is very tricky business at best. Cost-benefit analysis involves finding or guessing values for all kinds of numbers, including shadow prices, social rates of discount, income distributional weights for different groups of people, and values of nonmarketed goods and services. Sometimes the benefits are so difficult to quantify that some economists suggest that quantitative analysis should be done only for costs and not for benefits, in order to compare between different projects which yield (roughly) the same benefits. But a great deal of guesswork is required even to evaluate costs, especially if they incur nonmarket costs, such as the cost of displacing people from a project site (say a dam). Moreover, since some of the information (that is, information on marketed values, which we may call hard information) is available more easily than others (related to shadow prices, imputations for nonmarketed elements and distributional weights, which we may call soft information because they are not "out" there to measure) there may emerge a bias to emphasize the former over the latter. Accordingly, one may question if the approach is of any use for appraising projects from the point of view of social desirability. However, as Hubin (1994) argues, the approach does provide a framework, however flawed, to organize relevant data. The kind of information provided by a cost-benefit analysis is relevant for decision-making from the point of view of the different moral theories. It arguably provides a starting point from which economists can factor in other things, such as income distributional effects, and adjustments in the social discount rate. But in doing so, some additional problems of the method should be kept in mind. First, it evaluates the consequences of projects by using individual preferences regarding these consequences, and this opens up all the problems with this approach – such as the endogeneity of preferences and imperfect information – discussed earlier in this chapter. At the very least, for public projects there needs to be reasoned and public discussion about the consequences of projects rather than just using given individual preferences. Second, the approach can be thought of as commodifying goods and services provided by a project, that is, treating them as if they are traded in markets rather than provided publicly, and thereby failing to recognize the political values implicit in these goods and services in the sense discussed in Section 7.2. This problem becomes particularly acute when the projects have major effects on health conditions and the environment, where it becomes necessary to place a "market" value on human life (Anderson, 1993, chapter 9). In such cases, as Anderson argues, there is no alternative to involve robust democratic institutions in decision-making rather than trying to attach numbers to value such goods and services.

## 8.8 Conclusion

This chapter has examined the standard economists' approach of evaluating economic performance and the effects of policies in terms of individual utility. This approach is frequently adopted in the consumer and producer surplus "triangles" in the simple supply–demand approach, and in more general approaches, such as utilitarianism, the analysis of Pareto improvements and the social welfare function approach. The common feature behind these approaches is the use of individual utility to value social outcomes.

Although this approach has the appeal that they value social states in terms of what people want or seem to want, rather than imposing some preferences on them – like those of a dictator or a government that decides for them – it is problematic for a number of reasons. First, it sometimes overemphasizes efficiency and neglects distributional considerations. Distributional considerations are introduced in terms of social welfare functions or distributional weights in cost-benefit analysis, but their role is often minimized, perhaps because they seem to be imposed independently of individual preferences. Second, evaluating outcomes on individual utility and individual choices raises problems because of the endogeneity of preferences, the preferences of future generations, imperfect knowledge, and the possible disjuncture between individual choices and experiences. Third, relying on individual preferences neglects questions related to why people prefer some things to others, for instance, by focusing on wants rather than needs, and whether society should be concerned with the needs of other living beings, such as animals. Fourth, the approach is consequentialist and ignores issues such as individual freedoms, rights, and the character and nature of people and society (other than what can be inferred from outcomes).

Although economists frequently focus on individual utility in evaluating social outcomes, they also use other methods, such as income and production measures, and the extent to which people meet their basic needs, and many of them also pay attention to distributional issues. These issues will be discussed in the following two chapters.

# 9
# Production, Income, and Economic Growth

## Introduction

The most commonly used way in which economists and the general public evaluate economic outcomes is with accounting measures of income and production, that is, their levels and their growth rate. The levels of production and income per person – using Gross Domestic Product (GDP), Net Domestic Product (NDP), Gross National Product (GNP), and National Income (NI) – are some of the most widely available economic statistics for any country.[1] These figures typically measure the market value of all final goods and services produced in a country divided by total population. The statistic is used to rank countries in terms of how well they are doing in comparison to other countries. Countries which have high levels of production and income per capita are usually described as rich countries or developed countries while those with low levels of income per capita are called poor or less-developed or underdeveloped countries or, to put a positive spin on it, developing countries. Countries which experience high rates of increase in per capita income and product are praised as doing well, while low-growth countries are not.[2] Policies that supposedly result in high rates of growth of per capita income are often praised. Income and production are also used to examine how well individual people are doing. For instance, a person is usually called poor if his or her income falls below an amount or level called the poverty line, which is determined – often by the government – to be necessary to purchase some socially acceptable minimum amount of goods and services. Public programs are often called successful if they reduce the number of people who are considered poor according to this definition, or the percentage of total population that fall below the poverty line.

This chapter examines to what extent levels of income and production are good measures of how well countries or people are doing. Section 9.1 describes the most widely used reason for why income and product are used as a measure of well-being for individuals and for people in countries on average – as a measure of their standard of living – and briefly compares it to the concept discussed in the previous chapter, that is, individual utility. Section 9.2 discusses the many problems which are associated with income and product measures of well-being. Section 9.3 examines some recent research which suggests that income may not be associated with higher levels of utility or happiness, and discusses if these findings are of relevance for questioning the use of income and production for measuring well-being. Section 9.4 discusses briefly some proposed alternative measures which modify the income and production measures, but follow the same approach in spirit, and examine their problems. Section 9.5 then examines why, despite these problems, these measures may still be useful in telling us something about how people and countries are doing. Section 9.6 concludes.

## 9.1 Income, production, and well-being

The value of goods and services produced or income received is often justified as a measure of how well a country (or a person) is doing because it is a measure of its (or his or her) standard of living or well-being. The statistic tells us how much, in terms of goods and services, people can obtain. If people – on average – produce more goods and services, they can, on average, have more goods and services, either directly or by trading them for other goods and services from other countries. If people receive higher levels of real income they can have access to more goods and services. Higher income and production represents, to use Sen's (1999) term, a higher level of "opulence."

As noted in the previous chapter, economists often appraise economic outcomes in terms of utility levels. A person is better off if he or she obtains a higher level of utility. A society is better off if at least one person receives a higher level without anyone receiving a lower level. A society is in a good state – an efficient or Pareto-optimal one – if it is possible to obtain a higher level of utility for one person only by reducing the level of utility of some other person. Under certain conditions, a higher level of income for a person is equivalent to the person obtaining a higher level of utility. If we assume that individuals prefer more to less of any good or service, and an individual's utility depends *only* on the level of goods or services obtained or can be obtained by that person (for consumption or for saving), a higher level of real income – by shifting out the budget line of that person, as in Figure 4.1 – will allow the person to obtain a higher level of utility. The person will then be better off by his or her own reckoning. Thus, it can be argued that there is no necessary contradiction between the utility view and the income or production or opulence view.

In fact, it can be argued, there are some clear advantages that the income or production approach to measuring well-being has over the utility approach. First, income and production figures are routinely collected and available, while data for utility are not regularly collected, if at all. A measure of utility is sometimes collected by surveying people and asking them, for instance, on a scale of one to ten, how "happy" or "satisfied" they are. However, these surveys, as their name suggests, do not cover everyone, but only a sample of people. Moreover, they are not collected on a regular basis, as are income and production figures. Furthermore, since they use the recall method – asking people to evaluate how happy or satisfied they feel over the last year or so – the answers may well capture factors which affect them at the time of questioning (such as whether they are asked on a sunny day or a gloomy day), rather than being an unbiased measure of how they felt throughout the period in question. The Israeli psychologist and economics Nobel laureate Daniel Kahneman (b. 1932) has shown that the level of happiness people report when surveyed – that is, their remembered happiness – is not an average of how they report feeling over a period of time, say during a week, during which they are asked at closely repeated intervals their experienced happiness. Kahneman calls these the subjective and objective levels of happiness, respectively. Clearly, measures of experienced happiness are even more difficult to come by than survey measures – we do not have "hedonometers" that tell us how happy we are. Second, we cannot really compare utility levels of different people. Although we may say that a person is better off or worse off, how can we decide whether a person is better off than another person just by comparing their utility levels or their happiness levels? If one person reports a happiness level of 8 out of 10, is he or she better off or worse off than you when you report 7? The problem remains whether utility is ordinal or cardinal (the latter in the sense of being unique up to what is called an affine transformation).[3] If we cannot add levels of utility or happiness, how can we take averages for groups and countries? Finally, and related to this last point, we may prefer "objective" indicators "out there" rather than "subjective" indicators that are only in people's minds.

It should be noted that real income and product measures need not be used only as a measure of our well-being. For instance, we may be interested in output per capita to measure how "productive" we are in some sense, or the amount of resources that are available to us for doing whatever we are interested in doing with them. We will consider these alternative reasons for using income and product measures later on, but for now we stick with the well-being interpretation.

## 9.2 Problems with income and product measures for measuring well-being

There are many problems with income and product as a measure of well-being. Fundamentally, the problem is that just because we obtain more goods and income, we cannot really know that we are better off, or that our standard of living has gone up. Income and product provide us with the *means* of becoming better off, rather than a measure of our *actually being* better off. The question is, then, how accurate is it, at least as a proxy, as a measure of well-being?

Three issues are worth keeping in mind as we proceed to discuss this question. First, we need to assess production and income measures as they are actually measured, not in some ideal ways that they could be measured to correct for present shortcomings. There are differences between how they are or have been measured in different countries, but these details need not detain us here. Proposed modifications which improve on income and production measures will be discussed in the next section. Second, to assess how the means-oriented measure does in comparison to the end of well-being, we must have some agreement as to its definition or what we mean by the end of well-being. One meaning is how people themselves evaluate how well they are doing, that is, a utility or happiness measure. But there are well-known shortcomings of that measure, some of which were discussed in the previous chapter. We will discuss here, not only utility as an end, but also other concepts, including functionings, capabilities, and freedoms (as discussed, by Sen, 1999). Functionings refer to whether people achieve some things that are considered valuable, such as good health, education, self-respect, and dignity, and capabilities refer to not the achievement, but the ability of people to achieve these functionings. Finally, we should distinguish between measures for individuals and for averages for individuals within a country or other grouping of individuals since, in principle, different problems can arise depending on whether we are using the income measure for a person or for a country as a whole. Keeping these general issues in mind we now turn to the problems.

First, income and product per capita measure how much income or product an average person is obtaining or getting in a country, and does not examine how this total is distributed among the people of the country. Average per capita income and product may be going up in a country even when the richest among the population are experiencing higher incomes while the great majority of people are receiving no gain or even lower levels of income. This is, in fact, what seems to have been happening in many countries in recent years, so that this problem is a particularly important and relevant one. The measurement problem can be overcome by examining not only what is happening to average income or production in a country, but also keeping track of some measure of inequality or income distribution (see Section 10.1) such as the Gini coefficient or the proportion of income going to the poorest 40 per cent of the population, by looking at the average income of particular groups such as ethnic or religious groups, or by examining the absolute level of income per capita of the poorest 40 per cent of the population. Note that this problem relates to the average income or product measure, not to individual levels of income or production. Of course it applies to any averages within groups, not just countries. For instance, the problem relates to family income which, for instance, does not consider the internal family distribution of income by gender or age.

Second, the amount of goods and services produced or income earned as measured may not accurately represent the amount of goods and services available to an average person or even to individuals. Since production and income measures often refer to the market values of goods and services produced, they typically involve marketed goods and services. Goods and services produced at home for consumption are not included usually, although, especially for poor countries, food produced in family farms for consumption by the family – which can be a large amount in these countries on account of the presence of subsistence farms – is accounted for using some rough estimation and valuation techniques. Excluded from the figure is household production of goods and services, often performed by women, in the form of cooking, cleaning, and child care. Also excluded are goods and services produced or income received illegally, or in the unorganized sector, which are not recorded. Examples include production of illegal drugs and odd-jobs done for pay but not recorded, which may represent large amounts for countries in which illegal production is a major activity and provides the livelihood of a large number of people, as in

Colombia and Afghanistan. Individuals may also obtain goods and services by using up what are called common property resources, such as firewood and fish without paying for them. If they consume them they will not be counted as income or production, but if they sell them on the market they may be counted as income and production, and the reduction in the availability of these resources for the economy as a whole, and for individual people dependent on fish and firewood, will not be recorded. If a firm cuts down trees and causes deforestation, and this affects local climate reducing the ability of people to produce crops in the future, this will not be recorded. Moreover, if peasant farms overuse their land and the productivity of their land deteriorates, this loss will not be reflected in their income, although the depreciation of capital in firms is taken into account in net production and income accounts. In some cases in which goods and services are not sold in markets, as in the case of the government provision of goods and services, the valuation is done using income and expenditure measures, and not in terms of the value of output. It is not clear that these expenditures and income reflect "goods" in the sense of useful things; for instance, they could imply government waste and inefficiency, or projects which reflect corruption and lobbying. Even when goods and services are bought and sold in markets, it is not clear that they really are "goods" since they may solely reflect the manipulation of consumers by advertisers. It should be noted that these problems affect income and production figures for both individuals and for averages of individuals. Some other factors affect only individual measures, and not necessarily average measures. For instance, if people receive free or subsidized goods from the government or from nongovernmental organizations (NGOs), it will not be reflected in their income and production, but it will affect their ability to use goods and services. Thus, in some cases, as when governments and NGOs supply fewer goods and services, such as free education and health care and subsidized food, some people may have access to reduced amounts of goods and services while their incomes may not fall.

Third, the amount of goods and services is not the only thing that is relevant for the well-being of people. For instance, the utility obtained by people may depend on the amount of leisure they enjoy (which may include spending time with friends and family), with the natural environment (for instance, whether the air they breathe is clean and whether their health suffers because of water and air pollution), and with what is consumed by others (for instance, due to the fact that they may feel worse when other people wear fancy clothes and they do not). Problems such as these can imply that even when the value of income and production for individuals increases they may have lower levels of utility at the individual level and at the societal level. At the individual level, as people work more hours to obtain more income and produce more, their leisure time may go down, and their level of utility may be lower. It is possible that when people receive a wage cut they may increase their work time to keep their income unchanged, but may obtain lower levels of utility. Societal-level effects often involve what economists call externalities. When there is an increase in production and this causes environmental damage due to externalities, it is possible for the value of production to increase while utility falls. Note that we do not need to take the utility view to obtain the result that increases in production and income can accompany a lower standard of living if we take the view that the standard of living depends on people's health conditions and that the environmental problems cause a deterioration in people's health.

Fourth, in some cases "bads" (which may or may not be the result of increases in income and production) and resultant efforts to reduce them may imply increases in production and income without increases in well-being. For instance, when crime increases, people may need to buy more goods and services to protect themselves and their property from crimes, and environmental problems and deteriorating health conditions may require further expenditures and production to nullify their adverse effects on health and utility. Thus, these increases in production may not bring about any increases in well-being, rather they merely offset losses.

Fifth, how production and income translate into well-being as ends – whether in terms of utility or in terms of objective indicators such as health conditions and the availability of education and transport facilities – can vary across people, over time, and from place to place, variations Sen (1999, 70–1) has called individual, environmental, relational, and other heterogeneities. Different individuals may differ in how much of goods and services they may require to allow them to meet some given ends – in terms of utility or in terms of how they can function in society – because of some individual characteristics, such as physical or mental handicaps, or because of their gender, body size, and metabolism. The amount of goods and services people may need to survive with good health may depend on climate (which may require them to wear warm clothes in cold climates), health conditions (if they live in regions in which general health conditions are poor and where they are subject to health hazards they may need more medicines than people who live in healthier places), and whether these goods are provided by the government (for instance, people may need to own and maintain cars if public transportation is not available). The amount of income people need to maintain their dignity or self-respect may well vary across time and space depending on what consumption norms prevail, which in turn may depend on average consumption levels: people may not need to have shoes or braces in a particular time to not feel ashamed, if very few people have these things, but may be ashamed when most people do (see also Section 10.3.2). Other conditions may also affect what people may need in terms of income to satisfy some given ends – such as the extent of crime and pollution, or whether people have friends and family whom they can rely on for companionship and support, which depends partly on whether the society fosters such relationships or not (if friends help people in medical emergencies, then people may not require medical insurance, or if friends can entertain one another, the expenses on buying entertainment will be lower). Some of these considerations, of course, relate to some of the points already discussed, involving consumption and production externalities and the public provision of goods and services.

To conclude this section we need to point out that a focus on income and production implies a consequentialist perspective on what is good, since this approach relies on actual outcomes, in terms of real goods and services, in evaluating well-being. No consideration is given to processes by which goods are produced and exchanged, to the rights enjoyed by people, to the nature of people and institutions, or even to how variable over time are incomes and production levels which may be relevant to how vulnerable people may be or feel.

## 9.3 Income and happiness

We mentioned in the previous section that there are various reasons to doubt whether higher levels of income and production necessarily increase well-being in terms of people's utility, satisfaction, or happiness. Relatively recent empirical work – including the pioneering contributions of Easterlin (1974, 1995, 2001), and subsequent work by Oswald (1997), Deiner and Oishi (2000), and Frey and Stutzer (2002), among others – suggests that in fact people may not be better off as measured by happiness and satisfaction indicators (from survey evidence) when their income or average income increases. Time series data for individual countries do not reflect significant (and in some cases any) increases in the average level of self-reported happiness over time, despite significant increases in income and consumption. This is found to be true for the United States, where happiness levels have fluctuated without any upward trend despite significant increases in real income over several decades, and also for Japan, where in a period in which per capita income increased rapidly, the average level of happiness showed hardly any change. Data on specific individuals over their lives suggest that despite experiencing increases in income, these individuals usually do not show significant increases in self-reported happiness. Cross-sectional studies across countries suggest that countries with higher levels of per capita income and consumption do not have higher average levels of self-reported happiness beyond a certain level of income which is far below the income of the rich countries of the world. Even individuals who win lotteries have been found to report no greater happiness after a few years. To be sure, there is some support for the consumption–happiness connection. Cross-sectional studies within countries seem consistent with it: people in higher income groups with higher levels of consumption report higher levels of self-reported happiness than people in lower income groups; it seems that it is better to be rich than poor in a particular society at a particular point in time. Cross-country studies suggest a positive income–happiness link at low levels of income, up to the point where basic needs are met, and, some have suggested, even at higher levels of income. A few studies find that in some cases people are happier – even if temporarily – if their consumption and income increase. However, the bulk of the evidence seems to contradict the income–happiness relationship.

It has been suggested that one should not attach too much importance to these findings. For instance, Johns and Ormerod (2007) argue that they are misleading because while income and output can increase without limit, the way that happiness is measured – on a three- or ten-point scale – makes the measure have an upper limit, which makes it seem that there is very little variation in happiness, at least after a certain point. However, we would argue that there is still something interesting being shown in these findings, since they do not always show the absence of a positive income–happiness relationship. They do show such a relation in within-country cross-sectional studies, but do not show it in many time series studies of individual countries and in cross-country studies, at least beyond a certain level of income. Indeed, there are plausible explanations – backed by other evidence – for these apparently divergent findings. These explanations involve the idea that utility and happiness depends not just on people's absolute levels of consumption and income, but also their level of consumption and income relative to others in society (see Frank, 1999; Dutt, 2009), and that the importance of one's relative standing increases with increases in the level of income. At low levels of income, when people have needs which require a certain level of income to satisfy, increases in income have a major effect on utility. However, at higher levels of income, especially in rich countries, further increases in income increase utility if that income increases relative to others in that country. Thus, the rich in rich countries do feel better off than the poor in these countries. However, over time, as average income increases, if peoples' income relative to others remains unchanged, there is little effect on happiness. It appears that people obtain happiness from their relative position in society, for status reasons, and because of increases in socially acceptable levels of consumption based on what a great majority of the population are consuming at the time (see Dutt, 2009).

Do these findings imply that one should not rely on income and output as an indicator of well-being? They certainly do force us to think about whether ever-increasing levels of income and production are good for society, but one need not conclude that income and output are irrelevant. They do increase utility and happiness at low levels of income, when people are unable to fulfill what one may call their basic needs. And even if people don't report being too unhappy at low levels of income, this may be because they adapt (they have low expectations) to their poverty, despite being deprived. Happiness is not all that matters; a case can be made for the level of people's functionings and capabilities. Moreover, income and output can make possible other changes which improve the level of living, even if they do not by definition do so.

## 9.4 Some proposed modifications

There have been a number of attempts to modify income and production accounts to address some of the problems that afflict standard national accounts.

A number of ways of modifying the aggregate accounts have been proposed, such as the Measure of Economic Welfare proposed by Nordhaus and Tobin (1972). These measures add components involving leisure, nonmarket work, especially women's household work, and the services of government and consumer capital (such as government infrastructure and consumer durables), and subtract things such as commuting costs, regrettable necessities such as military expenditures, and an estimate of disamenities due to urban overcrowding and pollution, for example. Many recent efforts in this direction involve subtractions for environmental damage. While some of the issues addressed, such as household work and environmental damage are straightforward and noncontroversial their proper valuation raises all kinds of difficulties, which raises the question of whether one should aggregate all these into one indicator of well-being, or whether they should be tracked separately.

At the individual level, it has been proposed that resources available to individuals can be analyzed and measured in terms of the entitlements received by people. Sen (1981) focuses on direct entitlements (what is produced or gathered by the person or family, like subsistence crops, or from the commons), market entitlements (what is obtained through the market by the sale of the person's resources such as labor), and public entitlements (what is obtained from the government, such as health care and education). Later extensions include civic entitlements (what is obtained from other private persons and institutions, including nongovernmental organizations) and extralegal entitlements (what is obtained or lost through crime). These improve on standard income measures and also provide a simple way of analyzing how the resources available to individuals and families change over time, especially after some major event such as famines (the case analyzed by Sen, 1981) and wars. Sometimes the well-being of individuals and families have been measured using consumption, rather than income and production data, because they are more likely to be remembered accurately by survey respondents. However, these figures are misleading as indicators of the level of resources available, because they do not include saving and the problems due to borrowing and debt.

A problem with all these measures of income, output, resources, and consumption is that they focus on the means rather than the ends of what we mean by well-being or the standard of living. One way of viewing ends is in terms of utility or happiness, which has a number of problems, as discussed in the previous chapter. An alternative has been examined in view of the problems that beset the income-output and utility approaches, by Amartya Sen using the concepts of functionings, and especially, capabilities.[4] Functionings refer to what a person achieves, that is, what he or she manages to be or do, while capabilities reflects a person's ability to achieve these functionings. For instance, one functioning is the avoidance of hunger; Sen's focus on capabilities comes from the fact that what is important is that a person has the capability of avoiding hunger, because he or she can voluntarily go on a fast or a hunger strike. Other functionings and capabilities can include such things as being in good health and having adequate education, and broader and more nebulous things such as having dignity. This approach is not simply a modification of the production or income account, but focuses explicitly on the ends rather than the means of well-being.

This approach can be compared to the two other approaches – the income and production approach and the utility approach – in the following way: the availability of goods and services and income (and possibly other factors) allows people to have some capabilities, having these capabilities allows people to achieve some functionings, and their achievement can influence how people feel, that is, increase their level of utility. Sen focuses on capabilities because, as we have seen, focusing on goods and incomes is problematic since the amounts required to achieve particular functionings can depend on numerous personal, environmental, and societal factors, and focusing on feelings (or utility) is inappropriate since feelings adapt to circumstances. Sen prefers to focus on capabilities rather than functionings because he wishes to stress choices rather than actual outcomes in terms of what people obtain. The approach combines consequentialist and characteristics-based ideas, since functionings and capabilities may refer to not only some outcomes such as levels of education and health, and the ability to achieve them, but may involve having certain freedoms, such as the freedoms of choosing one's religion and one's place of work. The approach can be based on what individuals value, or what societies as a whole value, and can refer to what individuals or societies do or become. Finally, it is broad enough to encompass economic and noneconomic factors.

There are, however, a number of problems with this approach. What are the appropriate functionings and capabilities? Some analysts argue that there are some universal goods that they should refer to, while others believe that they should be chosen by societies, or even individuals. If we take the individual perspective, clearly not everything every individual may value can be included in a list, but then, how do we decide what will be included and what will not? How do we decide about who has the freedom to do what, or have what rights, since freedom for and rights of, some may be at the expense of those of others. Sen (1999, 2009) argues for the need of reasoning and public discussion to resolve these issues, or at least to narrow differences in points of view. When we have decided what to include and how, how do we aggregate over them to represent them by a single number? These problems may seem insurmountable, but there are ways of arriving at some numbers. The widely used Human Development Index in fact aggregates over three elements – income, education, and health – by giving equal weight to each in a way that many find more useful than focusing only on income.[5] Also, aggregation may not be necessary: we may focus on the achievement of a set of basic needs, as advocated by the basic needs approach that emerged in the 1970s, looking separately at education, health, and nutrition.

## 9.5 Other justifications for income, production, and economic growth measures

So far we have interpreted income and production to be a measure of well-being or the standard of living and found it wanting for a variety of reasons. An alternative way to interpret these measures is to focus on them as what they are, as a means to some ends, and argue that increases in production and income will result in improvements in other things which reflect well-being and the standard of living.

We have found that, at least beyond a certain level of income, it does not seem that increases in income have a significant positive effect on happiness, or utility. However, for countries at low levels of income – at levels which exist in many countries in the world today – increases in income and production per capita do in fact increase utility as shown by subjective welfare measures. Moreover, there are other "goods" that seem to be positively related to income and production.

First, increases in per capita income may be related to distributional issues. Increase in per capita income, given the distribution of income across income groups in a country, will reduce the number of people below a given poverty line in terms of real income, and will also increase the income of the worst-off people, thereby satisfying Rawls's difference principle in the commodities space. However, it may not necessarily do so, even with a given income distribution, if the real income which defines the poverty line shifts up because, for instance, poverty is to some extent a relative concept in terms of income, because more income may be needed to attain a given level of functioning when average income increases: for instance, at higher levels of income what is considered appropriate clothing may require more income to buy than at lower levels of average income.[6] Moreover, if income distribution worsens with increases in per capita income, the number of people in poverty may increase with increases in per capita income. This raises the question about the relationship between income and income distribution. This relationship is also of importance if we value improvements in income distribution as a "good" itself.

The relationship between per capita income and income distribution – measured for instance by the Gini coefficient or the Lorenz curve (discussed in Chapter 10) – is a complicated one. The American economist Simon Kuznets hypothesized that the relation between the two is an inverse U-shaped one: that initially increases in income increase inequality, but then reduce it. There is some evidence in favor of this based on cross-country data, but the relationship has increasingly come into question, especially examining what happens to countries over time. In some countries and at certain periods of time increases in income do in fact reduce inequality, but there are countries for which increases in per capita income tend to increase inequality, as has happened in countries as diverse as the United States, India, and China in recent years. It seems that government policies and the overall growth strategy have an important role to play in determining whether or not inequality falls or rises with income.

Second, levels of pollution and environmental damage in general are observed to be lower in countries with high levels of income than in poor countries and, moreover, rich countries have reduced their levels of pollution and improved their environment in significant ways as they have become richer. To examine the relationship between income and the environment some economists have examined cross-country and time-series data for rich countries to find that there seems to be something like an environmental Kuznets curve: pollution increases, and the environment deteriorates as income increases at low levels of income, but then improves. Thus, for countries at the positively-sloped part of the Kuznets curve, income increases do not improve environmental quality: overall growth leads to more production and more pollution. But the curve also implies that beyond a certain level of income further increases in income lead to improvements in environmental quality. As people become richer they desire cleaner air and water, and pressure governments into regulating pollution; as countries grow richer they are able to implement their pollution control regulations better and are able to develop technologies which emit less pollution: all of this reduces pollution and improves environment quality. While this is good news indeed, we cannot be confident that income increases around the world will in fact improve environmental quality. Although some measures of environmental quality do show improvement with rising levels of income (at least after a point), this is not the case for all measures. A notable exception is global warming. The environmental stock is not a homogenous thing: there are many different environmental stocks, and the relationship between them over time is not well understood. Things that get worse over time can have a negative effect on other aspects of the environment. Moreover, rich countries may have been able to reduce pollution by shifting some of their "dirtier" industries to poor countries with less strict environmental policies by moving firms there through what is called foreign direct investment, or by importing dirty goods from these countries. Thus, for the world as a whole the environmental Kuznets curve may not apply.

Third, there is a positive relationship between levels of per capita income and many indicators that measure levels of functionings. For instance, there is a general tendency for literacy rates, the percentage of people who have received high school and college education, and life expectancy at birth, and for infant and child mortality, to improve with increases in per capita income. However, there are countries at similar levels of per capita income which have very different performances in terms of functionings.

A related argument that can be made about income and production and these indicators of well-being is not that the two are necessarily positively related in all cases, but that, at least beyond certain levels of income, it is possible for countries to use their incomes to improve well-being in these senses. Whether or not they will do so will depend on the choices people, and perhaps more importantly, their governments make.

One can, of course, ask under what conditions countries will in fact increase their well-being when they are able to do so. Benjamin Friedman (2005) has argued that they are more likely to do better when their countries experience higher rates of growth. Friedman's argument is that growth has some important moral consequences. High-growing countries tend to be more tolerant toward minorities, devote more resources to social ends in general and be more generous toward their poor and disadvantaged, and devote more resources to environmental control. This is because when the "pie" is growing more rapidly people are less concerned about fighting over their share of a given pie. People may even be happier when their income is growing, because happiness is often determined not so much by levels of income (to which people adapt) but by the changes in it, and happy people tend to be more generous. While there is certainly something to be said for this, and Friedman culls historical evidence to make his case, what may be important for all of this is not just how fast an economy is growing, but what determines the rate of growth. In some cases, high rates of growth may be accompanied by rising aspirations and cutthroat competition which could exacerbate social tensions and inequalities and fail to have the favorable moral consequences. In departing from the views of Adam Smith and David Ricardo, who thought of the stationary state, in which economic growth ceased, as something to be dreaded, John Stuart Mill (1848) wrote that the absence of growth had its benefits:[7]

> I confess I am not charmed with the ideal of life held out by those who think that the normal state of human beings is that of struggling to get on; that the trampling, crushing, elbowing, and treading on each other's heels, which form the existing type of social life, are the most desirable lot of human kind, or anything but the disagreeable symptoms of one of the phases of industrial progress... Most fitting, indeed, is it, that while riches are power, and to grow as rich as possible the universal object of ambition, the path to its attainment should be open to all, without favour or partiality. But the best state for human nature is that in which, while no one is poor, no one desires to be richer, nor has any reason to fear being thrust back, by the efforts of others to push themselves forward... It is scarcely necessary to remark that a stationary condition of capital and population implies no stationary state of human improvement. There would be as much scope as ever for all kinds of mental culture, and moral and social progress; as much room for improving the Art of Living, and much more likelihood of its being improved, when minds ceased to be engrossed by the art of getting on.

Mill also movingly describes the benefits of the stationary state on the natural environment.[8]

## 9.6 Conclusion

The most popular way of evaluating how people and economies are doing is in terms of income and production. Income and product measures and their growth rates are also routinely used to guide and evaluate policies. This chapter has argued that for evaluating standards of living and the well-being of people these measures are highly problematic. Income and production may be a means to some desirable ends, but are not those ends.

We should be very cautious and careful to guard against the notion that increases in income and production are the goals of societies. Societies may have many goals, including those of making people happier, allowing people to flourish and have high levels of functionings and capabilities, increasing people's freedoms, creating better communities, increasing fairness, protecting the natural environment, and protecting people's rights. Having more goods and services and higher levels of income does not automatically translate into the achievement of these goals.

We end this chapter with three comments. First, even though income and production are not the ends, they may well be important means to satisfying these ends. Hence, there is no case for ignoring income and production and their rates of growth. Especially at low levels of income and production per capita, increases in income and production may be vitally important for making people better off in a variety of senses, including increasing happiness and functionings. Second, while one should evaluate how people, countries, and the world are doing in terms of income and production, such measures have to be supplemented by other indicators which are arguably far more important, including measures of poverty, income distribution, environmental quality, functionings, and freedoms. Third, although income and its growth may be important as a means to some ends, it would be misleading to take the view that increases in income will automatically imply improvements in well-being. It is necessary, therefore, to examine the relation between income and its growth on the one hand and growth of well-being on the other, both to improve the positive relation between the two, and also to check growth in some places and for some people when it conflicts with the attainment of some important ends.

# 10
# Fairness, Distribution, and Equality

## Introduction

Questions of fairness, distribution, and equality play an important role in economics and policy analysis. Broadly speaking, economists hold one of three views about these questions. One view is that efficiency and fairness are the two main goals for appraising how well an economy is doing and for devising, implementing, and evaluating economic policy. More specifically, every economic policy change – which usually impacts people differently – needs to be scrutinized for its distributional implications. A second view is that fairness necessarily involves value judgments and economists, as scientists, should concentrate only on efficiency, leaving judgments about fairness to society as a whole. A third view is that questions of equality and distribution are unimportant and divert attention from the important goals of efficiency and growth. The second view, we have argued in Chapter 2, is untenable, both because the notion of efficiency itself involves a value judgment, and because, more generally, one cannot avoid making value judgments in economics. Whether one subscribes to the first or third views, however, economists need to explain what they mean by equality, how it relates to fairness, and why distributional equality and inequality are worthy or not worthy of attention.

The two previous chapters have examined two major concepts that relate to evaluating efficiency and the overall well-being of economies, that is, utility and real income. These concepts are also relevant for the discussion of equality, that is, the equality of welfare or utility and the equality of income. This chapter turns directly to the questions of fairness and equality, analyzing the relation between equality and fairness, and discussing whether reducing or eliminating inequality is a good thing.

As we have already seen in earlier chapters (especially in Chapter 3), many ethical questions arise when we discuss equality. One relates to why equality should be considered a desirable goal. While, for some people, there is something intrinsically good about equality, others question whether it has any ethical value. For some others, while equality has no intrinsic worth, it may be related to other things that we value, either positively or negatively. Another question concerns what it is that we are discussing the equality of, that is, if we equalize, what it is that we should equalize or at least make less unequal? For instance, should we make less unequal people's incomes, or their happiness, their health conditions, or their opportunities in life? Yet another set of questions addresses among whom should we be equalizing, among people, groups, or countries, and if it is between people and groups, should we equalize between individuals who have more or are better off and those who have less or are worse off, or between people of different types distinguished by other characteristics, such as ethnicity, gender, and where they live? These questions, of course, are interdependent, because the validity of arguments about why equality is good may well depend on the equality of some things and not other things, and among some entities and not others. Despite their interdependence, we will introduce these three types of questions in turn. Section 10.3, will discuss the reasons for or against equality, Section 10.4 will address the issue of equality of what, and Section 10.5, equality among whom. Before we do so, however, by way of background, we will review briefly in Section 10.1 some measures of inequality and poverty and in Section 10.2 some determinants of distribution and inequality. Section 10.6 will make some concluding comments.

It is useful to start with the idea of fairness. Although it can be described in a number of ways, a central feature of it is the demand for impartiality and avoiding "bias in our evaluations, taking note of the interests and concerns of others as well, and in particular the need to avoid being influenced by our respective vested interests, or by our personal priorities or eccentricities or prejudices" (Sen, 2009, 54). This definition raises a number of issues. First, although we may argue that it is unwise to be fair in a world where most people are not fair, it is hard to argue against its overall desirability. Some sense or other of fairness appears to be universal among people everywhere. Even young children are often heard to emphatically declare "that's not fair!" Second, although it can tell us that certain things are unfair, it is not clear whether it can tell us what specifically it is to be fair, to act fairly, or to have a fair outcome. Third, and related to the second point, it is not clear what relationship equality (in some sense) has with fairness.

## 10.1 Measures of inequality and poverty

Inequality is often measured in terms of income or wealth within a country. Some simple and widely used measures examine the share of income going to say the top 1 per cent or 10 per cent of the population in terms of income, or to the bottom 40 per cent. Since there is nothing especially significant about these percentages (of the population), we may examine the percentage of income going to various percentage levels of the population, for say every 10 per cent or even every 1 per cent. The Lorenz curve (named after the American economist, Max Lorenz, who developed it in 1905), which provides a graphical depiction of this information, shows inequality of, say income, wealth, or expenditure, over certain units – say individuals or families – within a given population – say all individuals or all families in a country. Figure 10.1 is an example of the Lorenz curve for the distribution of income among individuals within a country, in which the horizontal axis shows the percentage of the total population, and the vertical axis shows the percentage of income they receive. Obviously, 0 per cent of the population must receive 0 per cent of the income, and 100 per cent of the population must receive 100 per cent of the income, so the curve will go through the points (0,0) and (100, 100), represented by the bottom-left and top-right corners of the square. If the Lorenz curve coincides with the diagonal, the distribution of

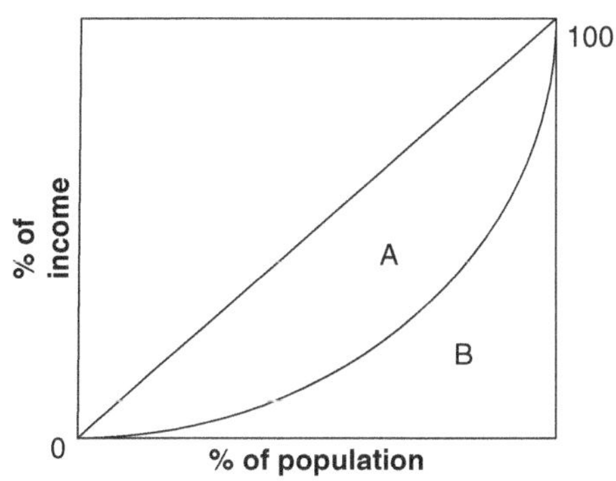


*Figure 10.1* The Lorenz curve

income is perfectly equal, while higher levels of inequality are shown by curves which are further away from the diagonal (other than at the two corners mentioned). Comparing Lorenz curves at two points in time or between two countries allows us to compare inequality levels between two situations. Since, in such comparisons, Lorenz curves may actually intersect, we cannot always rank inequality levels. The Gini coefficient (named after the Italian statistician Corrado Gini who developed it in the early twentieth century), which measures how far the curve is bowed away from the diagonal, and given by the area $A/(A + B)$ expressed in percentage terms, is one way of obtaining a clear ranking although, unless the curves do not intersect, the ranking is not unambiguous. There are other measures of inequality, including the standard deviation of income (or its logarithm, perhaps to take into account some notion of diminishing marginal utility of income), which can also be examined to explore the robustness of the measures.[1]

Inequality measures are sometimes used to examine how people who are at the low end of the income scale are doing. If per capita income is going up in a country and income inequality is not changing, we may conclude that the incomes of all people – including those at the low end – are increasing. However if, when per capita income is growing, inequality is increasing we cannot confidently come to such a conclusion. In such cases we may be interested in directly examining the well-being of those at the low end. A concept that is widely used for the purposes of doing this is poverty. Poverty is usually measured by first defining a poverty line, that is, an amount of income (per person or for a typical family) that is considered to be necessary for not being poor. It is usually specified as an amount of income or expenditure that is just sufficient to provide essential goods and services – such as food, shelter, clothing, health care, and so on – for this purpose. In practice, different countries define their poverty line in their own ways, and update it to take into account changes in the price of these essential goods and services. International organizations sometimes take the poverty line of a country to be at $1 or $2 a day, corrected for cost of living differences between countries. After the poverty line is determined, the number of people or families who live below that level of income is calculated as a measure of the number of poor people or families, and is called the poverty level, and the ratio of this to the total number of people or families is called the poverty rate. It should be noted that this is a measure only of the number of poor people, and not of how poor the poor people are (that is, the extent of their shortfall from the poverty line), or of how income is distributed among the poor. Additional measures of poverty, such as the poverty gap (which refers to the amount of income necessary to lift the poor out of poverty), exist to measure these things. It should also be noted that over time and across countries the poverty line is not adjusted to take into account changes or differences in how much income or expenditure is required to satisfy a given level of – say – functionings or need fulfillment.

The inequality measures discussed earlier in this section refer to what is called vertical inequality, that is, in terms of how a given thing – like income – is shared between different people ranked by that given thing, and not taking into account any other characteristics of these people. Sometimes it is of interest to compare how well different types of people are doing, for instance, people living in different regions, people of different ethnic or racial backgrounds, men and women, and the young and the old. This kind of inequality is called horizontal inequality. Thus, we may be interested in measuring the difference in average incomes of different ethnic groups, or in the (income) poverty rates of people in different regions.

Some illustrative facts about inequality and poverty are worth reviewing. The Gini coefficient of income for the United States has increased from 38.6 in 1968 to 46.9 in 2010. In the United Kingdom the Gini coefficient of household income increased substantially from around 26 in 1978 to over 36 in 1990, and has fluctuated since then. Measures of inequality also show increases in less-developed countries like China and India. The inequality across countries – treating each country as one individual observation – has also shown an upward trend over time since the 1960s, in terms of a variety of inequality measures, including the standard deviation of the logarithm of per capita GDP of countries. Poverty rates have fallen in many parts of the world, including countries in South Asia, East Asia, and many parts of Latin America, but not in all. In the United States, after declining significantly in the 1960s from 18.5 in 1959 to 8.8 in 1974, it increased to 12 per cent during the 1980s, and because of the recession beginning in 2008 the rate in 2011 rose to 15 per cent. In sub-Saharan Africa the poverty rate actually increased in the 1990s. Horizontal inequality measures remain high in several parts of the world, and even reveal increases in some. What are we to make of these trends?

## 10.2 What determines distribution?

Four preliminary comments about the determination of distribution are in order. First, although this question is primarily one of positive economics, addressing it provides a way of discussing some ethical issues and getting essential background to the more normative questions that are addressed in the subsequent sections of this chapter. For instance, what determines distribution and causes inequality obviously affects why we should be interested in the question of inequality and why inequality may be judged to be bad; as we have discussed earlier, if inequality arises due to choices some people make, one may argue that it is not something that society needs to address with redistributive policies. Second, without addressing questions such as the equality of what and among whom, we cannot conduct a full discussion of distribution. To understand the conceptual issues and because of the popularity of these issues, we will discuss mainly the distribution of income between the rich and the poor, that is, according to income groups, although we will have something to say about distribution between other groups, such as those who work and those who own property and people from different ethnic groups. Third, we will find it useful to distinguish between a microeconomic approach to the question – which examines why some people have higher incomes than other people – and a macroeconomic approach – which examines how aggregate income is distributed among people, although the two levels are clearly linked. Fourth, we can distinguish, especially at the macro level, the causes of inequality and the determinants of a particular pattern of distribution, although these issues are closely related. The distinction is useful because the two notions can be examined in two different ways: the former, by starting with a situation in which everyone has the same income and then analyzing why inequalities emerge; and the latter by starting with a situation in which inequality in distribution may already exist, but analyzing the factors which influence changes in that distribution.

### 10.2.1 A micro perspective

We start with the micro approach, having already briefly discussed it in Chapter 3, that is, in terms of luck, choice, effort, and birth. Some people have high levels of income and wealth because they are lucky: the simplest example is one in which some people win a lottery and others do not. Some people have high levels of income because they made choices that earned them riches: they chose to get a certain kind of education, they chose to move to a certain part of the world, or they chose to allocate their wealth in assets the value of which appreciated. Some people have high levels of income because of the effort they put into becoming educated rather than not going to school, working hard at their jobs rather than being lazy or enjoying spending time with family or friends, saving rather than spending, and so on. Finally, some people are born into rich families while others are born in poor ones, some are born in rich regions and others in poor ones, and some into families of ethnic minorities while others are not. Where one is born may be thought of as luck, but is usually treated in a different category because it raises different issues about the dynamics of inequality and the role of policy, and about incentives. One may also distinguish a fifth category, which is the use of illegal means, which may be incorporated into the choice or effort category (one chooses to do illegal things, or one decides to put more or less effort into illegal activities).

The distinctions made between these four (or five) reasons why people's incomes may be different can be justified in a number of ways. One is to apportion blame or responsibility: we may say that if a person makes some conscious choices, or does not exert enough effort in legal activities, they can be blamed for it, and must be held responsible, while someone who makes choices that result in higher income can be praised for it too.[2] A second is that income inequalities can lead to things that are good for society as a whole, for instance, by providing incentives that can lead to greater savings and investment and greater work effort which in turn increases economic growth A third, which may to some extent follow from the first two, is that the distinction may tell us about whether people who have less income or wealth should be compensated by other people, or by society as a whole, and whether some who get a large amount of income should be penalized. Also, we may think that people born into poor families should get help from society, but people who buy a lottery ticket and do not win or who slip and fall and lose their jobs, should not be compensated, because they exposed themselves to the risk by buying the lottery ticket and by not insuring themselves against risk, although both of these instances may be seen as matters of luck.

However, there are a number of problems with this classification, especially for addressing questions of the type discussed in the previous paragraph. First, it assumes that these four or five different categories are clear cut and mutually exclusive, which they may not to be. The effort that people will put into something, the choices they may make, and the risks they may take or avoid being exposed to, may be influenced by birth, determined by one's genes or one's environment as a child. Both nature and nurture can affect choices and effort. Moreover, what they do can also influence what they become, which implies that one cannot necessarily attribute effort and choices to one's genes and one's environments which are determined by birth. Also, choices may be made, or effort may be expended, that result in high or low incomes because of luck. One problem here is that effort and choices do not produce clear outcomes in terms of say, income, but only have some expectation of income. An expected value may be calculated if there is a given probability distribution, but in the case of uncertainty, people have to rely on what has been called animal spirits or their confidence in their expectations about the future. It is possible that blame and responsibility can be apportioned to people if they make actuarially inappropriate decisions, or if they do not insure themselves against risk. But in some cases they may not be able to insure themselves because insurance markets for that kind of risk do not exist because of moral hazard or adverse selection problems or because they cannot afford to pay the premiums for these reasons or because of restricted entry of sellers in these markets. Moreover, the decisions they make may be affected by their preferences in general, and their degree of risk aversion in particular, or the situation in which they find themselves (that is, whether they are close to subsistence or not) and these may not be something they choose. Another problem is related to the fact that it is not possible to evaluate these choices and actions in terms of assigning blame or responsibility if the consequences involve uncertainty in the sense of Knight and Keynes, as discussed in Chapter 4, in which case there is no objectively given probability distribution. In a world of uncertainty people may make decisions based on norms, and it is not clear why the act of following norms which have no ethical significance in themselves should be rewarded or punished.

Second, each category does not have a clear implication in terms of the reasons we have discussed for why the distinctions are made, because they leave out some dimensions within each category. For instance, if income is a reward for effort, should we distinguish between the type of activity in which that effort is expended. The legal/illegal distinction may be one way that such activities can be distinguished, but it is not always clear, in reality, what is legal and what is illegal, which may be affected by interpretations of the law and by the amount one can pay to hire a lawyer (both in terms of quality and the quantity of legal time). Moreover, there may be morally right and wrong laws, and activities which are not illegal but which are of bad or at least dubious moral status. Is it acceptable if someone in a company expends considerable effort in trying to capture a bigger share of production as in the game theory framework discussed in Chapter 5? An example may be activities by which people seek to take credit for things they did not do, or who try to curry favor with their bosses rather than contribute to the common good of the company. Is it acceptable if someone gets rich by expending effort in taking advantage of other people, such as by increasing the price of food during famines, or charging very high interest rates from people who are too poor to survive without loans? Or by selling products which are addictive for people, especially children?

Third, it leaves out some categories altogether. It does not distinguish between whether a person did not receive high income because he or she could not obtain a good job despite wanting it, or because he or she did not look for one. In other words, it does not distinguish between things that happen to someone because of what they do or what others do to them and what society as a whole does to them, or a combination of these things. The only way in which others or the environment can affect people, in this classification, is due to luck and birth, which do not, in fact, exhaust all possibilities. This problem arises because this perspective takes a strictly micro view, rather than a macro view in which people interact with each other and people may end up being constrained by their environments.

### 10.2.2 A macro perspective

From a macro perspective, which may apply to people in a society, groups within a society, or to people or countries in the entire world, we may first consider why some people or groups or countries became rich to start with, assuming, for analytical purposes, a starting point of equality in income. Some of the same factors that apply to the micro perspective apply to the macro one as well. There could be differences in effort, differences in choices the people make, it can simply be luck. Birth is not relevant here because we are starting with complete equality. Or, it can be that one person or country took resources by force or illegal means from another person or country. Or a person can have a higher level of income just because he or she got lucky. But if this higher income does not lead to an increased ability to receive more income in the future, such inequality will not be persistent and decline over time. However, if gains in income lead to further gains, inequality will widen over time due to this cumulative process, even if it started as a matter of luck, and we would need to know what factors cause such a process. If it is a question of different choices people make, we may ask what precisely these choices are about, and what explains why these different choices are made,[3] and the same applies to effort.

To understand the role of these different factors better, let us follow the standard neoclassical method of examining economic agents who have some initial endowments of resources, preferences, and technology, and who optimize. Imagine, more specifically, a situation in which there are two people who have identical amounts of a resource and who produce goods with these resources and their labor, given the technology available to them. They can trade with each other (if they produce different goods). They make choices to consume some goods and save and invest the rest to augment their stocks of resources. The augmentation of resource stocks allows them to produce more, both because they have more resources and because – as their resources increase so does their technology (especially if the resources are employed in the production of goods which result in what economists call learning by doing).[4] One can now consider two cases. In the first, the two people are completely identical in all respects, so that the only differences that could arise between them are due to different levels of initial endowments of resources. The person with a higher endowment or who produces goods which allow more technological change will be able to produce more in the future, and will be in a position to invest in more resources and enjoy more technological change. Provided we have increasing returns in the sense that an advantage allows more resource accumulation and more technological change, these gains will accumulate over time and the income gap between the two people will widen. Although luck (which gave one person more resources to begin with) started the process, it is the underlying structure of the economy, with increasing returns which makes the divergence continue over time. In the second case, there may be differences between the two people – for instance, one decides to work more and have less leisure, one decides to save and invest more rather than consume more now, or one decides to produce goods which allow more learning by doing, all of which can result in different levels of resource accumulation and technological change. The question then arises: why this difference in behavior? Let us assume, for simplicity, that they are purely matters of choice and not of given ability, and we hold the two people completely responsible for their actions. In the first case, one may ask in what sense we can justify inequalities. Luck may be outside anyone's control, but it is the structure of the economy which makes inequality accumulate. Should luck play such a strong role and bring about inequalities? In the second case, we may wish to reward choices and effort, but the increase in inequality over time is not just the result of choices and effort, but also due to systemic factors which result in increasing returns.

Issues become more complex if we extend this simple framework in two directions. First, to allow for different generations, we can assume that each individual is a family (which means that we are abstracting from distributional issues within families) and that each family has children. Assume also that the children inherit resources as well as technological knowledge from their parents – which may be linked to bequests and the passing of skills and other advantages over generations. In this case, the process generating inequality discussed in the previous section may continue over the generations. But now we have to ask if inequalities passed down from generation to generation are acceptable. Or should the advantages and disadvantages passed on between generations be considered as things that should not be rewarded? These are no longer issues of choice and effort, but the accidents of birth, although the bequest motive may give people strong incentives to produce more.

The second extension is to complicate matters even further by introducing many people, rather than two individuals, who can now, in addition to trading goods, borrow or lend to each other, hire or work for others, work together, and share technological knowledge. As soon as we allow many individuals we need to take into consideration market interactions between them, the nature of these markets, the possibility that they have a complementary role in production and the possibility of externalities. Let's start by considering externalities. When technology improves it is possible that this may not be the result of one person having more resources, but of others who have resources who then may share their technological knowledge. If some individuals share technology more than others,[5] those that they share with and who have more resources will have an additional advantage. Next consider markets which may not be perfectly competitive, but may involve asymmetric information in credit markets. If some individuals and families are richer, they may be able to borrow more for purposes of education and capital accumulation, and this will provide them with additional advantages. The poor may be left out of credit markets because they have lower endowments of resources and be left out of benefiting from knowledge because they "move" in different circles of people. These examples suggest that choice and effort become less important in determining inequality, since they are determined to at least some extent by how much income one has, and who one interacts with, and so on, which phenomena, in turn, are determined substantially by where one is born, and the general characteristics of the economy (for instance, the degree of imperfections in markets, and the nature of social and educational institutions). It is not at all clear to what extent people are entitled to the fruits of their endowments if they are the result of luck, birth, the nature of externalities, or whatnot.

Turning now to macro approaches to distribution which do not attempt to explain the emergence of inequality from an initial situation of equality, we may again start with a simple neoclassical framework, without insisting on explicit choice-theoretic foundations (for instance, by assuming that people save a fixed fraction of their income or devote a fixed fraction of their time to leisure), but merely allowing all markets to "clear" so that the economy always has all resources fully utilized. Personal income inequality then is determined by endowments and factor prices, and factor prices, in turn, are determined by the demand and supply of factors. An important determinant of factor demand is technology. For instance, if there is technological change which increases the demand for high-skilled workers and reduces that for low-skilled workers, high-skilled worker wages will rise and low-skilled worker wages will fall, thereby increasing the relative wages of high-skilled workers, and in that sense, increase inequality. Other determinants of inequality relate to the dynamics of endowments over time, and hence to personal characteristics (such as saving rates) or to systemic characteristics (as discussed earlier, such as market imperfections). The growth of international trade can also influence distribution, for instance by changing factor prices (reducing the earnings of those factors which are intensively used in the production of goods being imported). A demand-supply approach can result in the "winners" getting most of the income while the "losers" get very little, as in what Frank and Cook (1995) call the winner-take-all society. Suppose that there are many suppliers of a good or service, each supplier supplying a slightly different product or quality, among whose products buyers can choose. If the cost of obtaining products from sellers further away is high, then buyers will have fewer choices and buy more locally. If the cost of buying from sellers further way falls, buyers will have more choices in the type and quality of products allowing them to buy more from distant sellers whose products they like better than those they bought previously. A probable outcome – if there are some sellers whose products are generally preferred – is that buyers will buy from fewer sellers, who will become richer, while other sellers will lose their customers. Winners will take more and losers less. Now suppose that consumers prefer to buy from sellers who already have a large number of customers because their popularity makes them seem better or more desirable, and not necessarily because of their intrinsic ability. Then, sellers who get ahead initially – for whatever reason, including luck – will obtain more and more customers, and increase their incomes, while others will lose out. Sellers may be winners not because they are better in some sense, but only because for some reason they had more buyers initially.

Alternative approaches to economics focus on different determinants of income distribution. For instance: a Marxian approach highlights factors such as the relative bargaining power of workers and capitalists and the role of the state in mediating between them; a type of Keynesian approach emphasizes the role of animal spirits and business psychology in increasing aggregate demand, increasing the average price level and squeezing the real wage; a post-Keynesian one emphasizes the degree of competition or monopoly power in the economy and the strength of labor unions; an institutional one focuses on the role of institutions in affecting the power relations between different groups in society and their ability to shift the distribution of income in their favor by affecting prices and government policy or both; and a feminist one stresses the distribution of income, functionings, and capabilities between males and females, and on the nature of the family and its interactions with the outside world.[6] These theories not only examine what determines distribution, but also examine how the factors affecting distribution change over time. These theories stress external environmental factors while arguably neglecting issues such as choice and effort, but unlike the micro approach which does not adequately deal with these external environmental factors, they provide a way of analyzing the roles of different macro-environmental factors and understanding the effects of public policy on distribution.

## 10.3 Why equality?

It is standard practice in the discussion of ethics to distinguish between intrinsic and instrumental reasons for taking the view that something is good. Intrinsic reasons are those that assert that something is good or bad in itself, while instrumental reasons are those that assert that something is good or bad not in itself, but because it affects something else which is intrinsically good or bad. This distinction does not imply that something cannot be both intrinsically and instrumentally good or bad, or good in one sense or bad in another, but just clarifies two different senses in which things may be good or bad. When we say something is intrinsically good, we cannot just say that our intuition tells us that it is good in itself (because one person's intuition may be different from someone else's), but we have to defend its intrinsic goodness in some way.

In terms of this distinction, equality may be good in itself or it may be considered good if it affects something else that we value, for instance, how happy people are, whether it leads to higher levels of output, or whether it increases freedom. Let us consider each type of reason in turn.

### 10.3.1 Intrinsic arguments

It may be argued that inequality in the distribution of something is bad in itself. It is not clear, however, why this is so. There may be nothing intrinsically good about equality, because different people do not have to be the same, and that differences may be good because it promotes diversity.[7] For instance, Miller (1982, 73) states: "Why should equality be thought desirable? Equality after all means a leveling of differences; it means a smoothing down of irregularities or idiosyncrasies. Although I may from an aesthetic motive decide to trim my rose bushes to an equal height...,to treat people in such a way would be at best perverse and at worst immoral." While diversity may be good for a number of reasons, and homogeneity may be considered bad, especially if it is enforced, we can still defend equality in terms of equality of things that are considered to be good intrinsically or instrumentally. There may be nothing intrinsically good about the height of bushes, but there may be something intrinsically or instrumentally valuable about a resource available to people. Thus, if we think that there is something intrinsically good about the resources available to a person, or these resources improve a person's well-being in some sense, we may have the intuition that resource inequality is bad because it means that different people have unequal amounts of something that is intrinsically good. But what if people do not choose to obtain more resources in the usual sense, but wish to spend time with their family or friends or engaging in activities which do not increase their access to resources? To this, several responses are possible. First, we could restrict equality to those things people do not choose or are not responsible for. For instance, Cohen (1989, 916) argues for egalitarianism "to eliminate *involuntary disadvantage*," and Parfitt (1984, 26) describes the "The Principle of Equality" as the claim "that it is bad if, through no fault of theirs, some people are worse off than others." Second, we could restrict equality to broad concepts which may not be substituted by other things (like resources in a broad sense to include social relationships). Third, we could argue that it is possible that even if people choose less of some things, like good health care, they may be worse off in terms of their functionings, which society may wish to address.

Another set of arguments links up inequality to some other types of ends (which are not easy to measure empirically) which are so closely related to equality that we could refer to them as providing intrinsic arguments for it. Miller (1982) and Scanlon (2003) provide a number of arguments of this type.[8] First, if there are benefits and costs, it may be *unfair* (in the sense of deviating from fairness as discussed in the introduction to this chapter), other things equal, to distribute them unequally. Of course, other things may not be equal, because inequality may be caused by differential effort, in which case fairness may be inconsistent with equality. However, our discussion in Section 10.2.1 shows us how complicated these issues may be. Second, inequality in some spheres may exacerbate inequality in other spheres which, in turn, may exacerbate inequality in the former, and inequality in many of these spheres may result in overall unfairness even beyond what may be justified by things such as effort. Thus, inequality in income may imply inequality in political voice or in access to health and education, which may exacerbate inequality in each other. Third, high levels of inequality may result in a loss of self-respect as well as the failure to obtain the respect of others, and these may be valuable intrinsically and instrumentally (for instance, for having the capability of contributing to society, or being more virtuous individuals). Fourth, inequality can create obstacles to the achievement of social solidarity, and create obstacles to friendship and relationships. Finally, high levels of inequality may allow some people to subjugate and dominate others, which can be considered to be intrinsically bad.

### 10.3.2 Instrumental arguments

Turning from intrinsic to instrumental arguments, many variants of the argument have been made. One is that inequality reflects misery on the part of the worst off. In this argument, inequality is bad because it may imply that people toward the bottom of what is distributed unequally are absolutely miserable: if inequalities of income and the cost to access health care are high, people who are at the low end may be very poor and hence unable to buy the basic necessities of life, thus, may have a low life expectancy. This argument is an instrumental one and can be refuted. Inequality does not necessarily imply that people on the low end are absolutely miserable, because everyone may be quite rich and everyone may lead a long life, although there are inequalities among people. It is also possible that increasing the absolute position of the worst off may in fact require increases in inequality (for instance, because the rich save more, which leads to faster capital accumulation and the creation of jobs for the poor). Moreover, the instrumental argument may not convince some people because they believe that there is no justification for taking people out of poverty and early mortality if they chose not to work hard and attend to their health. However, it seems that some who take the view that inequality is acceptable, especially if it reflects people's choices and efforts, may accept the notion that everyone is entitled to some minimum absolute level of well-being, so that those who are worse off may have some priority over those who are better off, in terms of getting more of that in which there is inequality. As we saw in Chapter 3, Rawls's theory of justice gives priority to the least advantaged.

Although it is possible to argue in favor of priority of the poor and for people obtaining some absolute minimum level of well-being, it is not clear that these goals are independent of the argument for a certain measure of equality. First, it is not clear what is an absolute minimum level of well-being in a particular society. In evaluating how someone is doing we invariably make comparisons. For instance, we examine how someone is doing compared to how he or she was doing in the past, or with how that person can potentially do. Since potentials are difficult to measure precisely, one way of doing so is by examining how others are doing, so that inequality becomes an issue. Second, relative positions in some spheres may imply absolute positions in other spheres (see Sen, 1983). For instance, if there is inequality in income and the availability of resources, and if people who are worse off feel absolutely worse off, as mentioned earlier, they may not be able to maintain their dignity or self-respect. Adam Smith wrote in *The Wealth of Nations*:

> By necessaries I understand not only the commodities which are indispensably necessary for the support of life, but what ever the custom of the country renders it indecent for creditable people, even the lowest order to be without . . . Custom . . . has rendered leather shoes a necessary of life in England. The poorest creditable person of either sex would be ashamed to appear in public without them. (Smith, 1776, 351–2)

The need being fulfilled here, according to Sen (1983), is the need of not being ashamed; Smith is clearly arguing that the amount of commodities capable of satisfying this need depends on custom, and is therefore changeable as customs change, which in turn changes with average levels of income. This argument may be interpreted as being a subjective one, dependent on the feelings of people. However, a number of objective factors also play a role. For instance, the worth of a high school education in terms of getting "good" jobs depends on whether most people have secondary school education, high school education, college education, or post-graduate education, and the need for having a car to travel depends on whether most people have cars and on their willingness to support public transportation. In terms of the inequality between countries in the world, the income and hence technological gap between countries may determine the absolute ability of countries at the low end of the distribution to transfer technology from abroad, since this ability depends on their technological capability compared to the "frontier" technology.

Other instrumental arguments arise from theories of justice which are not necessarily egalitarian. Consider the case of utilitarianism discussed in Chapter 3. For example, take utilitarianism and add the assumptions that utility depends only on income and that marginal utility diminishes as income increases. Assume that each individual has the same relation between utility and their income shown by the total utility curve in Figure 10.2; the curve has a slope which falls as $Y$ increases because of diminishing marginal utility. Suppose we start from a situation in which everyone obtains the same level of income, that is, there is perfect equality of income, shown by $Y_E$. Now consider a change which increases one person's income to $Y_R$ and reduces that of another by the same amount, to $Y_P$. Because of diminishing marginal utility, the gain in utility for the person who obtains the increase in income (shown by the vertical upward-pointing arrow at $Y_R$) is less than the loss in utility of the person whose income is reduced, shown by the downward-pointing

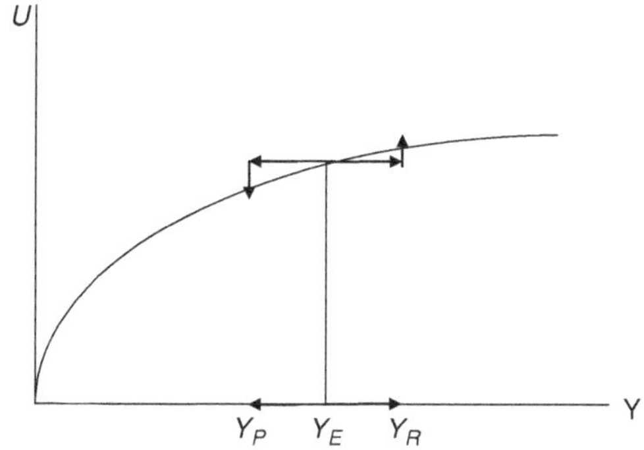


*Figure 10.2* Utilitarian argument for equality

vertical arrow at $Y_P$, implying a decline in the total utility of society. This utilitarian argument may, however, fail for a number of reasons. It can be used to justify income inequality if inequality leads to an increase in incentives which induces people to produce more, thereby increasing total utility. Moreover, the argument fails if it is not true that utility diminishes with income (which is possible even if there is diminishing marginal utility for the consumption of a particular good), or if some people derive much greater levels of utility from resources than others, or if interpersonal comparisons of utility are not possible.[9] A Rawlsian argument may also be made for equality on the ground that increasing the amount of primary goods going to the worst-off individual, consistent with the difference principle, may involve reducing inequality. However it need not since, as discussed above, improving the well-being of the worst-off individual may require greater inequality. Finally, a right-based libertarian argument may also be used to argue in favor of greater equality. Sterba (2010) points out that the libertarian view that the rich have the right to use their resources for any purpose they wish (for instance, on luxury consumption) even if the poor lack the resources to satisfy their most basic needs conflicts with the liberty of the poor to not to be interfered with when taking surplus resources of the rich to satisfy their needs. Given this conflict between the liberty of the rich and poor, Sterba uses the "ought" implies "can" principle to argue that the liberty of the poor, if some conditions (including the fact that the poor do all that they can to obtain resources to satisfy their needs through work) are satisfied, is morally preferable to that of the rich because the poor make an enormous sacrifice in relinquishing their liberty.

A final set of instrumental arguments regarding equality arise from connections between inequality of income and other things in the economy as a whole that we may consider valuable. Economists have been greatly concerned with the relationship between the distribution of income or some functionings on the one hand and the level of output of the economy or its growth rate on the other. An argument that has a long history in economics is that equality may have an adverse effect on the growth rate of the economy because the rich save a higher proportion of their income than the poor, so that inequality leads to higher saving, investment, and economic growth. Another argument relates to the efficiency–equity tradeoff discussed by Arthur Okun (1975) using the leaky bucket metaphor: if I try to distribute water between people, carrying it in leaky buckets, the total amount of water will be diminished due to the leaks. In other words, attempts at redistributing income may result in lower levels of total output due to the creation of disincentives (a tax on incomes may reduce the amount of work people want to do), or allocation inefficiencies (taxes on some kinds of activity may make people engage less in these activities and more in others which are not taxed). However, theoretical and empirical evidence suggests that although these tradeoffs may exist, they may not always do so, and there are a number of reasons why more equal distributions of income and other things may lead to higher levels of output and growth. As noted in Chapter 2, more equality can lead to higher levels of consumption demand (because the poor consume a higher proportion of their income than the rich), aggregate demand, output, investment, capital accumulation, and growth.[10] It is also possible for a more equal distribution of income to allow relatively poor individuals to have access to credit which they would not have with a more unequal distribution, because they lack collateral which they could offer creditors to allay fears of nonrepayment, and to thereby increase investment and growth. Improvements in health and education may also occur with a more equal distribution of income, or access to these resources, which can increase output in the economy by allowing the deprived to become more productive members of society in the usual sense. The existence of high levels of inequality may also lead to crime, conflict and violence,[11] as well as pressures to redistribute income through the political process, all of which could reduce output and income. Poor health conditions of the poor could result in epidemics which could affect the health of the entire population, or require higher levels of spending on health which may reduce the production of other types of goods. Inequality may also lead to an improper functioning of the democratic process with votes being bought and sold and obtained by domination and subjugation, rather than a fair process of discussion and debate which leads to good outcomes. These arguments do not automatically clinch the instrumental case for equality, since there is a fair amount of empirical controversy about the direction of effects, and because some arguments are about absolute levels of well-being and not necessarily inequality. However, the point remains that there are many possible ways in which greater equality may promote better aggregate outcomes for society.

## 10.4 Equality of what?

Whether we actually wish to equalize something across people or groups, or whether we want to evaluate whether we should equalize, we need to decide what it is that we should, or consider, equalizing.

Following our discussion in the last two chapters we can consider the equalization of income or resources, of welfare or utility, of functionings, and of capabilities. There is also some debate whether we should consider equalizing outcomes or opportunities: whether to allow people to get what they deserve or get what encourages effort, which is usually ignored by equalizing outcomes.

### 10.4.1 Income and resources

Discussions of equality and inequality are usually couched in terms of income and resources. Income equalization seems to be simplest, because it equalizes a type of easily measurable outcome. It is no wonder that when economists focus on inequality, they usually have income inequality in mind. There are, however, many problems with this form of equalization. If someone decides to work more and another person decides to have more leisure, why should we equalize incomes between the two and – assuming that both prefer more income to less – thereby make the second person better off in terms of welfare? Yet another issue arises if some people incur greater sacrifices to get something like more education or to save more. Should we not reward that person with higher income? Moreover, if one person has a health problem which requires higher medical expenses, should we not give that person more income to deal with a problem that he or she did not bring upon himself or herself,[12] an issue which is an example of personal heterogeneities discussed in the previous chapter. If a person happens to live in an area where there is greater availability of public goods like education and health care, should that person receive the same income as a person who lives in areas less well served – not due to the choices but because they happened to be born there and are unable to move. Finally, equalization may result in the removal of incentives, for instance, by rewarding those who work less and save less, which will, in turn, reduce welfare in some other sense (such as in a utilitarian or output sense), an issue to which we will return later.

To overcome some of these problems with income equalization, some egalitarians suggest the equalization of the resources that individuals have to pursue *their* ends, whatever they are. An advantage that may be claimed for resource equalization is that it does not involve some of the problems associated with desert, choice, and incentives, which afflict income equalization, because it simply provides the same resources to people who may choose to do with them as they like. This approach, however, is not free of problems either.[13] There is the problem of aggregating over different kinds of resources, since there is no reason to provide every person with exactly the same amount of every resource – because they may not need them all in every situation. Overall resource equalization after some aggregation is sometimes recommended using the no-envy criterion, which states that the allocation of resources should be such that no person will envy (or prefer) another person's resource endowment given his or her own preferences. There are problems that arise with this criteria, because of the possible endogeneity of preferences for the resources, but are not impossible to overcome. Other problems are more serious. First, it is not clear how heterogeneities of different kinds are to be dealt with, such as handicaps due to some heterogeneities beyond the control of the individual. Second, as mentioned earlier, choices and effort may not be entirely up to the individual, since abilities may influence effort, choices may be affected by preferences which depend on external norms and religious values, and luck may influence the outcomes of choices, and it is not clear why the consequences of luck should be left for individuals to bear or benefit from. Finally, there may be various external conditions which can affect the income that people can obtain out of their resources: for instance, it may be that a person is endowed with the ability to work, but for reasons outside his or her choice, the person cannot obtain employment, or may be subject to discrimination because of his or her religion, gender, or ethnicity. All of these problems could be dealt with by redefining resources in a way which takes into account all possible handicaps, problems, and heterogeneities but it is not clear which differences to compensate for and why, and whether one can actually do that without equalizing incomes which, of course, raises questions involving desert, choice, luck, and incentives.

### 10.4.2 Welfare or utility

Another approach, which focuses directly on a measure of well-being is welfare or utility. The goal here is to equalize the level of utility or happiness between people. Although this may seem more attractive than equalizing income or resources, because the equalization is one of ends rather than one particular means (for instance, it takes into account different choices people make between work and leisure, by not penalizing the person who works more), there are many problems with this approach. First, it requires that we can in fact make interpersonal utility comparisons, which is problematic, unless we can take pleasure and pain to be objective (which we will consider later), or if we derive some kind of common metric which forces each person to be alike; but in this case, equalization of utility will become equalization of some other concept such as functionings, capabilities, or resources in a broad sense. Second, if we do allow for pleasure and pain to be objective in some sense, it is not clear why we should reward those who do not have a sunny disposition with more resources at the expense of those who do, or how we can elicit information on who needs how much in terms of resources to attain a particular level of utility. In particular, if we compare a rich person and a poor person in terms of resources, if the rich person is unhappy because he or she wants even more (or at least says so), while the poor person is satisfied with his or her lot, should we give more resources to the former and less to the latter? Third, like other outcome approaches, it can result in problems in terms of desert and incentive considerations.

### 10.4.3 Functionings and capabilities

Another approach is to equalize functionings such as some indicator of good health, or being educated. This has the virtue of focusing on ends that are considered intrinsically valuable, rather than examining means to the end. However, it raises other problems. What functioning should be chosen for equalization? Why equalize all functionings and not leave some to individual choices; that is, why prevent someone from getting more education if he or she wants to obtain it, rather than working for a wage or enjoying leisure, or force someone to eat more if he or she voluntarily decides not to do so? If we decide to equalize overall functionings and not each and every kind of functioning, how would we weight them? The absence of envy is not likely to work here because it is not individual preferences we are concerned with, but something that people value with good reason and through public discussion. Also, how do we take care of problems of desert and incentives: why should all people have the same access to health care whether they work for it or not? A way out could be to equalize capabilities which provides access to functionings but does not ensure that a person does, in fact achieve them. Problems arise, however, with being able to distinguish between capabilities and the ability to make use of these capabilities. What if schooling is available to everyone, but children in some families are unable to acquire education properly, for instance, because of the lack of parental support for it?

### 10.4.4 Opportunity

A problem with any form of outcome equalization is that it does not distinguish between people who put in more effort, or who make different choices, than others. In other words, equalizing outcomes seems to go against the choice view and the desert or equity view. Another problem is that it may take away the incentives people have for doing better. Yet another problem is that it is exceedingly difficult to conduct public policy in a way that will equalize outcomes in some form or other: how does one make sure that everyone has exactly the same functioning in terms of education or longevity? One can decide to equalize things that are less outcome-oriented and which leave some room for individual choices, effort, responsibility, and incentives, such as the equalization of resources and capabilities, rather than incomes, welfare, or functionings. However, as we have seen, there are problems with these types of equalization as well. One can decide then to bypass both means and outcome variables, but instead make the "rules of the game" fair, so that each individual has an equal chance of doing well as defined generally or by the individual. The supposed benefit of this is that it will preserve incentives and allow people to earn what they deserve from what they choose. There are difficulties with this approach as well. First, how do we know that the playing field is really level and that the disadvantages some people have in terms of birth, luck, and societal constraints and other factors have in fact been eliminated? One can look at whether there is enough social mobility, but even then, perhaps the true test of equal opportunity is that incomes are at least made less unequal. Second, one can ask why one needs to promote incentives of certain kinds which do not really result in social improvements or even personal improvements. Hard work and saving, for instance, may not improve matters for society as a whole and for individuals. Many people are overworked because they are trying to consume more compared to others (with the result they are not better off by their own reckoning because others do the same and because they work more than they would like to). It is also possible that people save so much that consumption demand is low, and aggregate demand and output are too low to support full employment.

## 10.5 Equality among whom and within what?

Inequality is most commonly measured in terms of income by income groups, that is, vertical inequality. Such measures could also apply to expenditures, wealth, land holdings, and other indicators which can be added across people.

A different measure of inequality, called horizontal inequality, refers to inequality of income or some other valued thing among different identifiable groups in an economy, such as ethnic or religious groups, gender, class, or region. Thus, one may be interested in whether there is a difference between average incomes of whites, African-Americans and people of Hispanic origin in the United States, or between the average incomes of Hindus and Muslims in India, or between men and women who work for a wage, or between different provinces in China. We could also be interested in the levels of functionings – say in terms of education – of boys and girls. The reason why we may be interested in this kind of inequality is that it can be explained by causes which are different from those of vertical inequality, it may raise different kinds of issues about why we should care about inequality, and it may require different kinds of public policies to reduce the inequality.

An important cause of inequality of the horizontal kind is discrimination along ethnic, religious, regional, and gender lines. This discrimination may be the result of the beliefs and behavior of individuals and groups in societies – for instance, white employers may discriminate against blacks in their hiring or salary decisions – or there may be discriminatory policies by a group which controls the state apparatus against other groups, by excluding these groups from positions of power and influence, and through the allocation of resources. If there is discrimination by private people, one could examine why such discrimination exists: is it purely due to prejudice, or are there other underlying reasons such as competition for jobs.

We may be concerned about inequality because it may imply that people are being denied certain resources and rights purely based on prejudice which is difficult to defend as fair. But, is discrimination based on inborn characteristics – such as race – always bad? Clearly, if a firm does not hire someone, or pays a lower wage to someone, only because of reasons of race, the answer should be obvious. However, in some cases it is not (see Singer, 1978). What if an employer picks a person of a certain race or gender to play the part of a character of that race or gender in a play or a film, over people of some other race or gender under the plausible argument that that person suits the role better? This may not be considered ethically problematic, for instance, because the race or gender of the person can be argued to be of direct relevance to the job. However, suppose that a landlord refuses to rent an apartment to a person who belongs to an ethnic minority group because by renting to that person he or she would lose other tenants because of *their* prejudices? Or, suppose, an employer does not hire a person of a certain race because there is statistical evidence to show that on average people who belong to that race perform less well than others at their jobs, and it is too costly or impossible to obtain detailed information on how this particular person will perform? Although the landlord and employer are not necessarily prejudiced, these forms of discrimination may be considered problematic, partly because it is possible that if there is no discrimination, the prejudices of other tenants, and the statistical evidence of inferiority (because, given more chances, people from these categories could show that they are not inferior) or what is called statistical discrimination may disappear in the longer run. It is possible that even if employers weighed all the evidence about the characteristics of the person (such as his or her level of education and work history) and did not take into account the person's race or gender, and chose not to hire that person, people of that type would not be hired or be hired much less frequently than people of other types. Is that unethical? While it may not be unethical for individuals, it may well be argued to be unethical from a social perspective. The fact that people of that type have less education may be because they do not have the incentives, since they are less likely to obtain the jobs. This is an example of the cumulative causation mechanism that makes racial and other inequalities persist, without there being any fundamental difference between people of different types (see Myrdal, 1972). This is problematic, for instance, both because different people who are not really different in ability are being treated as belonging to different classes and because society would be better off in the sense of being more efficient if these people were hired because they would become more educated and more productive.

Moreover, such inequality may have effects which are different from vertical inequality. For instance, it has been found that although vertical inequality is not a major explanation for violent civil conflicts, horizontal inequality may well be, because solidarity based on common ethnic or religious background may make it easier for different groups to coalesce against other groups (see Stewart, 2008). Finally, some measures such as income redistribution through progressive income taxes may not be able to address inequality of this type; other methods, such as affirmative action in hiring and distribution of resources, proportional representation in government or seat reservations in legislative bodies may be called for. It has sometimes been suggested that no specific policies are required for the removal of discrimination. Nobel Prize-winning economist Gary Becker (1971), for instance, has argued that discrimination in labor markets would disappear due to the operation of competitive market forces. If discrimination occurs because of employers' "tastes" for discrimination, it would lead to lower profits because firms would make decisions not based strictly on profitability, so that those firms which discriminate would be driven out of business. The problem with this optimistic view – a view which adds another moral dimension to the market – is that sometimes discrimination may be good for profits, for instance, if it involves cost-efficient statistical discrimination on the part of firms, or if firms are able to reduce the bargaining power of workers with the policy of divide and conquer by treating people of different races differently and thus reducing their wage costs (see Reich, 1981).

Another dimension of inequality is the unit or domain in which it is measured. So far we have focused mainly on a country. But other units are relevant too. For instance, one may be interested in inequality at a larger level, such as at the world level, or inequality at smaller levels, say within a family or within an urban area. Inequality within a family between men and women may be extremely important for understanding the position of women in a society. Such inequality may need to measure not only income, but also the allocation of work time and differences in the levels of functioning, such as access to education and nutrition, and even life itself – given the reports of missing women due to the neglect, or worse, of girls (see Sen, 1999). Measures such as happiness may be quite misleading, because cultural norms may make women accepting of their subservient positions, making them believe that they are making sacrifices for their family. Moreover, apart from the intrinsic importance of the issue of inequality related to over half the population of most countries, there are instrumental reasons to be concerned about the position of women in the household, given their usually greater role in the health and education of children. Inequality at the world level may be important for a variety of reasons, especially in an increasingly interconnected world, and may refer to individual-level inequality or country-level inequality. We will briefly discuss some of these issues in Chapter 11.

## 10.6 Conclusion

The question of equality is a complex matter which raises many important ethical issues. Reasonable people can argue about whether or not equalization is a good idea, what should be equalized, and among whom equalization should take place. All of these questions raise a number of issues which are not very easy to resolve, but surely worth considering carefully. We end with four concluding comments.

First, there is no particular reason to expect the answers to these questions to be the same in all spheres of life. As Walzer (1983) has argued, the principles governing different aspects of social, political, and economic life may be different, so that the issues concerning equality may have to be different to reflect these different principles (see also Miller and Walzer, 1995). Although this observation may compound our general problem of dealing with equality, it need not, because more information about specific spheres may narrow debates about equality in those spheres.

Second, as noted earlier, inequality in some spheres may be causally related to inequality in other spheres, and these connections should be carefully borne in mind. For instance, inequality in education can lead to inequality in income and inequality in income can lead to inequality in political voice and social connections which in turn feed back into each other. Also, for instance, inequality between men and women inside the home may well interact with inequality in the workplace, because if women are not well paid at work their position at home may be adversely affected, and if women have an inferior position at home and have to bear the brunt of housework and childrearing, their opportunity to be equal participants in the labor market are adversely affected. This observation implies that there may be a case for stressing equality in some spheres which have stronger effects on equality in other spheres (if equality is considered to be desirable in both), and that one should not confine attention to examining inequality in each sphere separately, because of the possible spillover effects.

Third, sometimes debates about equality are couched in favor or against perfect equality. In fact, most relevant analytical and policy discussions in economics are not about removing inequality altogether (whatever that means), but about reducing inequalities. There may be more agreement about this incremental view of equality rather than about complete equalization. Thus, even if one believes that some inequality is justified because of the incentives and desert arguments, one may believe that the existing amount of inequality is too high in comparison to what is justified.

Finally, we have mostly discussed arguments about equality and inequality, and paid very little attention to the question of how to equalize whatever one is seeking to equalize. This may seem to be a matter just of implementation once the decision about equalization has been made. However, ethical (and other) issues arise about how one should actually equalize, and it may be possible to change income distribution and other measures of inequality in different ways, some of which are considered by some to be more ethical than others.

# Part IV
# Applications and Conclusion

# 11
# Ethics and Applied Economics

## Introduction

Throughout this book we have examined the role of ethics in different areas of economics. In this chapter we examine the role of ethics a little more systematically in a number of applied areas of economics or what are sometimes called sub-disciplines of economics.[1] It is not possible, in a short chapter, to examine the ethical issues related to these sub-disciplines in a comprehensive way, and we will do no more than make a few illustrative comments about how ethical issues enter these fields. Nor is it possible to traverse the entire range of sub-disciplines of economics. We will have to be content with a sampling of some fields which we consider to be particularly important both because of the issues they are concerned with and because of their relation with ethics. We discuss, in turn, development ethics, international ethics, environmental ethics, the ethics of labor and employment, and business ethics.

## 11.1 Development ethics

Development ethics is viewed broadly as an interdisciplinary field that reflects on, and is concerned with the application and practice of the moral analysis and assessment of the ends, means and processes of development. Rather than attempting to provide a review of the main issues in this field,[2] we will confine ourselves to a brief discussion of how ethical considerations enter the field of development economics. Development economics is a field of economics which emerged after World War II (although there was some work in this area for the economic problems of the early stages of the development of now-economically developed countries, and in terms of colonial policy) to conduct the systematic and specialized study of the entire range of economic problems of less-developed countries (LDCs).

The main issues and controversies in development economics can be examined by distinguishing between (1) methods of analysis, (2) analytical views of the economy, (3) the relation between analytical views and the "real" world, (4) strategies and policies of development, and (5) the meaning of development.[3] These dimensions can be clarified by examining how particular (possibly different) interpretations of neoclassical development economics and alternatives relate to them.[4] Methods of analysis refer to how explanation is organized, an example of which is the use of individual optimizing behavior, an alternative to which is the behavior of groups or classes based on observed behavior patterns. Analytical views of the economy refer to views on the key characteristics of the economy and how the economy as a whole functions, an example of which is smoothly functioning, competitive markets and the full employment of all resources, an alternative to which is to study the actual structural characteristics of economies, such as unemployment, distributional conflicts between groups, and the role of institutions.[5] The relation between analytic views and the real world refers to how – if at all – analytical views are constructed from information about the real world and how they are validated in terms of how they correspond to that world. An example of this relation is testing the empirical validity of theories by comparing their implications to real world data using statistical methods (called econometric methods), an alternative to which is the use of detailed case studies and observations from field work. Policies and strategies refer to whether, and what kind of, government policies are recommended – for example, the government should restrict itself to national defense and law enforcement, or should regulate and control the market. Finally, "development" can be defined in several different ways; for example, it could be understood as the growth of per capita income, or could stress income distribution and the well-being of the poor. Although some of these dimensions are in principle analytically independent of each other – for instance, one may define development as referring to growth *with* improving income distribution (and not just growth) without changing any of the other dimensions – in practice there may well be important relations between these choices.

In terms of these dimensions of development economics, development ethics is most closely connected with the meaning of development. Early development economics generally equated economic development with economic growth – that is, growth in per capita income and gross domestic product (GDP). Arndt states that from around 1950 to 1970, "economic development was often virtually equated with economic growth, although the former tended to be used mainly for poor, the latter for rich countries" (1987, 51), although it was recognized implicitly that economic growth was not good in itself, but valued because it made people, especially the poor, better off. The major change that has occurred in development economics (in the 1970s) regarding the meaning of development is the shift from the emphasis on growth to a focus on income distribution and poverty and on the fulfillment of basic needs. There has also been a shift in emphasis regarding the importance of environmental issues. These changes, however, do not really shift the focus of the meaning of development in a fundamental way. The focus on distribution and poverty maintains the earlier emphasis on measuring material means of development, although the focus has changed from average per capita income growth to how income is distributed among people and to the circumstances of people at the lower end of the income scale. The focus on nonmarket production and externalities such as the environment and the role of household production improves on the measurement of material production and takes into account the depletion of resources due to production. A more fundamental change in the approach to the meaning of development came with the basic needs fulfillment and "quality of life" approaches. Sen (1999), a major proponent of the change in emphasis away from material well-being, or "opulence," notes that GDP and GDP per capita, even after overcoming the problems of income and wealth distribution and nonmarket production and externalities, only relates to the means of achieving high levels of well-being during a certain period of time. As we have discussed in Chapter 9, he has emphasized the need for interpreting development in terms of "functionings" and "capabilities," which evaluate the ability of people to achieve certain things that are valued, and their freedom to achieve these things. While in many ways this approach presents a richer understanding of what development means, it leaves unclear how these different functionings and capabilities should be selected and weighted. Sen's (2009) reliance on the role of reasoned public discussion is certainly a useful and general way for addressing the problem, but development ethicists suggest more specific practical ways by discussing what may be considered valuable for people – like people's individual functionings and capabilities, but also what people may value collectively, such as the environment and community.

Some development ethicists, such as Goulet (2006), have focused on religious traditions because of the strong hold they have on many societies, but he has advocated an enlightened and critical borrowing of these traditions, such as that espoused by Mahatma Gandhi, rather than a fundamentalist one. More importantly, they recommend that development scholars and practitioners examine what people in developing societies, especially the poor who are not trapped by vested interests, want. If the opinions of people who are affected by development policies are to be taken into account when we consider the goals and meaning of development, how should one do so? Goulet and other development ethicists have stressed the importance of non-elite participation in development decision-making. As outside experts, development practitioners and scholars must take care not to impose their ethics on the subjects of development, and they should take pains to involve the poor in decision-making in a fundamental way at different levels, including local, provincial, national, and global ones and do so at difference-making phases of decision-making in meaningful ways (Crocker, 2008). Development ethicists have examined empirical cases in which non-elite participation has been an important aspect of development projects and those in which it had not in order to show not only how the former have been effective in terms of traditional development indicators but to examine under what conditions they successfully give voice to the poor (see Goulet, 2006).

These and other aspects of development ethics have enormous relevance for development economics even if they only have implications for the meaning of development. But given the relationship between the meaning of development and the other dimensions of development economics, development ethics has even broader implications. Most directly, it has important implications for development strategies and policies. In societies in which the government is expected to play a major role through direct activity and by indirectly affecting private decision-making, officials have to make choices among different strategies and policies. This involves judgments about the objectives of development, which not only have a bearing on the effects on growth, poverty, inequality (across income groups, social classes, ethnic groups, and genders), the environment, and meeting basic needs but also on the design of policies that take into account non-elite involvement. These decisions, in turn, have important implications for decentralization and popular involvement, not only in terms of making policies effective for standard development goals such as growth and distribution but also because of their intrinsic importance. Even in societies in which people prefer a smaller role for the government in economic activity, the government will need to take action to provide the sociopolitical framework necessary for the operation of markets, and this will require the discussion of development ethics. Moreover, development ethics may also be important for the strategies of nongovernment institutions and profit-making firms and how the government reacts to these strategies.

Development ethics also has a major role in terms of one's view of the economy – that is, whether one considers income distribution, poverty, and the environment as important elements in the analysis of the economy and whether one takes into account ethical and religious values as major factors affecting individual and group behavior. Whether or not (and how) one introduces these considerations as important elements of the analysis depends on their empirical importance rather than on whether one thinks that these issues are intrinsically important. But if one does think that they are intrinsically important, the development economist is more likely to start from the position that they are important and then make an effort to empirically examine their importance rather than just assume that they are unimportant. For instance, it may be argued that the focus on the relationship between poverty and growth came to be examined and incorporated into views of the economy only after poverty was considered to be an intrinsically important issue. Early development economists merely assumed that growth was a means to reducing poverty but did not explicitly incorporate it into their view of the economy, focusing instead on saving, investment, technological change, and growth. Furthermore, taking into account people's values and norms and how changes in the economy affect them opens up the question of whether changes in ethical and other values affect people – especially the poor – and their environment and whether the changes are desirable from the societal point of view. It is not that all changes in values have bad consequences – changes in values which condone discrimination against the poor and against women would be difficult to oppose – but they should be explicitly analyzed and their effects on societies assessed, thereby making us aware that the meaning of development has to take account of changes in values.

Development ethics also has important implications for the method of analysis and on how one views the relation between analytical views of the economy and the real world. Since development ethics is concerned with a number of value issues that are normally studied outside economics, it follows that development economics is multidisciplinary by its very nature. Moreover, the focus on values may require a critical perspective regarding the mainstream method of the optimizing agent, which typically ignores values and norms. Of course, these issues can be incorporated into the optimizing model as discussed in Chapter 4. But the bounded rationality of the analyst makes him or her focus too much on the technical aspects of optimization and ignore arguably more important aspects of behavior involving values, norms, and institutions. The analyst should give more attention to carefully examining how people actually behave rather than simply making up optimizing models of their behavior. In doing such empirical work, it may be necessary for analysts (foreign and domestic, since the latter are frequently influenced by foreign ideas and methods) to immerse themselves in societies they wish to understand – rather than relying only on secondary data – while taking care not to see only what they want to see in terms of their preconceived "scientific" notions and change reality in their own image. Jeffrey Sachs (2005) argues that development economics training should be more like medical education and practice, and it requires clinical experience and apprenticeships for economists before they go out into the field. He argues further for more attention to ethical issues; as he says "the development community lacks the requisite ethical and professional standards" (2005, 80). William Easterly adds that "The best rule of all for Western helpers is, first, do no harm" (2006, 336).[6]

## 11.2 International and global ethics

International and global economics raise many ethical issues of which we briefly examine two. The first relates to trade policies and protectionism and the second concerns the inequality between rich and poor countries and whether rich countries should do anything to help poor countries.

A central doctrine of international economics is that free trade is good. In fact, one of the issues on which there seems to be most agreement among economists is that restrictions on trade through protectionist policies, such as import tariffs and quotas, are bad. This argument is usually made using the so-called theory of comparative advantage, according to which under conditions of free trade a country will gain from trade and will export goods in the production of which it is relatively more productive (in the sense of having a lower opportunity cost) and import goods in the production of which it is relatively less productive (in the sense of having a higher opportunity cost).[7] There are actually two separate ideas here. One is that free trade will result in countries trading according to their comparative advantage and the other is that when they do so the countries will be better off compared to what they would be had they not traded at all, or restricted their trade through government protectionist policies. Under some conditions (including the absence of monopolistic firms which dominate international markets and restrict production to obtain higher prices, and the absence of transport costs) free trade and competition will lead to trade according to comparative advantage: firms and countries will in fact export goods which they can produce at lower cost.[8] The question of whether countries will benefit from free trade (according to comparative advantage) is a more controversial issue.

If countries happen to specialize in trade according to current comparative advantage, some countries may export simple goods which are technologically not very demanding, and others may export more technologically sophisticated products (for instance, textiles versus computers). The latter is then likely to learn how to better produce these technologically sophisticated goods, while the former, since they produce less of these goods with trade (not having a comparative advantage in them), will be denied this experience. Thus, the latter is likely to develop technologically, and experience further growth, while the former falls further behind. Thus, even if both countries benefit when they trade by obtaining goods more cheaply compared to restricted trade, over time one country will grow faster and the other will fall behind.[9] Since the country which has a comparative advantage in the technologically sophisticated products is economically more developed, trade is likely to lead to uneven development in the sense that the gap in development between rich and poor countries will increase. Thus, free trade may hurt the poorer country, and it is likely to benefit from trade protectionist measures which allow them to produce technologically more sophisticated goods than what they could produce with free trade, when they are open to competition from more experienced foreign producers. It is not surprising that most countries which developed from low levels of technological capability did so by protecting some industries which allowed them to gain technological experience. Such countries included the United Kingdom, the United States, Germany, Japan, and South Korea. In fact, countries which were colonized by others were not allowed to protect their industries, and this may be an important explanation for the low level of their economic development.[10]

It is claimed that this argument does not clinch the issue against free trade. First, if firms in poorer countries who are at a comparative disadvantage know that they can develop their comparative advantage over time by production experience, why don't they produce making losses which they can recoup later? Why do they need government help? This argument overlooks the fact that in an uncertain world firms are unlikely to be willing to invest resources in products in which large current losses can be expected. Moreover, firms which do invest are unlikely to reap all the benefits of their investment, since other firms in the country can benefit from their experience; in the presence of externalities such as these it is well known that free markets do not deliver. In addition, countries may always need to protect these industries to benefit technologically, and one cannot expect private firms to invest while making losses forever. Second, if firms do need government help, it is better to provide production subsidies rather than tariff protection, because the latter raises prices for consumers whereas the former does not do so. What is overlooked in this argument is that it is typically far more feasible for governments in poor countries to impose taxes on imports than to provide subsidies to producers, both because of the availability of finance and because of administrative reasons. Third, governments may not know which specific industries to protect, and when it does protect particular industries, producers will lobby the government for protection and the government will essentially be captured by these producer interests who will get rich by producing internationally uncompetitive products at the expense of the consumers. Problems such as these may in fact arise in particular countries in which the government is weak in relation to industrial firms, but there is nothing to suggest that these conditions prevail in all poor countries. In fact, there are countries which have developed with tariff protection in which governments have been able to "pick winners" – South Korea, Taiwan, India, and China come to mind. It is well known, in general, what kinds of industries can help in the development processes (ones which are technologically sophisticated, which have strong technological spillover effects to other sectors, and for which demand can be expected to grow with increases in world income), even if the precise sectors which are best likely to promote development may change over time and space. Whether or not governments can protect industries without being captured depends on the details of the political economy situation of the country, about which little can be said in general.

All of this does not imply that there is no case which can be made in favor of free trade. Sometimes free trade may be more efficient (than trade protection) and may help growth and development, especially if countries can import foreign technology and develop its own technological capabilities to adapt and use this technology in the production of their own sophisticated products. Free trade can be defended in terms of the right people have to trade with whoever they want, or to expand their freedom of choice. It can also be defended in terms of the idea, due to the English philosopher John Locke, that trade between nations is more likely to lead to world peace, although this claim has to be empirically defended. It can also be defended in terms of the positive effect it may have in the distribution of income within the country: if a country has a large amount of unskilled labor, free trade will imply that it will export goods which intensively use this unskilled labor, and the wage of unskilled labor would be increased due to trade. This result follows from a standard theory of international trade known as the Heckscher–Ohlin–Samuelson theory, but its implications clearly need to be checked against real world data. It should also be noted that apart from the first argument of this paragraph, the others do not invoke the concept of efficiency on which the standard argument for free trade is typically based.

There are many more specific ethical questions in international trade policy but we will analyze just one. Suppose at a point in time there are two countries, one rich and one poor. The rich country has high tariffs against the importation of textiles and employs many low-wage workers in the industry. The poor country is starting a textile industry in hopes of employing its large unskilled work force. Because of its poverty the main market for its products must be exporting to the rich country but the high tariffs prevent this from happening. The poor country appeals to an international "ethics board" that these tariff walls are an unfair trade practice. The rich country argues that it must protect its poor workers. The poor country argues that the rich country can afford to retrain those workers and move them to other industries while it, the poor country, has no alternative but to export. This case illustrates the complexities of the ethical issues of international trade policy.

Turning to the question of international inequality, one of the major facts about the international economy is the vast differences between levels of development, however measured, between the rich and poor countries of the world. There are many ethical issues surrounding this question.

One set of issues relates to how one should measure levels of development, something we have discussed in the previous section: should we measure development in terms of production and income, utility, or some other method, perhaps using functionings and capabilities. We may use production and income as a measure of well-being or as a broader index of economic dynamism. Even if we decide on a measure of development, say real income, and decide to examine whether the inequality between nations is going up or down, there is no agreement on the issue. Some economists find that the extent of inequality between countries has been increasing, while others find that it has been falling. How can these different findings both be correct? The reason is that although both groups use the same measure of inequality – say the variance of the logarithms of per capita GDP, or the Lorenz curve and the Gini coefficient – they use different units of analysis. Those who find that inequality across countries is rising – so that they find divergence – treat each country as one single observation, that is, they treat China and Cambodia each as one observation. Those who find that inequality across countries is falling weigh countries according to their populations, so that large countries like China and India receive a much higher weight than small countries like Cambodia and Haiti; since China and India have been growing at high rates in the recent past, it is not surprising that they find convergence. So what really is going on between countries: convergence or divergence in per capita real income? That depends on the question one is asking. If we are interested in how countries are doing relative to each other – how poorer countries are doing relative to rich ones, which is something we may want to know because we wish to evaluate how poor countries are doing in comparison to how they could if they were rich – then treating each country as one observation seems reasonable. If, on the other hand, we are interested in changes in inequality across people in the entire world, it may be reasonable to consider weighted averages. But doing so assumes that everyone in each country actually gets that country's average income, and ignores the fact that inequality within a country may be changing over time, as it appears to be increasing in both China and India. Milanovic (2005) discusses different concepts of inequality to show how inequality at the global level has changed over time.

Whether or not world inequality has actually been growing, there is no doubt that there is a wide disparity across both countries and people around the world. Another set of issues concerns whether rich countries should help reduce inequality between countries by transferring resources to poor countries. Unlike governments of individual countries, there is no world government which redistributes resources across countries to reduce regional inequality. However, individual rich countries and institutions do provide foreign development aid to poor countries, although the amount of this transfer has become less significant over the years. What are the reasons, however, why rich countries should be transferring resources to poor countries? Are they obligated to do so? Or are there reasons why they should not give foreign aid? To some extent these questions can be addressed by examining, empirically, whether foreign aid actually helps development – in whatever sense – in poor countries, and there is considerable debate about this (see, for instance, Sachs (2005), and Easterly (2006), for opposed views).

But the question is also an ethical one: do rich countries bear a moral responsibility to provide such assistance? Various arguments have been made to support the case that rich countries have an obligation to help poor countries. One argument is based on some historical wrongs (for instance, due to colonization and plunder, an argument that could be consistent with Nozick's views). A second is based on some present problems in the global economy which hurt poor countries now because of their economic and other interaction with rich countries. Examples include environmental damage due to the movement of "dirty" production industries to poor countries, the losses poor countries face due to international trade with rich countries (although these effects of interaction need to be shown), or even because of the disproportionate and not fully compensated use of natural resource from a single resource base, that is, the world environment (see Pogge, 1998). One could also justify such resource transfers – without making rich countries morally responsible for making them – from the perspective of a bargaining contract between countries which could make all countries better off, because of externalities and global public goods such as the global environment, global health, and world peace. Rawls's difference principle could also be used as a justification, although Rawls (1999) explicitly rejects its application to global justice with the argument that the moral agents of international justice are not individual human beings within a society, but peoples. It should be noted that some arguments that have been made against egalitarian approaches at the individual level, discussed in Chapter 10, do not apply at the level of countries, where the governments of poor countries, and not necessarily all individual residents of these countries, can be blamed on desert and equity theory grounds. However, variants of these arguments have been used in some economic analysis by treating countries as single individuals, or by arguing that foreign aid only helps corrupt government leaders, fuels civil conflict, reduces saving, and discourages institutional reforms which could help development.

## 11.3 Ethics of the environment

At various points in the earlier chapters we have had occasion to discuss issues about the natural environment. We discussed them in the context of the preferences of people who have not yet been born in Chapter 10; in the context of valuing the production of goods and services in Section 9.2; and in discussing the relationship between economic growth and the environment in Section 9.5. This discussion was conducted using the consequentialist and instrumental logic of evaluating the environment in terms of how the environment affects utility of society as a whole and how the environmental stock affects production and growth. In the discussion on production we discussed the environmental stock both from the point of view of how to value output (net of environmental degradation) and how the environment interacts with output and growth as traditionally defined (not net of environmental degradation). In the discussion on utility we could make the environmental stock affect utility directly because people feel worse off by environmental degradation, quite apart from what this does to the availability of goods and services. Economists traditionally examine the environment in terms of production, growth, and utility. They typically view the problem of pollution and environmental degradation more generally as resulting from externalities: self-interested firms and people do things that result in pollution because these generally affect other people, not themselves directly, and do not reduce this damage because it is costly to do so – it lowers profits to reduce pollution because higher prices mean people consume less. Thus, they recommend remedies such as pollution taxes and standards to restrict the quantity of pollution, and introduce tradable pollution permits which allow firms to pollute according to the value of permits they hold. Many economists show a preference for pollution taxes and especially pollution "cap and trade" markets over quantitative restrictions for the sake of efficiency: they provide the least-cost method of reducing pollution. Firms which pollute have to pay fees for doing so, and those firms which can reduce their pollution cheaply can choose to do so, while those for which this is more costly can pay the fees. Marketed permits introduce a market where none existed. The authorities can impose a cap on the total amount of pollution and distribute these to firms, who can then trade these permits depending on whether they can more cheaply reduce their pollution with cleaner technology (in which case they can sell their permits) or buy permits which allow them to pollute more.

One set of ethical issues arises from how to evaluate the environment. If, following our discussion in Chapters 8 and 9, we have misgivings about evaluating what is socially desirable in terms of utility or production and income, we can examine the environment in terms of how it promotes functioning and capabilities or how it affects rights. If pollution causes health problems – such as respiratory problems due to air pollution, diseases due to water pollution, and cancer due to ozone layer depletion – or even threatens our very survival, due to problems caused by global warming, clearly environmental problems have an adverse effect on our functionings and capabilities in terms of a healthy life. If pollution taxes and other government regulations are viewed as interfering with a person's rights to do what they want with what they own, they can be criticized for infringing on people's rights. If, however, we extend the notion of rights to deal with the right to enjoy one's property or environment without infringement by others who pollute, we may justify government interventions which infringe on some rights to protect other rights. If we take a desert view we may find it acceptable to punish with fines those who impose a negative externality on others. If we take an egalitarian perspective we have to be particularly concerned about how pollution affects the rich and the poor. It may be argued that poor people are often less able to reduce the adverse effects of pollution on their health than the rich do because, for instance, they often live in polluted neighborhoods (because they cannot afford to live in more expensive and less-polluted regions), and they cannot afford suitable health care. Thus, we have additional reasons to control pollution, especially of the kinds that adversely affect the poor. However, we also need to be cognizant of how the livelihoods of poor people are affected by pollution control policies.

All of these ways of thinking about the environment view it as being instrumental in promoting some other good. Alternatively, we can take the ethical view that the environment is intrinsically valuable and should not be destroyed. Many religious traditions, including Christianity, Judaism, Hinduism, and Buddhism, take such a perspective. Jewish commentators stress the Biblical injunction "You shall eat from the tree but you shall not cut it down," interpreting it to refer to the fact that the tree is self-sustaining and can produce more fruits.[11] In Hindu traditions, the earth and natural objects are often revered as gods, which are to be respected and preserved, and Buddhists and Jains follow the path of nonviolence or *ahimsa* toward all animals and many kinds of plants. The environment may also be considered to be intrinsically valuable from secular perspectives which argue that nature is good in itself and should be preserved.

Indeed, the field of environmental ethics (as distinguished from the intersection of ethics and economics) takes a variety of different approaches to the environment, including human-centered, animal-centered, and life-centered (which includes plants) ethics, even the ethics of inanimate objects (such as rocks), and ecological holism which stresses the conservation of the biosphere or ecosystems.[12] The discussion of ethical issues in environmental economics is clearly human centered in terms of these distinctions: there may be concerns for animals, plants, and the biosphere and ecosystems, even for land and the soil, but these concerns are due to the fact that these aspects of the natural environment are instrumentally important for human beings. Environmental ethicists extend their concerns to the environment independent of human interests. Human-centered ethics takes the view that humans are morally considerable because they have interests which can be advanced or harmed, that is, they can experience pain or pleasure or have a capacity for free actions. Less obviously, they are considerable because they possess the property or characteristic of being complex living things, and they have beauty. Many ethicists argue that to avoid arbitrary moral distinctions environmental ethics should be animal centered because, for instance, they have feelings, they are complex livings things, and they have beauty. The case for the ethical consideration of animals may in some ways be stronger, because humans are more powerful than animals, as argued in Buddhist ethics. Some have argued for the extension of ethical consideration to all living things, inanimate objects and especially the biosphere and ecosystems because of their characteristics such as complexity and beauty. Because of the uncertain and complex interdependencies involved between these different aspects of the environment, and because of their relation to human interests, the environmental ethicists and economists concerned with ethical issues may well come to similar policy conclusions about environmental issues, although for different reasons.

While the requirement that there should be no damage to the environment may be difficult to justify for the case of exhaustible resources (such as the stock of petroleum, which cannot be regenerated in the longest runs that are relevant for us) which are essential for production and for maintaining life, it may be justifiable for renewable resources which can regenerate naturally (such as clean air, clean water, and forests). It should also be noted that valuing the environment intrinsically may have the effect of ensuring that environmental degradation does not do instrumental harm. Economists and policymakers can form a judgment about the optimal amount of pollution after evaluating and quantifying the benefits and costs of pollution (the benefit being that of not incurring the cost of controlling pollution), but because of the enormous uncertainty involved in estimating especially the costs of pollution, they may make large mistakes. Economists may even exaggerate the benefits of pollution in terms of higher levels of consumption, not taking into account the possibility that people may be no better off in terms of utility with higher levels of consumption beyond a certain level (for instance, because after a certain level utility depends mainly on what people consume relative to other people). Thus, they may not sufficiently conserve the environment to prevent catastrophic consequences. An attitude that intrinsically values the environment may then be more likely to protect it and make us better off by making growth more sustainable and by making us (and future generations) happier.

Another set of ethical issues arises from the motivations of people whose activities result in environmental degradation. As noted earlier, economists, who assume that individuals and firms are self-interested, typically view the problem of environmental degradation as an externality. However, people are not necessarily just self interested, and often have ethical values and follow codes of conduct. Thus, sometimes people may not want to harm others and nature by degrading the environment (especially if the costs to them of not polluting are relatively small, as is often the case of littering in public places), but nevertheless do so because they are too poor to be able to not pollute, or because they do not fully understand the adverse effects of their actions. Thus, poverty and destitution may make people pollute their environments (even at major costs to themselves), and cut down trees and overuse common lands and even their own lands. People may not know the details of how their actions, like consuming large quantities of things, and consuming particular kinds of goods, may adversely affect the natural environment. The solutions to these problems lie not so much in government regulation (although they are certainly relevant for many kinds of polluters) but in anti-poverty measures and in spreading information and encouraging public discussion about the consequences of people's actions. It is even possible that imposing fines and markets in permits may have perverse effects of making people and firms pollute with a clear conscience as long as they pay for it. The environment is seen more as something one can pay to damage, rather than something that is intrinsically valuable. Here again is an example of the need to recognize the importance of ethical values in people's motivations. Only focusing on self-interest can lead to wrong predictions.

## 11.4 Ethics, labor, and employment

Ethical issues are particularly important in the field of labor economics because of the fact that it deals with not just a factor of production, but with human beings. There are numerous ways in which ethical issues enter labor economics, some of which have been discussed in the course of this book. Thus, the fact that workers, as human beings, have ethical beliefs has implications for labor market outcomes, wage rigidity, and unemployment, as discussed in Chapter 6. Furthermore, labor markets have a crucial role to play in determining the overall personal distribution of income through its effects on the labor share of output, and thus have an important bearing on the question of distributive justice, as discussed in Chapter 10. In this section we briefly discuss two additional issues concerning labor economics.

First, we discuss the ethics of the minimum wage. Standard micro principles textbooks usually stress the fact that introducing a binding minimum wage (that is one which is above the market clearing wage) reduces employment (by raising the cost of hiring workers for firms) and causes unemployment, making the economy less efficient. In Figure 11.1 the demand and supply curves of labor are shown by the curves marked $N_d$ and $N_s$ (as in Chapter 6, although here we are dealing with a single localized labor market, so that we can ignore the price level, taking it to be exogenously given), so the market clearing wage is $W_e$. For the minimum wage to be binding, it has to be set above that level; suppose it is set at $W_m$. As a consequence, employment will fall by $N_1N_e$, as employers reduce their labor force due to the increase in the wage. From an initial position in which the labor market cleared we now come to a situation in which there is unemployment, given by $N_1N_2$ (since, apart from those who lose jobs, some people who were not willing to work before are now induced to do so by the increase in wage). Thus, the standard story – which makes some people critical of minimum wage legislation – argues that the minimum wage results in inefficiency. There may be additional problems which result from this. Firms who face higher wage costs may increase the prices of their products, which can

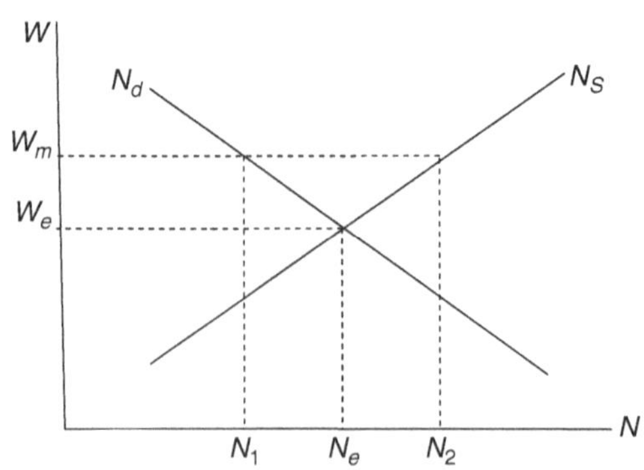


*Figure 11.1* Effect of a minimum wage in a supply–demand model

make consumers worse off. Moreover, if profits are squeezed, business firms will experience a reduction in their cash flow, which could reduce their rate of expansion due to lower investment. The minimum wage reduces profits and prevents such growth from occurring.

The conclusion that the minimum wage or its increase reduces employment and causes or increases unemployment is usually demonstrated using a simple perfectly competitive framework in which both firms and workers are wage-takers, that is, they are such small parts of the market that when they decide how much to work or how much to employ they do not think they will have any effect on the wage. If, however, firms are large in relation to the labor market, they may realize that if they increase the number of workers they hire, they will increase the wage and cut into their profits. This will induce them to reduce their level of employment in an effort to keep the wage down and increase their profits. In the case of a monopsony, where there is only one firm hiring labor, the imposition of a minimum wage above the profit maximizing wage in effect makes the firm a wage taker, removing its incentive to reduce employment and reduce the wage. Hence, employment will actually increase, and unemployment will fall. Although the practical relevance of the one-firm monopsony idea may be limited, large employers in small towns and the costs of job search can result in monopsonistic features which drive wages down. Beyond monopsony issues, if the wage rate is, in fact increased, by the minimum wage, and this translates into increases in the real wage, the redistribution from profits to wages may increase consumption spending, both at local and macro levels, which may increase employment and output, and even increase profits and investment. Thus, even the growth effect may not necessarily be negative. Empirical evidence on the effects of the imposition or increases in the minimum wage on employment and unemployment do not clinch the issue, although it suggests that the textbook view about a necessary increase in unemployment seems to be incorrect. Card and Krueger (1995) examine the effect of an increase in the minimum wage on low-wage jobs in US states and find that unemployment does not rise, but very likely falls. Other studies, however, find mixed results (see Bazen, 2000, 124–30 and Becker and Becker (1996, 37–8).

With the efficiency and growth effects being inconclusive, evaluations of the minimum wage have turned to other ethical considerations. It has been defended on the egalitarian ground that it increases the wage of the lowest-paid workers and increases, overall, the wage share because it sets a floor to the wage, and given the relative wage concerns on account of fairness issues, pushes up wages for other jobs as well. Others argue that its distributional consequences are negative if one is interested in improving the position of the worst-off members of a society and the labor market (Wilkinson, 2004). Many poor people are in fact not minimum wage workers and sometimes outside the labor force, and employers sometimes blunt the effects of the minimum wage by making minimum wage jobs more onerous. The minimum wage is criticized from the rights perspective because it adversely affects the freedom of contract. Brittan (1995, 244), for instance, argues that "minimum wages are a denial of the human right to sell one's labor to a willing buyer and to make one's decisions about whether or not to take paid work at the going rate." Wilkinson (2004) does not find this argument convincing because, if as a result of the minimum wage, unemployment falls and the earnings of low-paid workers increase, then no workers lose from the minimum wage, and it is implausible to conclude that the workers have lost some rights. Thus, if the workers lose, they do so from the consequentialist ground that they lose their jobs, or the lowest-paid workers are worse off. From the rights perspective Arthur Okun (1975) writes that minimum wage laws can be defended with the argument that no one should be forced to sell their labor for less than a living wage. A fundamental human right, at least in a prosperous society, is the right to earn a minimum livelihood. If markets do not yield minimum wages that provide for this living wage then society has a moral right to intervene and enact minimum wage laws. Without these laws human life is corrupted in the sense that life itself is threatened. It is a similar argument to the one against indentured servitude.

Second, we consider the role of labor unions. There is a fairly widespread view among economists that labor unions are bad for the economy. The issues are in some respects similar to the arguments against the minimum wage, and on them our discussion can be brief. The labor union is viewed as introducing a monopoly element in the labor market: when workers form unions they become in effect a single seller of labor, restricting their supply of labor to obtain a higher wage, so that, compared to the perfectly competitive situation shown in Figure 11.1 by the intersection of the demand and supply curves of labor, the wage is higher and the level of employment lower. The result is a deadweight loss in the market and in the economy as a whole implying economic inefficiency. Moreover, by raising wages unions squeeze profits and slow down growth, at least to the extent that profits drive investment, technological change, and growth. Paralleling the discussion of the minimum wage, the counterarguments are that unions do not create inefficiency, but merely correct it, since labor markets typically have monopsonistic elements which make the wage low compared to the perfectly competititve one, and unions bring the wage closer to it. Moreover, at the macroeconomic level, it is possible that the increase in the wage share expands markets (under the plausible assumption that workers have a higher propensity to consume than profit recipients), increases sales, and in fact increases profits, which in turn may increase investment, technological change, and growth, rather than reducing it. A higher wage share may also be considered good from an egalitarian view, if labor unions actually increase the wage and do not increase unemployment.

Labor unions, however, introduce additional elements that are not present in the discussion of the minimum wage. First, since not every sector of the economy is unionized, if unionization raises the wage and reduces employment in the unionized sectors, these unemployed workers will increase the labor supply in non-unionized sectors, exerting downward pressure on the wage in those sectors. Since wages are likely to be relatively low in those sectors, wage inequality will increase in this case. The position of the worst-off in society, in fact, may be worsened, as in the case of the minimum wage. It is argued, in fact, that unions represent insiders, and do not represent the interests of outsiders, who are unemployed, in the wage bargaining process. Second, unions not only bargain over wages, but also change power relations in the workplace and give workers a voice. The effects of this on efficiency are not obvious. On the one hand, they may make workers more aggressive, less productive because of work norms and opposition to technological change, and create industrial strife. On the other hand, they may increase cooperation between workers and supervisors, who meet on relatively more equal terms and therefore trust each other more. This can increase labor productivity and productive efficiency, and also help to improve technology as workers, with their direct knowledge of production shop-floor practices, can contribute to improving technological and organizational methods. By providing voice as an option, and not just exit, as discussed by Hirschman (1970), unions can improve overall efficiency, since decisions will reflect the views of all workers, and not just the marginal worker who is most likely to leave. Participation in unions can build community among workers which may increase worker cooperation and efficiency, in addition to being good for developing fellow-feeling and fraternity. In some contexts labor unions and their associations represent the interest of all workers, and not just their members, and extend fellow-feeling to a wider level, sometimes even at a global level. Third, unions can provide a check on unethical business practices, such as arbitrary dismissal and noncompliance with regulations about working conditions and safety. Labor unions can have a countervailing influence on the power of big business, not only at the firm level, improving efficiency, but also at the broader political level thereby making the political playing field more even and fair (Galbraith, 1952).

## 11.5 Business ethics

Business ethics deals with questions such as the following: Do business firms actually behave in ethical ways? Should they behave ethically? If so, in what ways should they act ethically? How can they be induced to be ethical, or more ethical than they are? Business ethics is not normally considered to be a part of applied economics, but rather an aspect of business management, concerned with the multiplicity of decisions business firms have to make about product development, research and marketing, especially advertising, pricing, investment and financial decisions, financial accounting and representation, hiring policies and compensation standards, conditions of employment and codes of ethics, effects on the natural environment, relations with the government, and managerial styles and corporate culture. In an increasingly globalized world corporations have also to deal with foreign governments, employ poor people in LDCs, and adapt to foreign cultures. Rather than address how ethical questions are related to all these decisions and more,[13] we will examine a few general issues about business ethics which are related to the issues discussed in this book.

The traditional view of the firm is that it maximizes profits and does not have any other concerns. Nor should it, since by maximizing profits it promotes overall economic efficiency. Moreover, if they did not maximize profits, firms would be unable to compete with their competitors, and would soon be driven out of business. All of these claims are questionable. First, firms are constituted by people, and as we have seen, people have ethical values and act ethically. Thus, it is likely that firms would reflect some of these ethical values, even though there are many instances of unethical and illegal behavior by firms and their leaders. Indeed, firms do seem to do things which are ethical: for instance, they recall products which are problematic even when they are not legally required to do so, and they make charitable contributions. Although it may be argued that firms do these good things because it helps them maximize their profits, the motives behind such behavior are worth examining more carefully. Second, in a complex business environment, it is not obvious that there is a unique and known way to maximize profits and compete successfully with other firms. Firms may choose among different possible ways by pursuing more ethical practices which, may, indeed, be good for business as well. Third, we have seen that the single-minded pursuit of profits by firms need not produce efficient outcomes. Even if markets are perfectly competitive, externalities and imperfect information, among other things, can result in inefficiency. Firms with market power can also result in social inefficiency. Breaking laws can result in problems in markets. Moreover, efficiency is not the only ethical issue that societies are concerned with, since they may value fairness and the protection of rights, which are concerns separate from efficiency which itself may be questioned as a good. The first two issues raise questions on whether firms actually do behave ethically and whether doing so is good for business. The third issue has been addressed throughout this book, and we need not repeat the discussions here. However, it should be noted that if firms appear to behave ethically, for instance, by pursuing environment-friendly practices, paying ethically fair wages, and by not breaking contracts and other laws, questions arise about what precisely it means for firms to be acting ethically and being ethical, toward whom and about their motivations for such behavior.

Firms sometimes do things which reflect concern for ethical values. For instance, firms sometimes pay workers more than the wage which would just induce them to work. We have seen earlier, in Section 6.2, firms do this in part because they are involved in a gift exchange with their employees, responding to feelings about fairness that workers may have, and they also may do this because – at least in part –it does well for themselves. This is because it has a positive effect on their profits by increasing their employees' work effort and productivity. There are some other things firms do which even more strongly suggest that they act ethically; an important example of this is business philanthropy. Firms make a significant amount of charitable contributions to a variety of causes either directly, or through foundations they support. They also provide their products (such as computers) – sometimes free – to customers who may not be able to afford them. Some of this may be done with the intention of increasing their profits, but that underscores the points made above: firms do at least seem to act ethically, and this behavior may in fact increase their profits and not drive them out of business (Kotler and Lee, 2004).

The literature on business philanthropy suggests that there may be a number of reasons why firms may contribute to charity (see, for instance, Porter and Kramer, 2002). One reason is that firms are composed of individuals, and since individuals have values, the activities of firms are likely to reflect such values. Managers of firms may have ethical views which make them want to donate to charity because they believe that this it is a good thing to do. A second reason that also attributes business philanthropy to managerial decisions is that managers may engage in it for personal benefit and for increasing their social status. Both these explanations rely on some degree of managerial freedom. But are managers actually free to do these things or are they restricted by shareholder interests? Managers are constrained, but depending on the extent of shareholder control and supervision, they may still have some wiggle room. Moreover, shareholders may also have some values, for instance, which make them wish to "invest" in socially responsible firms and shun firms which reflect undesirable values, such as creating environmental problems, have poor working conditions, etc. A third reason is that firms may engage in ethical activities because it increases their profits, at least in the long run. If firms give away products, or do good things like donating to charities, consumers may become more favorably disposed toward them, and buy their products, increasing their profits. Making charitable contributions to causes that workers like increases the firms' chances of attracting more productive workers even without directly paying them more. Finally, charitable giving is likely to increase the goodwill of the firm with government regulators, and make them act less strictly with the firm, which can also be good for profits. It is possible that managers of the firm may do such things because they take a long-term view of profits, rather than the possibly more short-term interests of stockholders, many of who may be more interested in quick gains through increasing stock prices, so that more managerial freedom may induce more ethical behavior. However, it is also possible that, if managerial compensation is tied to short-run profits and shareholders have strong ethical values (as noted earlier), more managerial freedom may reduce business philanthropy.

Regarding what is meant by ethical behavior, there are at least three broad ways of interpreting it. The first is simply not to break laws. This meaning of ethical behavior is unclear and incomplete, because, given gray areas in the law, it is not clear what not breaking it means. Also, laws may not be ethical and more likely, there will be unethical behavior which would be legal, especially because in many cases firms, through lobbyists, can influence laws which keep the obligations of firms at low levels (such as, for instance, laws regarding credit, which are affected by the lobbying efforts of financial firms). The second refers to not engaging in behavior which is unethical, that is, not harming others (by polluting, or with unsafe working conditions), not paying reparations for harming others (for example, not compensating customers for products which harm them), not lying or misrepresenting (as in deceptive advertising). The third refers to doing positive things, such as helping the community by organizing and financing health campaigns in poor countries (on the part of pharmaceutical companies), making charitable donations which help the poor or in communities where they operate. Clearly, the second is a necessary aspect of ethical behavior, but the third is also important.

Regarding toward whom firms should be acting ethically, or what can be called the constituencies of ethical business, the traditional focus was that the firm should represent the interests of its owners or stockholders, which is to maximize profits for them, so that it is unethical for firms to do anything that does not do so. We have seen, however, that stockholders may have other interests, and may express a preference for "socially responsible investment," for instance, by not polluting the environment. Moreover, as mentioned already, there may not be one clear strategy that maximizes profits, so that managers may choose to act ethically while making profits. The narrow focus on the stockholder has, in any case, been superseded to a large extent by recognizing that there are multiple constituencies of the firm, that is, its "stakeholders" include, in addition to stockholders, its customers and clients, suppliers, workers and managers, and the community in which the firm operates. While adopting this stakeholder approach may well have the result of making the firm behave more ethically, at least two problems with the approach, especially in the case of large corporations in an increasingly globalized world, should be borne in mind. First, ethical behavior does not imply that the firm should merely represent and balance the interests of what it considers to be its various stakeholders, since these interests need not necessarily represent what is good. Second, enumerating and balancing the interests of some groups may result in doing things that are not in the best interests of society as a whole, or even for the world as whole, and firms should take into account its effects on, and interests of, all who they may affect. For instance, locating "dirty" production in poor countries may appease people from the neighborhood from which they move, but may have consequences which are worse for the world as a whole, due to the effect on poor people who may be less able to protect themselves from the dangers of pollution, and because of the overall effect on global warming.

Finally, we may briefly discuss how firms can be induced to act (more) ethically. We may think of changes that can be made at the societal or macro level (and even at the global level), at the institutional level of the firm or what can be called the meso level, and finally, at the level of the individual, or micro level (Enderle, 2003). A focus on the meso level of the firm actually allows us to enrich the discussion of levels at which ethics is relevant since most of our analysis so far has been at the macro level of society or the world or at the micro level of the individual. At the macro level, firms can be affected by many kinds of government interventions and regulations, including laws which introduce pollution fees, promote product safety, quality control, and influence hiring practices. While such interventions are good for setting standards and encouraging certain kinds of behavior, it is important to realize that firms do have ethical values which should not be ignored (for instance, introducing laws about pollution may result in the tendency of firms "buying" pollution rather than acting ethically to reduce it), and that laws and regulations are not enough, because they often create gray areas, and they need to be implemented, which requires the cooperation of the firm and the individuals who represent it. The government can have a more positive role in encouraging firms to make changes within their institutional structure which promote ethical behavior, for instance, by spreading the practice of firms announcing their ethical codes of conduct and goals and providing verifiable information on their degree of compliance with them. Governments and non-government institutions can also promote ethical behavior by verifying and disseminating information about the ethical and unethical practices of firms more openly. This would allow people who may be workers, shareholders, customers, and others to become more aware of how firms are doing. At the institutional level, in addition to this, firms can encourage practices and develop internal rules and corporate cultures which encourage managers to become institutional citizens – who give more weight to honoring their own individual conscience than to simply following what they think of as their orders – by providing an environment which cultivates the habit of thinking and judging independently as a basis of acting civilly with others – employees, customers, suppliers, owners, and civic representatives – and resisting the behaviors and phenomena of what Nielsen (1983) calls the Eichmann, Richard III, and Faust management types. Such an institutional setting can reduce deaths from harmful pollution which causes cancer, unsafe products sold to customers, and from unsafe working conditions. Firms may also promote virtues along communitarian lines, which emphasize building communities within them and with those outside the firm – like suppliers – with whom they interact, in order to build trust, act ethically and succeed in business along the lines pursued by Japanese firms for a long time and other exemplary firms which can be found in many countries (see Stewart, 1995, who explicitly draws on Aristotelian virtue theory). At the individual level, business education can stress the study of the field of business ethics, so that aspiring managers and other workers can learn about how to think of ethics and apply it to the business world, and how to relate ethical behavior with profitability. It is possible that if firms and their managers were more aware of these issues, they would be more likely to adopt ethical behavior for themselves and for the firms whose culture and internal rules they can affect.

Finally, it needs to be emphasized that ethical behavior by corporations and government regulations can work together. Business executives often comment that they should not be asked to do what their competitors are not asked to do because even if they want to behave ethically they can be undermined by competitors who do not do so. They say that government regulations requiring all companies to follow the same rules – such as providing safe working conditions, cleaning up their toxic waste, etc. – will allow companies to exercise the ethical behavior they actually prefer without being punished by competitors.

## 11.6 Conclusion

In this chapter we could do no more than discuss how ethical issues are relevant for a few questions in some applied fields in economics. We hope that these examples will encourage the reader to reflect on how incorporating ethics into the analysis of other issues in other fields of economics can help enrich our understanding of these issues and policy discussions concerning them.

# 12
# Ethics and the Global Financial Crisis

## Introduction

A financial crisis erupted in the US in 2007–8 and then spread to global financial markets and the global economy. The causes, nature, and consequences of the crisis have been extensively examined and debated in the academic literature, policy discussions, and the popular press, and the story is fairly well known.

A widely held view is that the stuff of crises – arrogance, greed, unacknowledged conflicts of interest, unethical behavior, lack of transparency, failed leadership, and insufficient accountability – fueled "an industry out of control." Banks and other financial institutions got themselves, and the whole economy, into trouble by overleveraging, that is, they borrowed heavily, used relatively little of their own capital and bought extremely risky assets. In doing so, they used confusingly complex instruments. The prospect of high returns and thus high compensation led account managers to accept excessive risk, rather than seek more prudential investments. Banks made all these mistakes unknown to the public, because so much of what they were doing was "off the books" financing. And the regulators appeared to be asleep, failing to use what little power the waves of deregulation had left them.

Beyond the discussion of these mistakes, which have received the greatest popular focus, attention has also been given to several other issues: the nature of the financial sector; the role of the economic profession and economic analysis in failing to predict the crisis and creating conditions increasing the likelihood of its occurrence; the implication of macroeconomic imbalances involving increases in debt and income inequality; and the political economy of changes in government policy resulting from the increasing influence of powerful interest groups.

Despite the plethora of issues that have been discussed, very little has been said specifically about ethical issues in economics and their relation to the global crisis, apart from some references to the role of 'greed' in popular discussions.[1] To us, this provides another illustration of how economists and others think that economic and financial issues are separate from ethical considerations. We would argue, on the contrary, that ethical issues are very relevant for understanding the causes and effects of the crisis and subsequent recession and for reducing the possibility of their recurrence in the future. While it is beyond our scope to provide a comprehensive discussion of the issues involved, this chapter will comment on some ways that the material in this book is relevant for understanding the crisis. We devote a separate chapter to the crisis because of the dramatic way in which this major recent event illustrates some of the issues we emphasize in this book.

Section 12.1 will provide a brief review of some relevant features of the crisis by way of background. The following two sections will focus on how ethical issues affect the behavior of individuals and groups in the context of the crisis. Section 12.2 will examine the notion of greed, which has been emphasized in the popular discussion, and relate it to social norms. Section 12.3 will examine more broadly the role of changes in social norms in creating conditions which made the crisis more likely. The next two sections will discuss how the neglect of ethical issues in economics is at least partly responsible for bringing about the crisis. Section 12.4 will focus specifically on finance, and section 12.5 will comment on more general economic issues.

## 12.1 The crisis

While many economists view financial markets as being self-adjusting and efficient, as shown, for instance, in the efficient markets theory, others point to their inherent instability. A long view of financial history (see Kindleberger, 1978) and analytical approaches (see Keynes, 1936, and Minsky, 1986), which take the future to be fundamentally uncertain (in the sense that there is no objective basis to determine the probabilities of future events and returns on assets), suggest that financial markets alternate between bouts of exuberant optimism, when asset prices and credit increase, and forlorn pessimism in which asset prices tumble and credit freezes. According to this view there is nothing special about this crisis.

However, its severity and broad reach has been explained by the deregulation and inadequate regulation of US financial markets; the appearance of new financial instruments, including derivatives such as mortgage-backed securities, collateralized debt obligations, and credit default swaps; bank and leveraged buyouts of unregulated private equity funds; and remuneration policies in financial institutions that encouraged lending irrespective of future returns. All of these led to a huge increase in lending because banks were making loans and passing them on to other financial institutions which sold them by splitting them up in the form of derivatives. It also led to an increase in house prices which fueled borrowing and lending further, linking the fortunes of large numbers of financial institutions. When the loans could not be repaid, there was a ripple effect throughout the financial system, which then froze lending. Since there are large movements of financial capital internationally, due to the removal of restrictions on international financial transactions (as different financial centers had relaxed their regulations to compete for funds) the financial crisis moved across national borders. Moreover, several other countries had their own financial bubbles based on real estate loans.

## 12.2 Greed and the crisis

Blame for the crisis has often been placed on the greed of bankers and financiers. Following a 2009 speech on Wall Street supporting financial regulation, it was reported widely in the press that US President Barack Obama's message was that the "[d]ays of reckless greed are over."[2] He is reported to have said that "We will not go back to the days of reckless behavior and unchecked excess that was at the heart of this crisis, where too many were motivated only by the appetite for quick kills and bloated bonuses." Other US politicians, including the former presidential candidate Senator John McCain, have also used the word greed in describing the behavior of Wall Street and corporate executives.

In Chapter 6 we mentioned greed as a vice which can affect how economies operate and which can result from, and be increased by, engaging in some types of social activities, but we did not define it precisely. Given its importance in discussions of the crisis, it is worthwhile trying to make the concept more analytically precise. Despite the attention that the concept has received, especially in religion, a clear definition is not easy to find.[3]

One approach is to use the neoclassical concept of the *homo economicus*, according to which individuals are seen as maximizing utility given the constraints that they face, and where individual utility depends on what affects people directly (rather than on what affects others); is affected only (or at least primarily) by material goods and money (rather than, say, leisure time spent with others); and is insatiable (that is, more is always better). While this kind of individual behavior can be called greedy, it can lead to the view that greed has positive consequences if the conditions of the first welfare theorem of neoclassical economics (as discussed in Chapters 1 and 7) are satisfied. In this case, "greed ... is good," as the character Gordon Gekko famously stated in Oliver Stone's film *Wall Street*. If all that went wrong is that during the financial crisis the conditions of that theorem were not, in reality, satisfied, then greed led to bad outcomes and that is why it is bad, in a consequentialist sense. Surely, greed is more appropriately conceptualized as a character trait or behavior which is ethically problematic independent of its consequences.

A second way to conceptualize greed is that it is behavior which breaks laws and regulations. During the crisis this could include insider trading and knowingly providing false accounts. This approach can even be formalized using the concept of *homo economicus*, but adding a constraint which states that people do not break laws. However, this approach is problematic because it is not clear when a law is being broken and when it is not, given that laws unavoidably have many gray areas and require interpretation in a given context, interpretations which can and do vary, and because greed is usually thought to go beyond breaking laws.

A more reasonable approach is to interpret greedy behavior as those that violate some socially accepted norms regarding what is permissible and what is not. Although this conceptualization may appear to be vague, it does not have the problems of being consequentialist or requiring an objective interpretation of what it means to break a law. Using this approach, greed can be interpreted as a characteristic of people that leads them to not internalize and adhere to norms that are socially acceptable, and greedy behavior is behavior in which individuals break these norms for personal gain. Examples range from providing information that one considers to be untrue or withholding true and relevant information to doing things which increase one's income without adequately taking into account how those actions affect others or society as a whole.[4]

Interpreted in this way, how is greed responsible, even if only in part, for the financial crisis? We confine ourselves to a few illustrative comments. First, greed led financiers to conceal information in order to increase loans and sell assets, which contributed to the increases in indebtedness and the instability in financial markets. Although greedy behavior is not logically necessary for such instability – indeed, fundamental uncertainty can feed asset bubbles and debt expansion and subsequent busts – it can clearly exacerbate it. Second, greed led financiers to devise compensation systems – bonuses for short-term profits – that allowed them to gain from activities which created incentives to engage in these kinds of destabilizing behavior, so that greed fed greed. Third, greed arguably led financial elites to pressure the government into relaxing and preventing financial regulations with the purpose of increasing their incomes, which made the financial system more vulnerable. Greed is not the only factor, since the power of academic ideas, as we will argue later, also had a role to play in financial liberalization, and greed did not necessarily result in making all financial elites better off although some certainly benefited. Fourth, more generally, greed on the part of the rich arguably had an important role in bringing about increases in overall income inequality in countries like the US, for instance, by engaging in business practices that depressed wages and by supporting tax breaks for themselves. The result was a stagnation of the real incomes of others, which, in addition to other factors which increased vulnerability, led to large increases in consumer debt. While this arguably maintained consumption and aggregate demand in the short run, it proved to be unsustainable in the longer run as debt burdens grew and asset bubbles burst.

But doesn't greed always exist and, if it does, can one argue that greed has had a role in specifically bringing about the crisis? Although there is no doubt that greed – in the sense of breaking social norms in the pursuit of personal aggrandizement – is present to some degree at all times and places, its role is likely to increase in some circumstances. Two major aspects of the current crisis are its financial source and its international scope. Changes in the structure of economies have increased the size of the financial sector compared to that of the non-financial or "real" sector in many counties, and changes in communication technology and changes in policies regarding international capital flows have increased the importance of international financial transactions. It can be argued that both of these changes have given greed a more important role. The financial sector is arguably more likely to be a fertile ground for the conduct of greedy behavior. The financial sector deals in assets which are intangibles – rather than goods and services whose properties are more easily perceived by buyers and sellers – the characteristics of which are not well understood by market participants, thus, there is greater scope for obfuscation and prevarication by those who are in a position to do so and gain from (see Reddy, 2011). Second, the fact that many market participants are working in isolation using computers instead of dealing face-to-face with people makes social restraints on greedy behavior less effective. Third, the fact that financial actors often work in organizations or are competing with other such actors makes it more likely for greedy behavior to become infectious, due to its acceptance in organizational culture or in the culture of the financial community at large. Finally, the fact that the amounts that are traded in a very small period of time in these markets can be very large, because they do not require the physical movement of goods and people, makes the effects of greedy behavior more pernicious. Regarding international transactions, it is possible that interactions between people from different countries can lead to their being less constrained by the social norms that are sometimes shared within a country (see Reddy, 2011).

All of these factors can explain why greedy behavior in the form of violations of social norms for private gain increased during the run-up to the crisis. Such behavior, over time, is likely to change norms as well. A cumulative dynamic was arguably created which made the crisis more likely.

## 12.3 Social norms and the crisis

In addition to the specific characteristics of financial markets and international financial transactions which, we have argued, increased the role of greed, there were general socioeconomic changes which altered social norms. In 1980 the elections of Ronald Reagan in the US and Margaret Thatcher in the UK represented an alternative social consensus to the prevailing Keynesian welfare state – a return to less government and freer markets. The result of these political changes has been the growth of an economic philosophy dominated by an ideology fixated on competition and success as the measure of a person's worth. Although many will deny that this describes the essence of US economic philosophy, daily events are reminders of its sway, as reflected in the exaltation of sports and movie stars and Wall Street and corporate executives; the negative attitude of Congress and the business community toward welfare legislation; the downsizing of corporations in which the managers and stock holders get richer while the employees get fired; and the whole philosophy of success which measures the value of people by their income.

The promotion of financial success and self-interest first became epitomized in the 1980s by Wall Street stock brokers and merger specialists and the goal of newly minted Harvard MBAs to make $1 million a year before their thirtieth birthday. By 2000 it was hedge fund managers and derivatives traders.

Businesses close industrial plants, create unemployment, devastate whole communities, and call it an efficient reallocation of resources. They, who have prospered from free market policies, caution that nothing can be done because natural economic forces are at work. Not only are these changes desirable, but they are inevitable, dictated by the natural forces of globalization and competition; without them, costs will be too high and the economy will become uncompetitive. The poor, the unemployed, and the underemployed are the ones who bear the burden of this free market ethic.

Government social programs established during the previous 60 years were attacked because they supposedly reduced incentives and thus productivity. Reduce welfare, minimum wages, and unemployment benefits so that the poor will have greater incentives to work. Lower taxes and remove regulations on business so that the resulting higher profits will encourage corporations and wealthy individuals to save and invest. Increased productivity and growth in GDP will be the result. Eventually, the benefits will trickle down so that even those on the bottom will be better off than before.

The philosophy and set of values embodied in a society's institutions and policies help shape the character of the people in that society. It is most revealing to examine the character of powerful elites, people in our society, such as CEOs, and Wall Street brokers, who are considered successful. R. H. Tawney's thoughts are illuminating[5]:

> The types which it [the industrial system] carries to power tend to be not unlike those produced by war. They must have energy, self-control, foresight, a willingness to take risks. They must be undisturbed by pity for the weak, by doubts as to the value of the immediate ends at which they aim, by reverence for the finer and more delicate human qualities and achievements, by humility or consciousness of personal deficiencies. They are essentially a conquering race. Like other conquerors they leave a trail of wreckage, consisting of the weak, the exceptionally scrupulous and honourable, the unconventional, the merely gentle and kindly who "dare not have the lives of others on their conscience" (1972).

If one believes that the natural order of society is one in which the strong win their way to power over the ruin of the weak, they will find nothing fundamentally wrong with these attitudes, behaviors, policy changes, and outcomes. It is an easy step to understand, if not condone, the greed-driven behavior within the financial sector that crossed the line to unethical insider trading, excessive risk taking, and the ignoring of their prudential obligations as custodians of other people's money. Since the movers and shakers of the financial world were seen as the Masters of the Universe, it is clear how government regulators were easy to convince that all was well. And given everyone's acceptance of the economics profession's teaching that markets know best, there was little reason to question what appeared to be unending success. Thus this social consensus led to an atrophy of the normal legal, institutional, and social mechanisms which, in earlier times, might have countered those ethical lapses and their consequences.

## 12.4 The ethics of finance and the financial sector

From a discussion of greed and changes in social norms, and their effects on individual and group behavior in bringing about the crisis, we turn to the problems that arose out of the economists' neglect of the ethical aspects of the financial sector and the economy as a whole.

Although there has been some discussion of the effects of a rise in the financial sector, in general the ethics of finance have escaped attention.[6] Financial activity, like any other kind of activity, if done voluntarily, is not something on which "scientists" can or should pass value judgments. But if we reject this claim (following our discussion in Chapter 2) and delve into the ethics of finance, a central question we need to ask is whether the financial sector – especially as large as it has become – is good for the society as a whole and whether such large profits for financial activities are justified?

There has been a tendency in the past to denigrate financial activities such as money lending. Religious traditions, including Jewish, Christian, and Islam, all looked down upon usury, and some denounced and even forbade charging interest. Aristotle opined that money is barren and that usury, among all the businesses, "is most contrary to nature."[7] Many other classical Greek and Roman writers agreed with Aristotle on this.

However, Aristotle's argument was ridiculed by later writers, including Jeremy Bentham (1790), by drawing attention to the positive consequences of financial activity (see Sen, 1993). They have a point. Indeed, there is no question that the availability of finance can make possible many kinds of activities, including production, innovative, and consumption activities, and has the possibility of having major positive consequences for people, in terms of increasing production and income, increasing utility and happiness, improving functionings and capabilities, and expanding freedoms. The provision of finance to low-income farmers can increase production by the use of purchased inputs, which can increase the income of the farmers and in turn increase food production and increase food security for others. The extension of finance to large firms can increase production and investment, increasing the rate of growth of the economy and increasing employment growth.[8]

But these possible *consequentialist* benefits do not address the *deontological* perspective, discussed in Chapter 3, to which Aristotle and others draw attention, that is, whether the activity of financing, which does not involve the creative activity that innovation and production does, deserves the rewards it gets in terms of interest or other returns (see Sen, 1993). In terms of the desert perspective on justice (see Section 3.5), such considerations raise the question of what kinds of activities are worthy of reward and of how much. In terms of the egalitarian perspective, it raises questions about whether deviations from equality due to the returns from financial activity are justified in terms of effort or choice, when the effort involved is simply making finance available, rather than in terms of some activity like labor, or whether the returns to choices are uncertain, perhaps more so than the returns to other types of activity (see Section 2.2.1).

Moreover, the idea that financial activity invariably has good consequences is questionable, especially when the financial sector becomes very large in relation to the rest of the economy. Many writers in the history of economic thought have been concerned with the problems that can arise from financial markets. Sen (1993) discusses the views of the Indian politician and philosopher, Kautilya (who flourished 300 BC), Aristotle, and even Adam Smith, among others. Mainstream neoclassical economics, when it allows for asymmetric information, also implies that market failures can arise from informational problems, leading to inefficient outcomes (see, for instance, Stiglitz, 1985). In addition to inefficiency, the large size of the sector which is subject to financial fragility makes the entire economy more crisis prone and people more vulnerable. When asset prices tumble and credit freezes the real sector is adversely affected as investment, output, and employment drop, and unemployment rises, leading to reductions in income, functionings, and capabilities. These effects were felt during the recent recession, when many people lost their jobs due to the recession and their homes due to foreclosures. Also, large increases in income and asset inequality have occurred with the rise in the importance of the financial sector that, as we have argued, are difficult to justify in terms of several approaches to justice, and can therefore be considered as a bad consequence. This rise in inequality also increases the power of financial interests to affect legislators and push for policy changes which are intended to bring about further increases in their income.

The neglect of these issues has led to the failure to ask what the financial sector does for society and whether and why the high rewards to financial activity are justified. This, in turn, has led to an uncritical acceptance of the growing size of the financial sector, an acceptance which arguably had consequences which made economists in general fail to recognize the crisis and what it could do, and also to support policies which made the crisis more likely.

## 12.5 The neglect of ethics, economic analysis, and the crisis

The failure to examine the ethics of the financial sector is of course a reflection of the general tendency of many economists to neglect ethical issues. This neglect does not imply that ethics are left out of economic theory and policy analysis, which we have argued in Chapter 2 to be impossible, but that particular goals of a good society have been emphasized by default, that is, the goals of promoting individual freedom and economic growth and efficiency.

In the analysis of the financial sector, this bias is reflected in the use of terms like the *efficient* market hypothesis, capital market *liberalization,* and financial *liberalization* as opposed to financial *repression*. This choice of words, as pointed out by Myrdal (1954) and discussed in Chapter 2, suggest hidden values in the apparently value-free terms.

The removal of regulations on banks, of the type embodied in the US Glass-Steagall Act of 1933 that limited commercial banks' ability to engage in transactions involving financial securities and their association with securities firms, and the decision to not regulate markets for new securities including derivatives, can be traced to this problem. The efficient market hypothesis basically suggests that financial markets operate efficiently, in the sense that they fully use all the information available at the time financial investment decisions are made, so that it is not possible for someone to make consistently higher returns on investments than the average returns in the market when risk is adjusted for. This hypothesis has been widely taken to provide a justification of deregulation: if the market operates efficiently by itself, why regulate it? Without going into the problems regarding the assumptions on which the hypothesis is based – such as utility maximization, objectively calculable risk rather than uncertainty, the rational expectations which states that individuals take into account all information available, and the empirical tests of that approach – we wish to stress here the implied focus on efficiency for supporting market freedom. The lack of regulation, of course, was caused by a variety of reasons, including the strong political pressures imposed by financial interests[9] and by the role some economists played as their "hired guns."[10] However, the acceptance of these pressures arguably had something to do with the views of the economics profession in favor of relatively unregulated markets, especially financial markets, and to a large part this can be seen to be the result of the failure to take ethical issues seriously.

These attitudes are relevant not only for the financial sector but for the economy as a whole. The bias that economists and policymakers have shown toward efficiency and growth have made them support neoliberal policies, some of which we mentioned earlier, and have neglected other goals such as fairness, equality, the enhancement of functionings and capabilities, and the reduction of poverty and vulnerability. This neoliberal approach has been implemented through using the state to increase the efficient functioning of markets by increasing market flexibility, for instance by weakening labor unions, by reducing government support for the poor and the unemployed, and by reducing the costs of firing workers. It has also arguably had the effect of policymakers not giving sufficient attention to unemployment and being more concerned with the problems of government debt and thereby reducing the ability of governments to pursue expansionary fiscal policies sufficient to reduce unemployment. All of this is not just the consequence of not taking ethical issues seriously, it also is undoubtedly related to the nature of rewards in the economic profession, and also – as mentioned in our discussion on financial market policies – to the power and influence of those who believe that they benefit from such policies. Nevertheless, the failure to take ethics seriously arguably has had some role.

In contradiction to our argument, it has sometimes been claimed that the crisis in the US is largely a consequence of government attempts to increase lending on housing for low-income households, to provide a salve to address their economic plight, so that it was government concern for equality that led to the crisis. Apart from the empirical question as to how much of the housing bubble was caused by lending to low-income households, and to what extent this lending was the result of government policy rather than loan pushing by deregulated lenders who were unconcerned with the quality of their lending because they were able to securitize their loans, this criticism does not negate the basic problems of irresponsible behavior in the financial sector, slack regulation by the public sector, and an overall policy stance which tolerated increasing inequality in the name of efficiency and market freedom.

## 12.6 Conclusion

This chapter has complemented the previous one by showing how the general ethical issues discussed are relevant for analyzing many concrete economic issues, not just in terms of applied fields of economics but also in the sense of understanding particular events. Given the importance of the recent global financial crisis, we have used it as the event to examine.

This chapter has argued that an analysis of ethical considerations that affect norms which influence the behavior of actors in financial markets and other sectors of the economy can increase our understanding of the genesis, spread, and continuation of the crisis. We have also examined how the role of greed, which has attracted a fair amount of popular attention, can be given clear analytical foundations. The chapter has also argued that neglect of ethical issues by economists in the study of finance and financial markets, and the economy in general, have created conditions which made the financial crisis more likely to occur. However, since norms and behavior on the one hand and how economists neglect or view ethical issues on the other are not independent, many issues discussed in these sections are closely interrelated, and our division of the chapter into these sections has been somewhat artificial.

# 13
# Conclusion

We have argued in this book that it is impossible to do economic analysis and conduct public policy by leaving out ethics. Efforts to purge ethics from economics by separating positive and normative economics and by appealing to the value neutrality thesis are unwarranted. Economists make explicit and implicit value judgments when they do what they call positive economic analysis in choosing what questions they examine and what assumptions they make in their analysis and their models. These questions cannot be swept aside by appealing to brute facts and to empirical testing.

When economists examine how the economy functions, they have to analyze what the individuals who populate the economy are like and how they behave. While for some purposes the view of individuals as *homo economicus*, the self-interested and optimizing agent, may have served economists well, for many purposes that conception of individuals is flawed and provides a misleading analysis of individual behavior and how the economy functions as a result of the interactions of individuals. Individuals are not just self-interested optimizers, because they have concerns for others, they follow norms, and in general they have ethical values. These features of human beings affect how they behave, how they interact in institutional settings, and what outcomes occur in the economy. Ethical values can improve the working of markets and the economy as a whole in some cases, and they may result in unfavorable outcomes in some senses, and these features must be kept in mind for analyzing the workings of the economy.

When economists try to evaluate what happens in the economy and what policies to adopt, they often do so by examining individual utility and satisfaction, and by examining income, output, and economic growth. These approaches are often used in the conduct of government policy interventions in the economy and in evaluating the implications of policies, using notions of efficiency and equality, cost-benefit analysis, and macroeconomic policy. These approaches, however, are limited in the amount of attention they give to ethical issues. Many important issues are relevant in discussing whether and to what extent markets and other economic institutions are moral, whether efficiency based on individual utility, and income and output and their distribution among people are appropriate ways of evaluating outcomes. Since most economic policies affect different people in different ways, it is particularly important to evaluate the distributional consequences of policy changes, and economists need to do so much more carefully by incorporating ethical issues, than they usually do.

These ethical issues pervade every aspect of economics. This book could do no more than discuss some general aspects of these issues and illustrate their role in chapter 11 for a few subfields of economics, such as development economics, international economics, environmental economics, labor economics, and business economics; and in chapter 12 discuss ethical issues related to the financial and economic crisis that exploded in 2008.

Economists were not always doing economics without ethics. The economist who is widely considered to be the father of the subject, Adam Smith, examined both the economy and ethical issues. While in *The Wealth of Nations*, Smith described how the invisible hand leads self-interested people to achieve unintended outcomes which are good for society as a whole, in *The Theory of Moral Sentiments* he was concerned with other motives and why they were also important for good social outcomes. Many great economists of the past and the present, including William Petty, Francois Quesnay, John Stuart Mill, Karl Marx, Jeremy Bentham, and Amartya Sen, to name just a few, have examined both economic and ethical issues and their intersection. Economists generally would be well advised to follow their examples.

Although one may concede that ethics and economics are intrinsically interrelated, it may still be argued that it is unnecessary for economists to become more familiar with ethics. Partha Dasgupta (2005, 224–5), a well-known economist in general and development economist in particular, has reacted to criticisms of development economics made by some economists and philosophers who argue that most economists do not show an adequate appreciation of ethical issues. He counters that responses to many practical questions development economists have to face require "a good dose of modern economics, with all its technicalities... [T]hey require in addition involvement with anthropology, ecology, demography, epidemiology, psychology, and the nutrition and political sciences. Ethics, on the other hand, would appear to have little to offer." He argues that this is because

> [M]odern economics is built on broad ethical foundations, capable of being reduced as special cases to the various ethical theories that are currently on offer... [S]ince the foundations themselves were settled decades ago, research economists don't find it necessary to rehearse them over and over again. They know that to do so would be to plough diminishing returns, possibly even negative returns. So, the ethical foundations of modern economics are regarded as unspoken assumptions in research publications. Moreover, ethicists are not firm guides for choosing among ethical theories.

For Dasgupta (2005, 222), the main debates among economists on public policy matters relate not to values, but about their readings of facts. Although Dasgupta's argument mostly refers to development economics, it is clear that he believes that it applies generally to all of economics.

However, Dasgupta goes too far in arguing that economists should leave aside ethical questions because they have already been settled. In fact, ethical issues continue to be heatedly debated, and many, if not, most economists seem to be unaware of the ethical issues involved. This impoverishes their economics because they evaluate the performance of economies and public policy in terms of narrow goals of efficiency and growth, and leave out of consideration the fact that people actually have ethical values which affect their behavior. It is also not the case that just because economists argue about the facts, they are not implicitly arguing about values, because it is not clear how facts alone – not least because empirical work, as discussed in Chapter 2 is often inconclusive – can resolve arguments about policies. Finally, it is not clear that all economists do have the same values – there are many who argue that efficiency and growth are all that matters, and that one should not worry about inequality at all, even if one worries a little about poverty and unemployment.[1]

But if they need to become more aware of ethical issues can economists possibly do this? Isn't there so much in economics that leads one to specialize within economics, let alone be knowledgeable about ethics (and sociology, and political science, and so on)? There are undoubtedly benefits from specialization, but it is possible that in this case specialization has gone too far and along a wrong direction. In their narrow search within their specialized areas, and in trying to ape the methods of scientists who study the physical universe, they often seem to lose track of what is really at stake: the betterment of people, communities, societies, and the world (including its natural environment) as a whole. How can one seek to do this without a conception of what is good and what is better? Not only do they risk losing track of what is really important, but they may also risk doing badly the things that they do in their specialized ways by portraying people in the caricatured form of the *homo economicus*, rather than how they really are.

The stakes are high indeed. Keynes ended his *General Theory* with the words:

> The ideas of economists and political philosophers, both when they are right and when they are wrong, are more powerful than is commonly believed. Indeed, the world is ruled by little else. Practical men, who believe themselves to be quite exempt from any intellectual influences, are usually the slaves of some defunct economist. Madmen in authority, who hear voices in the air, are distilling their frenzy from some academic scribbler of a few years back. I am sure that the power of vested interests is vastly exaggerated compared with the gradual encroachment of ideas. Soon or late, it is ideas, not vested interests, which are dangerous for good or evil. (Keynes, 1936, 383–4)

Economists, through their writing and teaching have a major effect on policymaking and the lives of people all around the world. DeMartino (2011) writes, emphasizing the role of ethics, that:

> Their [that is, the economists] authority to affect the lives of others entails ethical challenges that are exceedingly difficult. They need the help of the best minds of their profession in sorting out how to act ethically. At present, they receive none. I will argue that the failure of the profession to recognize (let alone engage) these challenges is itself ethically indictable.
>
> Economics operates on the presumption that its field is somehow beyond ethics or that the answers to the ethical questions that arise in economic practice are so obvious that they require no sustained attention... [Thus] at no point in their professional training will they have been trained to confront the ethical dilemmas that this enormous responsibility entails.

What needs to be done? In general, economists need to pay much more attention to ethical issues when they do economics, and need to be much more aware of the ethical implications and underpinnings of their theories and policy prescriptions. They need to inculcate these values when they spread their ideas and influence future economists by their teaching and popular writing.[2] There seem to be some signs that things are moving in this direction.[3] We hope this book will add to the momentum of getting economists to take seriously the role of ethics in economics, and also help others to take economists to task when they fail to do so.

# Notes

## 1 Introduction

1. It is actually called the Sveriges Riksbank Prize in Economic Sciences in Memory of Alfred Nobel, since the prize was not actually established by Alfred Nobel, but first awarded in 1969. In 2011 the Nobel family went public and disassociated themselves from this Bank of Sweden Prize, calling for it to be delinked from the real Nobels.
2. There are many views about what science is and what science does, and given these definitions, about whether or not economics is a science. We need not go into these issues here.
3. Sometimes, however, a distinction is made between the two in terms of whether one is referring to individual or societal ethics.
4. There is, of course, a great deal of disagreement about how to be unselfish and how to help others. For instance, it may be argued that it is not good to give money to the disadvantaged, because it will not help them remove their disadvantages, while others may argue that giving money will help them overcome their disadvantages.
5. Lionel Robbins's (1932) statement that "economics is a science which studies human behavior as a relation between ends and scarce means which have alternative uses" has also proved to be influential, and is adopted in many introductory economics texts. We do not find this definition very useful for our purposes because it defines it as a science, does not take into account that some means may not be scarce (such as labor, which may be unemployed, or capital, which may not be fully utilized), and seems to leave out many issues with which economics is concerned, such as how income is distributed among people and groups.
6. Sometimes such equilibria may not exist (that is, the conditions are such that there may be no state of the economy in which all markets clear at economically relevant values and in which individuals do not want to change their behavior because they prefer doing something other than what they are doing). Sometimes there may be multiple equilibria.
7. Some also make this argument because of the difficulties involved in aggregation across individuals and markets.
8. Sometimes applied economics is distinguished from theoretical economics: the latter is defined as examining abstract theoretical principles while the former is concerned with applications of these principles to the real world, usually with quantitative analysis using empirical data. Here we use the term "applied" differently. Both microeconomics and macroeconomics can deal with empirical analysis using data, while applied analysis applies the general ideas of microeconomics and macroeconomics to specific aspects of the economy, such as labor markets, public policy issues, international

aspects, growth, monetary aspects, and development issues. These subfields may have both microeconomic and macroeconomic aspects.

9. At this stage of our analysis it is not necessary to rigorously define specifically such terms as smoothly functioning markets, distortions, and imperfect competition. Roughly, we refer to smoothly functioning markets as those in which prices are flexible, so that if there is excess demand or supply, the price will go up or down to restore the equality of supply and demand, and by imperfect competition we mean a situation in which, for instance, there are a small number of sellers, or even one seller, which can influence its price rather than accept that the market price is beyond its control.
10. A state of the world is a full description of the state of all possible variables over which individuals (or society as a whole) have preferences. Thus, a state of the world may refer to quantities produced of all goods and services, quantities of goods and services consumed by each person, the wages and incomes of each individual, the amount of hours each person works, how much each person saves, and so forth. The state of all these variables may not be of interest to every person. For instance, a person who is self-interested may only be concerned with what he or she consumes, and how much he or she works, and not with what others consume. In this case the person may still have a preference ordering over all aspects of the state of the world, but will be indifferent between states in which levels of consumption of other people are different, as long as the variables which directly concern them (such as their own levels of consumption) are the same between the states.
11. The rationality aspect is usually stressed less by economists than by other social scientists who adopt the "rational choice" approach.

## 2 Economics Without Ethics?

1. We say that these questions usually start in these ways because sometimes a positive question can be asked in the form "what level of output should a firm produce in order to maximize its profits?" And a normative question can take the form of "what is the best policy for reducing unemployment?"
2. See Krugman and Wells (2005, 34), emphasis in original.
3. For a discussion of differences in perceptions of trends in the inequality between nations, see Milanovic (2005).
4. See Blaug (1990). Also see Nagel (1961).
5. See Dutt (1984, 1990) for examples of macroeconomic models which incorporate such distributional affects.
6. Popper's own ideas are far more complex and sophisticated, showing an awareness of many of the problems that occur in implementing his prescriptions, including the defensive mechanisms that protect theories that are discussed below; what is caricatured here is the standard mainstream economists' view of Popper, which is rooted in some of Popper's ideas.
7. For a fuller discussion and analysis of methodology in science in general and in economics see, for instance, Kuhn (1970), Blaug (1990), and Caldwell (1982), and for useful collections of readings, see Caldwell (1984) and Hausman (1984).
8. For instance, a macroeconomic model may assume that the economy is a closed one which does not trade with other countries, but it will need to be extended to consider an open economy.

9. For instance, the results depend on the assumption that wages are perfectly flexible, but may not follow if wages are rigid.
10. This thesis is so influential that we have heard many noneconomists *define* inflation as the phenomenon in which "too much money chases too few goods and makes prices increase."
11. For the supply of money, there have been numerous definitions, according to whether it refers to a narrow definition, referring to currency in circulation and checking account deposits – called M1 – or more inclusive measures like M2, M3, M4, and so forth, with some of these even having A and B versions! For an overview of these issues see Wilber (1979).
12. See, for instance, Sims (1996).
13. Some of the comments in this section may seem to be critical of neoclassical economics. However, our intention here is not to criticize the approach, but to argue that it is value-laden, that is, it makes numerous value judgments even when it claims not to. This does not mean that we have no opinions on neoclassical economics. Since we are arguing in this chapter that value judgments should be made explicit, we better come clean about our opinions on that approach. We personally have reservations about many aspects of neoclassical economists, and we are very troubled by what we see to be the domination of economics by that approach (however it is precisely defined). However, we believe that the use of the optimizing approach – perhaps with modifications which allow people's utility to be affected by habits and the well-being of others – which is widely used in neoclassical economics may be very useful for some purposes, provided that it is not considered to be a requirement of proper economic analysis. Further, we believe that, since it is the dominant approach to economics, it is something that people, especially students, should understand before they criticize it.
14. See Boland (1981).
15. See, for instance, Frank et al. (1993).
16. We will see later, in Chapter 9, that this may not be the case in reality.
17. Suppose that the equilibrium is not unique. Then, since both are efficient, it must be the case that when one compares them, some individuals must be better off at some and others better off at others. Then we have the difficult problem of having to choose between different equilibria which would necessitate value judgments regarding fairness. If the equilibrium is not stable, it has no practical significance, because the economy will go further and further away from it, without converging to it from a particular starting point.
18. Roughly speaking, if there are two "distortions," say an externality and a situation of imperfect information, taking care of the first (say, with a tax which makes the originator of the externality pay a fee for causing it) may remove the problem of inefficiency caused by that distortion, but exacerbate the problem caused by the other distortion. In economics this kind of issue is addressed by the literature on the theory of the second best.
19. It should be clarified that what is implied here is that if neoclassical economists are making the value judgment that all the assumptions mentioned here are satisfied, they are in effect making the value judgment that free choice in free markets is good. However, they may believe that free choice and free markets are good because of other reasons. For instance, they may think that individuals have the right to buy and sell what they want

(within the limits of laws), or they may think that government intervention makes things worse in terms of efficiency. Thus, they need not necessarily be making value judgments in support of these assumptions when they support free choice in markets. In other words, making the judgment that all the assumptions mentioned in the text are satisfied is sufficient, but not necessary, for supporting free choice in markets.

20. Krugman and Wells (2005, 35). Earlier in the text they define efficiency as a situation in an economy in which all opportunities to make some people better off without making others worse off have been taken (2005, 14).
21. The following discussion draws in part on Weston (1994).

## 3 Approaches to Ethics and Justice

1. This account is based on Solomon (1998).
2. Italics in original omitted. MacIntyre takes this to be a provisional definition in need of amplification and amendment. By practice he means "any coherent and complex form of socially established cooperative human activity through which goods internal to that form of activity are realized in the course of trying to achieve these standards of excellence which are appropriate to, and partially definitive of, that form of activity, with the result that human powers to achieve excellence... are systematically extended" (MacIntyre, 1984, 187). For instance, in the practice of chess or football, internal goods are those in which people try to excel, while external goods are things like status and money.
3. These quotes are from Kant (1785).
4. For instance, Kamm argues that while it would not be permissible to kill somebody for his or her organs to save the lives of five others, it would be permissible to divert a runaway trolley that will kill five innocent and immobile people on the track onto a side track where one innocent and immobile person will be killed.
5. Suppose that individuals 1, 2, ..., $N$, obtain utility levels $U_1$, $U_2$, ..., $U_N$, from a particular state of the world which fully specifies the relevant aspects of the world (what gives them pleasure and pain), that is, what each person gets, what they get collectively, etc. Then total utility is given by

$$W = U_1 + U_2 + \ldots + U_N = \sum_{i=1}^{N} U_i.$$

6. Thus, even if total utility can be increased by a driver running through a red light in a particular instance when there is no one else at the intersection, it will be better to follow the rule of stopping at a red light if it increases utility overall in general. Note that the act is still being justified in utilitarian consequentialist terms, not in terms of the goodness of the action as such.
7. These problems can be overcome if individual utility depends negatively on the existence of the institution of slavery or if the act of killing is considered bad by individuals. These extensions of utilitarianism, however, stretch the meaning of utility far beyond the intention of its proponents who were concerned with outcomes, not acts and rules as such.

8. For instance, if a person chooses to buy one bundle of goods over another bundle which she could have bought, that person is better off (and obtains more utility) buying the former bundle. This is true by definition. If she didn't get more utility she wouldn't have chosen that bundle.
9. For good, brief, discussions on justice and contractualism, see Kymlicka (1991) and Hausman and McPherson (2006, 198–213).
10. See Sterba (1998) for a critical discussion of communitarian and other approaches to social justice.
11. The rest of this section relies heavily on Held (1990), which provides further references to the literature.
12. See Gilligan (1982).

## 4 Individuals, Norms, and Ethical Values

1. No distinction is usually made between the act of purchase or the act of use (like eating or reading). There is a time dimension involved here – say a day or a week – since the number consumed obviously depends on the amount of time being discussed.
2. There are other constraints in this example. Since the consumer cannot buy negative amounts of these goods (we assume that she does not have any apples and books to start with which she can sell, and therefore "buy" negative amounts), the quantities of these goods are constrained to be positive. The consumer does not necessarily have to obey the budget constraint if he or she can beg, borrow, or steal. If time is needed for consumption, total time may be another constraint faced by the consumer.
3. For simplicity, we assume that the consumer can buy any quantities of books and apples, not just integers. In other words, she can buy fractions of an apple or a book.
4. Balanced bundles refer to those in which both goods are well represented, while extreme ones have large amounts of one and small amounts of the other good. In economics textbooks this is expressed by the assumption of diminishing marginal rate of substitution which states that as a consumer has more and more of a good, the amount of that good she will require to compensate her (that is, leave her with the same utility) for giving up a unit of another good will increase.
5. However, since the firm is not an individual, it is not quite clear who exactly is making decisions and therefore who is rational. The same problem exists for consumers if we interpret them as a household with multiple individuals.
6. We do not insist that the bundle chosen provides more utility than other bundles because there may be several bundles which provide the same level of utility in a more general framework than the one depicted in Figure 3.1. This possibility is ruled out in that figure by the assumption that individuals prefer more balanced bundles to extremes.
7. In these two assumptions we are distinguishing between information about the current characteristics of the goods and services, and information about the future, that is, what choosing them will imply in the future. In reality, it may not be possible to distinguish between these two assumptions about knowledge very clearly.

8. Note that this is not the same thing as the utility of the expected value of the lottery, that is, $U(\frac{1}{4} A + \frac{3}{4} B)$. This is the utility a person gets by getting the bundle $\frac{1}{4} A + \frac{3}{4} B$ for sure. If a person is risk averse, this utility will be greater than the expected utility the person gets from the lottery, that is, $\frac{1}{4} U(A) + \frac{3}{4} U(B)$.
9. See Hausman and McPherson (2006, 51–55) for a brief discussion.
10. For further discussion of games, see Chapter 5.
11. See Hausman and McPherson (1996, 58).
12. It may be argued that these behaviors are self-interested because people can tell other people about them and then derive some material benefits. But this is not entirely convincing, because this amount of self-interest may be consistent with fibbing about one's good deeds which are not actually performed. Some economists argue that people get "psychic satisfaction" from doing these things, but this explanation becomes tautologous, since it is consistent with any kind of behavior unless there is some independent means of verifying this, perhaps based on surveys.
13. We do not consider here (1) what it is that standard neoclassical theory has done well in comparison to and (2) whether its wide use and popularity are for reasons completely unrelated to how accurate it is (for instance, because people are not taught about alternative approaches).
14. The following discussion draws heavily on Konow (2003), which provides the relevant references and details of some of the vignettes, surveys, and experiments.
15. The dictator game is different from the ultimatum game discussed earlier. In this "game" the counterpart does not respond at all, whereas in the ultimatum game the respondent does actually take or leave the offer.
16. For a fuller discussion of the literature the Kahneman et al. (1986a) contribution has spawned regarding context-dependent notions of fairness, see Konow (2003, 1215–22).

## 5 Social Interactions and Ethical Values

1. Some games examine the interaction between groups, such as countries, and some examine how an individual interacts with some inanimate object such as nature.
2. For simple but more extended treatments of noncooperative game theory see, for instance, Dixit and Nalebuff (1991) and Kreps (1990).
3. Repeated interaction between two people may not involve repeated games with the same payoffs. For instance, if one player is hurt in some way (like, for instance, he or she loses an eye), the payoffs in the next round may not be the same. This example refers to Gandhi's quote about an eye for an eye making everyone blind.
4. For instance, if a player's payoff in each move is 3, the total payoff in a game repeated four times is $3 + 3d + 3d^2 + 3d^3$, where $d$ is the time discount factor which is less than 1 to reflect the fact that the player prefers payoffs now to payoffs in the future (that is, they are impatient).
5. If this strategy involves playing one particular chosen move, it is called a pure strategy. Sometimes the Nash equilibrium may involve a mixed strategy,

in which the player plays different strategies with some probabilities. For those who know the rock–paper–scissors game the Nash equilibrium requires each player to play rock, paper, and scissors, each with a probability of 1/3. There is, in fact, no Nash equilibrium pure strategy in this game. For instance, if in a one-shot game, someone always plays "rock" the opponent will always play "paper."

6. This kind of game is called a Prisoner's dilemma game because it is associated with a story in which two prisoners – say Bonnie and Clyde – are being held in two separate cells in a jail and not allowed to communicate with each other, accused of breaking and entering and armed robbery. There is enough evidence to convict them both of breaking and entering, for which they will be given a year in prison each. They are told that if they confess and give evidence against the other which proves that the other one committed robbery, they will be allowed to go free (for good behavior they will not have to serve the year in jail) if there is no evidence against them, and the other will be given 8 years. If they both confess and provide evidence against the other, they will be jailed for 5 years for good behavior (for cooperating with the law). What will the two prisoners do? The objective of the prisoners, here, is to minimize their jail term. The payoffs are shown in the following table. In the Nash equilibrium they will both confess. If we are only concerned with the utility levels of the two accused robbers which falls with the length of the jail term, the Pareto optimal outcome (in which both are better off) will occur if they both do not confess. Since they cannot communicate with each other (and even if they could, if they are looking out for themselves), they will not risk not confessing, fearing that the other will confess.

| | | Clyde | |
|---|---|---|---|
| | | Not confess | Confess |
| Bonnie | Not confess | 1, 1 | 8, 0 |
| | Confess | 0, 8 | 5, 5 |

7. Social nonoptimality can also arise from situations in which there are many players and there is no strategic interaction in the sense that each player can ignore the reactions of others to their actions. This is because some of the other assumptions made in proving the result that perfectly competitive equilibria are Pareto optimal may not be satisfied. An example of this will be discussed later in the text.
8. Note that the payoffs in the first game shown in Table 5.5 and the second game shown in Table 5.6 are not comparable because the first refers to income and the second to utils. Even if we interpret the payoffs in the first game as showing self-interested utils, the same player in the two games

is not in fact the same person, because in one he/she is not envious and in the other he/she is, and thus we cannot compare utility levels of these two incarnations of the same player.

9. A problem with this analysis is that in this game "tit for tat" is not evolutionarily stable, since mutants who follow the strategy of "always cooperate" may spread in the system because they do just as well against those following the "tit-for-tat" strategy, since everyone always cooperates. When the share of players who always cooperate becomes large enough, the system can be subject to attack by players with other strategies who may do better, on average, than the others.
10. This model is described in Skyrms (1996), and a brief outline is contained in Hausman and McPherson (2006, 244–5).

## 6 Markets and Ethical Values

1. That is, if traders do not like the terms of the trade they may not buy or sell at all, or switch to other buyers or sellers, rather than communicate to each other about which aspects of the trade and product they are dissatisfied and how to improve matters while staying in their buyer–seller relationship (Hirschman, 1970).
2. See, for instance, Shapiro and Stiglitz (1984).
3. However, those who believe that the money wage is completely flexible argue that the economy is always at the full-employment level of employment, but output fluctuations occur because workers and other sellers supply more or less because they make incorrect forecasts about the general price level (than they would had they made forecasts that turned out to be correct). For instance, if there is an unexpected negative demand shock (a fall in the aggregate demand due to a lower level of planned investment by firms), the money wage will fall if wages are flexible, but workers may not expect the price level to fall. Thus, they will expect a lower real wage than the one that actually prevails (because the actual price level also falls, unbeknownst to the workers) and supply less labor, thereby causing output to fall.
4. Another way of stating this is that the Phillips curve – showing the relationship between the inflation rate and the unemployment rate – may be negatively sloped in the short run, but vertical in the longer run.
5. See Yuengert (1996) for a good review of some of these debates.
6. Sometimes the critics and advocates of markets seem to define markets as everything in modern society. Since it is not clear what everything is we will not employ this definition either.
7. McCloskey's (2006) long, erudite, entertaining and very readable discussion on "bourgeois virtues" is summarized in the concluding part of her book, especially on pgs. 507–8, which is the source of the following quotations in the text.

## 7 The Morality of Markets and Government Intervention

1. The fact that unlike the robber, the market need not have placed the person in a coercive situation, is not of relevance here. A robber could still be

coercive even if the situation of the victim is brought about by someone else or by natural causes.

2. For instance, we might not like our choice to buy ice cream denied to us even if we never buy.
3. See Sen (1985, section 4) for a fuller discussion.
4. See Leibenstein (1966).
5. Calling these values economic values arguably excessively narrows the meaning of the term economic, and can lead to the problem of believing that other values are not affected by goods which are often thought of as economic goods.
6. Anderson (1993, 151).
7. Note that there may not be a complete correspondence between nonexclusivity in the sense of a property of goods and a property of the nature of social arrangements for exchanges. Goods that promote political values and thus appropriately distributed through public provisioning, which Anderson calls "political goods," do not in principle have to be nonexcludable. For instance, health care may be excludable, yet be considered a "political good."
8. Sandel (p. 95) distinguishes two objections to prostitution and says: "Consider two familiar objections to prostitution. Some object to prostitution on the grounds that it is rarely, if ever, truly voluntary. According to this argument, those who sell their bodies for sex are typically coerced, whether by poverty, drug addiction, or other unfortunate life circumstances. Others object that prostitution is intrinsically degrading, a corruption of the moral worth of human sexuality. The degradation objection does not depend on tainted consent. It would condemn prostitution even in a society without poverty and despair, even in cases of wealthy prostitutes who like the work and freely choose it."
9. This problem is sometimes avoided by allowing a limited number of people to enter during a particular period of time.
10. An argument can be made that education and health care create positive externalities, because of the general overall benefits of education and health (for instance, because education creates better citizens who make better democratic decisions, and because better public health reduces the incidence of infectious and contagious diseases), which implies that markets result in inefficient outcomes. But the argument made here is independent of this one.
11. See also the discussion of Titmuss's work in Hausman and McPherson (1996, 215–6). The validity of Titmuss's claim continues to be empirically tested. Mellström and Johanesson (2008) find strong support for Titmuss's claim (at least for women) in field experiments in which the subjects were asked to give blood with and without compensation. Interestingly, the blood donations did not fall if the subjects received compensation but were allowed to donate them to charity.
12. Anderson (1993, 169) states that in the 1980s a typical gross payment to a broker is about $15,000 from which the surrogate mother typically receives $10,000. In 2006 the payments to surrogate mothers ranged from $22,000 to $30,000, increasing with the number of pregnancies a surrogate mother contracted, with $5000 in additional fees and allowances, health

and life insurance, and all surrogacy related expenses; see, <http://www.surrogateweb.com/content/pdf/Surrogate_Benefit_Package_IVF_1st_time_3994_6_1_748.pdf>

13. The following discussion draws heavily on Anderson (1990a, 1993), which may be consulted for a fuller analysis.
14. For instance, it may seem that in a monopoly or oligopoly situation with one or few sellers, price discrimination – the practice by the seller of charging different prices to different buyers – may be inefficient, but under certain conditions, it may imply an improvement in efficiency.

## 8 Individual Preferences, Efficiency, and Cost-Benefit Analysis

1. More generally, social welfare is nondecreasing with each person's utility, and increasing with the utility level of at least one individual. Specific examples of social welfare functions include a Benthamite one, for which $W = \sum_i U_i$, where welfare is the sum of individual utilities, and a Rawlsian one, for which $W = \min_i U_i$, where social welfare increases when the worst-off individual increases his or her utility.
2. Sometimes economists do not use a social welfare function, but use the concept of the compensation principle in evaluating states which cannot be Pareto-ranked. The basic idea here is that one can rank two states, *A* and *B*, and say that *A* is socially preferred to *B* even if there are some worse off at *A* compared to *B* if the winners can compensate the losers to make them no worse off than at *B* and yet themselves be better off. Since this criteria does not require compensation to be actually paid, this method focuses on efficiency and is not concerned with fairness. The compensation criterion may not be able to rank all states since, as noted by Scitovsky, it is possible for *A* to be preferred to *B* by this criterion, and also for *B* to be preferred to *A*, since different individuals may have different utility functions.
3. Cognitive dissonance refers to the pain people feel when they are in states of the world which they do not like (especially if, some reason or other, they have chosen to be in that state). In such cases they may wish to reduce their pain by making themselves like the state in which they find themselves. Thus, if one chooses to live in a particular neighborhood, they may force themselves to like it, since not to do so creates cognitive dissonance.

## 9 Production, Income, and Economic Growth

1. Gross Domestic Product and Gross National Product differ according to whether what is being measured is production within the geographical boundaries of a country or production by nationals of a particular country. Net Product takes depreciation of capital out of Gross Product figures. Production measures evaluate goods and services according to market prices while income measures do it in terms of the incomes people actually receive, the difference being explained by indirect government taxes and depreciation (when gross production figures are considered). These differences need not detain us here. Per capita, or per person, figures are used to correct for population size: a

country with a large number of people may have a much higher level of total production than a country with a small number of people, without people in the large country having a higher average income or production level than the small country.
2. Comparisons over time for a country require adjustment to take into account average price changes or inflation. Thus, real per capita income or production figures are considered, rather than nominal figures. Comparisons between countries require conversion in terms of the prices of goods and services which can be actually purchased, or what is called Purchasing Power Parity (PPP) terms, rather than in terms of exchange rates (since, for instance, the same amount dollars can buy very different amounts of goods and services, especially services in different countries). There are many problems with both kinds of adjustment, especially the latter, which we will not discuss here, although they are relevant for discussions about ethics, because of the technical issues involved.
3. An affine transformation of one variable into another changes the origin and slope of the variable, but keeps the slope positive. Thus, $V$ is an affine transformation of $U$ if $V = a + bU$ where $b > 0$. Utility is cardinally measurable if it can be represented simultaneously by $U$ and all $V$ for any $a$ and $b > 0$.
4. For an accessible discussion of Sen's views on this see Sen (1999), chapters 1 through 3.
5. An alternative is the Physical Quality of Life Index (PQLI) which aggregates basic literacy rate, infant mortality, and life expectancy at age one, all equally weighted on a 0–100 scale. While many others things are also important, infant mortality, life expectancy from age one, and basic literacy are central to well-being of the very poor. Thus it may be more appropriate for poor countries than for rich countries.
6. See the discussion of this earlier in the chapter, in Section 9.2 and in Chapter 10.
7. See Mill (1848, 754, 756), Book IV, Chapter VI, "Of the Stationary State."
8. Mill (1848, 756), Book IV, Chapter VI, states that there is no "satisfaction in contemplating the world with nothing left to the spontaneous activity of nature; with every rood of land brought into cultivation, which is capable of growing food for human beings; every flowery waste or natural pasture ploughed up, all quadrupeds or birds which are not domesticated for man's use exterminated as his rivals for food, every hedgerow or superfluous tree rooted out, and scarcely a place left where a wild shrub or flower could grow without being eradicated as a weed in the name of improved agriculture. If the earth must lose that great portion of its pleasantness which it owes to things that the unlimited increase of wealth and population would extirpate from it, for the mere purpose of enabling it to support a larger, but not a better or a happier population. I sincerely hope, for the sake of posterity that they will be content to be stationary, long before necessity compel them to it."

## 10 Fairness, Distribution, and Equality

1. Other well-known measures include the Theil index and the Atkinson index. See Sen (1973) for a discussion of these and other measures.

2. This is not necessarily moral blame or praise, since it does not say that having more income is a good thing – it is simply something that they chose or made an effort to obtain.
3. In seeking for explanations of choices we are not taking a position on the debate on free will and determinism. We can take the position that in actual fact both free will and the constraints faced by the decision-maker determine what people do, and yet ask, within a macroeconomic framework or model, what explains or determines what decisions a person makes. It is in the latter sense that we are looking for explanations.
4. The production of some goods like agricultural products may not result in much technological learning, especially of a kind which can be transferred to other sectors, but that of some goods like cars and computers, may have such a result.
5. This may happen because they are in similar income brackets, and therefore have (through clubs, schools, etc.) stronger connections.
6. For discussions of these theories see, for example, Kaldor (1955–56), Galbraith (1952) and Ferber and Nelson (2003).
7. This and the following few quotes, although not the basic argument developed here, are taken from Hausman and McPherson (2006, 178–9).
8. See Hausman and McPherson (2006, 182–3) for a fuller discussion.
9. However, a variant of the veil of ignorance argument can be made in the form that in the absence of knowledge of who we actually are in a society (and hence about the precise nature of our utility functions), we may take everyone's utility function to be the same and comparable to justify the argument for equality.
10. One may wonder how it is possible for an increase in inequality to both increase growth through the savings argument mentioned earlier and reduce it by reducing aggregate demand, as just mentioned. Both effects are possible, but which one will prevail in a particular situation will depend on whether there is some degree of slack in the use of resources (like capital and labor) and whether technological change responds positively to the pressure of higher aggregate demand.
11. An impeccably mainstream neoclassical analysis suggests that there is a perfectly "rational" alternative to going hungry or doing without the basic goods needed for survival. After weighing all of the probabilities, costs, and risks, a person can choose to allocate part of his or her labor to such anti-social activities as selling drugs, burglary, shop lifting, and mugging. This is not to argue that when wages fall below some minimum level every such person threatens the peace by becoming a criminal. Rather the argument is that to some extent the amount of crime committed by an optimizing agent is a function of its opportunity cost. If there is no legal work available or only at less than subsistence wages, then the opportunity cost is low. Whether you believe desperate people are driven to crime by poverty or that weak people are enticed into crime because the risks are not high enough, the fact remains that crime creates enormous costs for the community in the form of negative externalities – loss of life and property, costs of law enforcement, and the psychic costs of fear and insecurity. See Schotter (1984).
12. For instance, the person has a congenital illness, or contracted a disease from exposure to substances which are not known at the time to cause that illness.

Difficulties arise when people choose to smoke or engage in physically dangerous sporting activities. Overeating and drinking can also bring about health problems, and one can debate endlessly about whether one is choosing to become ill or not. The claimed connection of HIV with some kinds of lifestyles, such as drug use and homosexuality, has also caused enormous controversies. It is possible to debate whether persons should be responsible for some problems that could be due to addiction or genes, or whether even completely free choices should go "unpunished." Notice that even if one argues that choice may have some role to play, there may be other reasons, such as compassion for others, or considerations related to infection and contagion and other externalities (such as those related to driving accidents or effects on the families of the person with poor health) which could still call for equalization to some degree.

13. See Hausman and McPherson (2006, 185–90) for a fuller discussion.

## 11 Ethics and Applied Economics

1. Applied economics is sometimes referred to as the economics which applies economic theory to the real world. This is not the sense in which we use the term applied economics in this chapter. Sub-fields of economics involve the use of both abstract "theory" and empirical information about the "real" world. Indeed, it may be argued that the definition of applied economics according to the theory-real world dichotomy is problematic because theory involves abstractions regarding the real world, and empirical applications are closely connected with theories.
2. For discussions of development ethics, see Crocker (1991, 2008), Goulet (2006), and Wilber and Dutt (2010).
3. See Dutt and Wilber (2010), on which this subsection draws.
4. Development economics, perhaps because it deals with economies which are so very different from each other, and especially from economically advanced countries where mainstream economics developed, admits of different approaches to the field, including, in addition to different types of neoclassical economics, Marxian-radical, institutionalist and structural approaches.
5. These views, of course, are related to preanalytical visions, but we here actually refer to how the economy is explicitly portrayed in the analysis.
6. For a discussion of professional ethics in relation to economics see DeMartino (2005 and 2011).
7. The simplest model in which this can be shown is the textbook-Ricardian model, named after the English economist David Ricardo (1772–1823), in which there are two countries, two goods, and one factor of production, labor. Suppose that there are two countries, England and Portugal, which can produce two goods, textiles and wine with fixed labor-output ratios. Suppose that Portugal requires one worker to produce one unit of textiles, and one worker to produce one unit of wine, while England requires two workers to produce one unit of textiles and four workers to produce one unit of wine. In this example, Portugal has an absolute advantage in producing both textiles and wine (it requires less labor to produce both), but Portugal

has a comparative advantage in producing wine (since to produce one more unit of wine Portugal's opportunity cost – the amount of textiles production it must forego – is one, while that for England it is two units of textiles), and England has a comparative advantage in producing textiles (since to produce one more unit of textiles England's opportunity cost is half a unit of wine while for Portugal it is one unit). According to the theory of comparative advantage, Portugal is better off producing and exporting only wine and England is better off producing and exporting only textiles. This can be seen as follows. Suppose that both countries initially produce both goods. Now suppose that Portugal produces two more units of wine, to do which it must produce two less units of textiles. To consume the same amount as before and therefore be just as well off, Portugal can export the two units of wine and import two units of textiles. Suppose that England produces two more units of textiles to supply Portugal with them, but for that England will need to produce one less unit of wine. Portugal can export one of the two units of wine to England, and make England just as well off as before. But as a result of this trade, we have produced one extra unit of wine. This wine can be consumed in one of the countries or both, making one or both of the countries better off under the assumption that more is better. Examples of this type are shown graphically and in more detail in economics principles textbooks.

8. Lower opportunity costs, it is argued, will lead to lower absolute costs, at least in the long run. For instance, if a country has a higher cost of production of a good in which it has a comparative advantage because of high wages, unemployment will result in a reduction in the wage till it has a cost advantage in the good in which it has a comparative advantage. Similar adjustments can result through changes in the exchange rate. These adjustments may not take place in the real world if wages cannot be reduced further (because they are already at or below subsistence levels) or because of fixed exchange rates. In such cases countries may be unable to export and undergo persistent balance of payments problems. We abstract from such complications here to focus on the gains from trade issue.
9. It is interesting to note that Ricardo's example of trade between England and Portugal, in which England exported textiles and Portugal exported wine, was of this type. Textile production led to many kinds of technological improvements – including the spinning jenny, the water frame, and the power loom – which not only increased productivity in textiles but in other industries, and wine production did not. It is not surprising that England became the leading industrial nation in the world, and Portugal one of Europe's poorest. It is also interesting to note that the pattern of specialization that did occur was more due to political and military power which allowed England to dictate the terms of trade treaties to Portugal, than to competition and trade according to comparative advantage. See Sideri (1970).
10. See Chang (2008) for a discussion of these issues.
11. The quote is from Deuteronomy, 20:19. See Diamond (1998).
12. See Elliot (1991) for a brief review.
13. For a recent discussion of the ethics of these decisions which draws on different ethical theories, see Audi (2009).

## 12 Ethics and the Global Financial Crisis

1. For exceptions, see Dobos, Barry, and Pogge (2011) and Reddy (2011). Note, however, that the contributions in the first book are mostly by ethicists and public intellectuals who are not economists, and the second book is by a policymaker rather than an academic economist.
2. See, for instance, the report in *The Christian Science Monitor*, September 14, 2009.
3. See Tickle (2004) for a discussion of religious perspectives and, for a wide-ranging examination following the crisis, see Brassey and Barber (2009).
4. This approach can be seen as incorporating additional elements into the optimizing approach, but can also be seen as being independent of it. Indeed, the focus on optimization can be argued to be a diversion from the more important questions of how the norms actually affect behavior under specific conditions, what determines these norms, and how they change.
5. The late Richard Henry Tawney, Christian, socialist, Professor of Economic History at the London School of Economics, was the author of *Religion and the Rise of Capitalism*, *The Acquisitive Society*, *Equality*, and many other works on the origins, nature, and reform of modern industrial economies.
6. A notable exception is Sen (1993), on which this section draws.
7. Aristotle (350 BC, b), I, 1258B, 49–50, quoted from Sen (1993). Sen also provides an excellent and wide-ranging discussion of attitudes toward usury and finance in early writers on antiquity, in both the West and the East, and their later critics.
8. It has been argued, along similar lines, that unlike the purpose of "real" sectors, which provide material goods to people, such as food, housing, and clothing, the social purpose of the financial sector is unclear (see, for instance, Dobos et al., pg 17). This line of argument is problematic both because it ignores the fact that material goods may not necessarily satisfy only social "needs" but at least to some extent "wants" created by the sales promotion efforts of firms and because it does not take into account the fact that the financial sector may facilitate the real sector's ability to produce goods and services.
9. The newly released report of the Financial Crisis Inquiry Committee reports that the financial industry spent $2.7 billion on lobbying from 1999 to 2008, while individuals and committees affiliated with it made more than $1 billion in campaign contributions. In addition, government regulators often move back and forth between the private sector and government. As a high-level example, Goldman Sachs paid Larry Summers $135,000 for one speech just before he was appointed to be President Obama's economic adviser. The Citizens United decision by the Supreme Court allowing corporations themselves to make unlimited political contributions will magnify the banks political clout making it even more unlikely that Congress or the administration will enforce a banking reform that includes breaking up large banks.
10. Some of these issues are discussed in Charles Ferguson's film, *Inside Job*; see also Ferguson (2012).

# 13 Conclusion

1. This does not seem to apply to Dasgupta himself who, though being a hard-headed economist with little patience for ethical hairsplitting, nevertheless has worked extensively on issues of poverty, malnutrition, and environmental degradation, and clearly thinks these issues are of enormous importance.
2. DeMartino (2011), for instance, argues more specifically that the only solution to the problems is to develop a new field of professional ethics for economists. At the minimum this would entail, required courses in ethics during graduate training, encouragement by the professional organizations, such as the American Economic Association, for revamping curricula to teach ethics, emphasize humility in policymaking, openness to alternative views, emphasis on the importance of getting informed consent of those effected by recommended policies, and always to remember "first do no harm."
3. In 2007 economists working for the US federal government organized a new association called the Association for Integrity and Responsible Leadership in Economics and Associated Professions (AIRLEAP). The association is designed to focus attention on the ethical questions that face the practicing economist. The association has begun running a session on economic ethics at the annual Allied Social Science Association (ASSA) annual meetings in the United States.

# References


Akerlof, George A. (1970). "The market for 'lemons': Quality uncertainty and the market mechanism", *Quarterly Journal of Economics*, 84(3), 488–500.

Akerlof, George A. (1982). "Labor contracts as partial gift exchange", *Quarterly Journal of Economics*, 97(4), 543–69.

Akerlof, George A. and Rachel E. Kranton (2000). "Economics and identity", *Quarterly Journal of Economics*, 115(3), 715–53.

Akerlof, George A. and Rachel E. Kranton (2002). "Identity and the economics of organizations", *Journal of Economic Perspectives*, 19(1), 9–32.

Akerlof, George A. and Robert J. Shiller (2009). *Animal Spirits*, Princeton, New Jersey: Princeton University Press.

Amsden, Alice (1991). "Diffusion of development: The late industrializing model and greater East Asia", *American Economic Review*, 81(2), May, 282–6.

Anderson, Elizabeth (1990a). "The ethical limitations of the market", *Economics and Philosophy*, 6(2), 179–205, reprinted in Wilber, Charles K. (ed.), *Economics, Ethics and Public Policy*, London: Rowman and Littlefield.

Anderson, Elizabeth (1990b). "Is women's labor a commodity?" *Philosophy and Public Affairs*, 19, 71–92, reprinted in Wilber, Charles K. (ed.), *Economics, Ethics and Public Policy*, London: Rowman and Littlefield.

Anderson, Elizabeth (1993). *Value in Ethics and Economics*, Cambridge, Mass.: Harvard University Press.

Archibald, G. C. (1959). "Welfare economics, ethics and essentialism", *Economica*, November, 26(104), 316–27.

Ariely, Dan (2008). *Predictably Irrational. The Hidden Forces that Shape Our Decisions*, New York, NY: Harper.

Aristotle (350 BC, a). *Nicomachean Ethics*, in *The Works of Aristotle Translated into English*, vol. 9, trans. W. D. Ross, Oxford University Press, 1925.

Aristotle (350 BC, b). *The Politics*, translated by Carnes Lord, Chicago: University of Chicago Press, 1984.

Arndt, H. W. 1987. *Economic Development*, Chicago: University of Chicago Press.

Arrow, Kenneth J. (1951). *Social Choice and Individual Values*, New Haven: Yale University Press, 2nd ed., 1963.

Arrow, Kenneth J. (1972). "Gifts and exchanges", *Philosophy and Public Affairs*, 14, Summer, 343–62.

Audi, Robert (2009). *Business Ethics and Ethical Business*, Oxford and New York: Oxford University Press.

Axelrod, Robert (1984). *The Evolution of Cooperation*, New York: Basic Books.

Barry, Brian M. (1989a). *Democracy, Power, and Justice: Essays in Political Economy*, Oxford: Clarendon Press.

Barry, Brian M. (1989b). *Treatise on Social Justice*, vol. 1, *Theories of Justice*, Berkeley, California: University of California Press.

Bauer, P. T. (1981). *Equality, the Third World, and Economic Delusion*, Cambridge, Mass.: Harvard University Press.

Bazen, Stephen (2000). "Minimum wages and low-wage employment", in Mary Gregory, Wiemer Salvedra and Stephen Bazen, eds, *Labour Market Inequalities*, Oxford: Oxford University Press.

Becker, Gary S. (1971). *The Economics of Discrimination*, Chicago: University of Chicago Press.

Becker, Gary S. and Guity Nashat Becker (1996). *The Economics of Life: From Baseball to Affirmative Action to Immigration, How Real-World Issues Affect Our Everyday Life*, New York: McGraw-Hill.

Bentham, Jeremy (1790). *In Praise of Usury*, London: Payne.

Binmore, Ken (1994). *Playing Fair: Game Theory and the Social Contract*, Cambridge, Mass.: MIT Press.

Blackburn, Simon (2001). *Being Good: A Short Introduction to Ethics*, Oxford: Oxford University Press.

Blank, Rebecca M. and William McGurn (2004). *Is the Market Moral?*, Washington DC: Brookings.

Blaug, Mark (1975). "Kuhn vs. Lakatos, or Paradigms vs. Research Programs in the History of Economics", *History of Political Economy*, 74(4), Winter, 399–433.

Blaug, Mark (1990). *The Methodology of Economics: Or How Economists Explain*, Cambridge: Cambridge University Press.

Boland, Lawrence A. (1981). "On the futility of criticizing the neoclassical maximization hypothesis", *American Economic Review*, 71, 1031–6.

Boland, Lawrence A. (1982). *The Foundations of Economic Method*, London: Allen and Unwin.

Brassey, Alexis and Barber, Stephen (2009), eds., *Greed*, Houndmills, Basingstoke, UK: Palgrave Macmillan.

Brittan, Samuel (1995). *Capitalist with a Human Face*, Aldershot, UK: Edward Elgar.

Buchanan, James M. (1986). *Liberty, Market and State: Political Economy in the 1980s*, New York: New York University Press.

Caldwell, Bruce (1982). *Beyond Positivism. Economic Methodology in the Twentieth Century*, London: George Allen and Unwin.

Caldwell, Bruce (1984). Editor, *Appraisal and Criticism in Economics. A Book of Readings*, London: Allen and Unwin.

Card, David and Krueger, Alan (1995). *Myth and Measurement*, Princeton, NJ: Princeton University Press.

Chang, Ha-Joon (2008). *The Bad Samaritans: The Myth of Free Trade and the Secret History of Capitalism*, New York: Bloomsbury Press.

Cohen, G. A. (1989). "On the currency of egalitarian justice", *Ethics*, 99, 906–44.

Cowen, Tyler (1993). "The scope and limits of consumer sovereignty", *Economics and Philosophy*, 9(2), 253–69, reprinted in Wilber, Charles K. (ed.), *Economics, Ethics and Public Policy*, London: Rowman and Littlefield.

Crocker, David (1991). "Toward development ethics", *World Development*, 19(5), 457–83.

Crocker, David (2008). *Ethics of Global Development: Agency, Capability and Deliberative Democracy*, Cambridge, UK: Cambridge University Press.

Cross, Rod (1982). "The Duhem-Quine thesis, Lakatos and the appraisal of theories in macroeconomics", *Economic Journal*, June, 320–40.

Dasgupta, Partha (2005). "What do economists analyze and why: Values or facts", *Economics and Philosophy*, 21, 221–78.

David, Paul A. (1985). "Clio and the economics of QWERTY", *American Economic Review*, 75(2), 332–37.

Deiner, Ed and Shigehiro Oishi (2000), 'Money and happiness: Income and subjective well-being across nations', in Ed Deiner and Eunook K. Suh, eds, *Culture and Subjective Well-being*, Cambridge: MA, MIT Press, pp. 185–218.

DeMartino, George (2005). "A professional ethics code for economists", *Challenge*: July–August, 88–104.

DeMartino, George (2011). *The Economist's Oath: On the Need for and Content of Professional Economic Ethics*, Oxford: Oxford University Press.

De Quervain, Dominique J.-F., Urs Fischbacher, Valerie Treyer, Melanie Schellhammer, Ulrich Schnyder, Alfred Buch, and Ernst Fehr (2005). "The neural basis of altruistic punishment", *Science*, 305, 1254–64.

Diamond, Eliezer (1998). " 'The earth is the Lord's and the fullness thereof': Jewish perspectives on consumption", in David A. Crocker and Toby Linden, eds, *Ethics of Consumption. The Good Life, Justice and Global Stewardship*, Boston, Mass., Lanham: Rowman and Littlefield, 501–36.

Dixit, Avinash K. and Nalebuff, Barry J. (1991). *Thinking Strategically. The Competititve Edge in Business, Politics and Everyday Life*, New York and London: Norton.

Dobos, Ned; Barry, Christian; and Pogge, Thomas (2011). *Global Financial Crisis: The Ethical Issues*, Basingstoke, UK and New York: Palgrave Macmillan.

Dworkin, Ronald (1981). "What is equality? Part 2: Equality of resources", *Philosophy and Public Affairs*, 10(1), 283–345.

Dworkin, Ronald (2000). *Sovereign Virtue: The Theory and Practice of Equality*, Cambridge, Mass.: Harvard University Press.

Dutt, Amitava Krishna (1984). "Stagnation, income distribution and monopoly power", *Cambridge Journal of Economics*, 8(1), 25–40.

Dutt, Amitava Krishna (1990). *Growth, Distribution and Uneven Development*, Cambridge, UK: Cambridge University Press.

Dutt, Amitava Krishna (2009). "Happiness and the relative consumption hypothesis", in Amitava Krishna Dutt and Benjamin Radcliff, eds, *Happiness, Economics and Politics*, Cheltenham, UK: Edward Elgar, 127–50.

Dutt, Amitava Krishna and Charles K. Wilber (2010). "Development ethics and development economics", in Charles K. Wilber and Amitava Krishna Dutt, eds, *New Directions in Development Ethics: Essays in Honor of Denis Goulet*, Notre Dame: University of Notre Dame Press.

Easterlin, Richard (1974), 'Does economic growth improve the human lot? Some empirical evidence', in Paul David and Melvin Reder, eds, *Nations and Households in Economic Growth: Essays in Honor of Moses Abramovitz*, Palo Alto, CA: Stanford University Press, 89–125.

Easterlin, Richard (1995). "Will raising the incomes of all increase the happiness of all?", *Journal of Economic Behavior and Organization*, 27, 35–47.

Easterlin, Richard (2001), 'Income and happiness: Towards a unified theory', *Economic Journal*, 111, July, 465–84.

Easterly, William. (2006). *The White Man's Burden: Why the West's Effort to Aid the Rest have done so Much Ill and so Little Good*. New York: Penguin Press.

Elliot, Robert (1991). "Environmental ethics", in Peter Singer (ed.), *A Companion to Ethics*, Oxford: Blackwell, 186–96.

Enderle, Georges (2003). "Business ethics", in N. Bunnin and E. P. Tsui-James, eds, *Blackwell Companion to Philosophy*, Oxford: Blackwell, 531–55.

Etzioni, Amitai (1987). "Toward a Kantian socio-economics", *Review of Social Economy*, XLV (1), April, 37–47, reprinted in Wilber, Charles K. (ed.), *Economics, Ethics and Public Policy*, London: Rowman and Littlefield.

Evans, Peter B. (1989). "Predatory, developmental and other apparatuses: A comparative political economy of the third world state", *Sociological Forum*, 4(4), December, 561–87.

Evensky, Jerry (1993). "Ethics and the invisible hand", *Journal of Economic Perspectives*, 7(2), 197–205, reprinted in Wilber, Charles K. (ed.) *Economics, Ethics and Public Policy*, London: Rowman and Littlefield.

Evensky, Jerry (2005). *Adam Smith's Moral Philosophy*, Cambridge, UK: Cambridge University Press.

Fehr, Ernst, and Gächter, Simon (2000). "Cooperation and punishment in public goods experiments", *American Economic Review*, 90(4), 980–94.

Fehr, Ernst and Gächter, Simon (2002). "Fairness in the Labour Market: A Survey of Experimental Results", Working Paper No. 114, Institute for Empirical Research in Economic: University of Zurich, Switzerland.

Ferber, Marianne A. and Julie A. Nelson (eds) (2003). *Feminist Economics Today: Beyond Economic Man*. Chicago: University of Chicago Press.

Ferguson, Charles (2012). *Predator Nation: Corporate Criminals, Political Corruption, and the Hijacking of America*, New York: Crown.

Frank, Robert H. (1999). *Luxury Fever. Why Money Fails to Satisfy in an Era of Excess*, New York: The Free Press.

Frank, Robert H. and Philip J. Cook (1995). *The Winner-Take-All Society: Why the Few at the Top Get so Much More than the Rest of Us*, New York: The Free Press.

Frank, Robert H.; Gilovich, Thomas; and Regan, Dennis T. (1993). "Does studying economics inhibit cooperation?" *Journal of Economic Perspectives*, 7(2), Spring, 159–7, reprinted in Wilber, Charles K. (ed.), *Economics, Ethics and Public Policy*, London: Rowman and Littlefield.

Frey, Bruno S. and Felix Oberholzer–Gee (1997). "The cost of price incentives: An empirical analysis of motivation crowding-out", *American Economic Review*, 87(4), 746–755.

Frey, Bruno S. and Alois Stutzer (2002). *Happiness and Economics*, Princeton, NJ: Princeton University Press.

Friedman, Benjamin (2005). *The Moral Consequences of Growth*, New York: Alfred A. Knopf.

Friedman, Milton (1953). "The methodology of positive economics", in Friedman, Milton, *Essays in Positive Economics*, Chicago, Ill.: University of Chicago Press.

Friedman, Milton, and Rose Friedman (1990). *Free to Choose. A Personal Statement*, New York: Harvest Books.

Galbraith, John Kenneth (1952). *American Capitalism. The Concept of Countervailing Power*

Gauthier, David (1986). *Morals by Agreement*, Oxford: Oxford University Press.

Gilligan, Carol (1982). *In a Different Voice: Philosophical Theory and Women's Development*, Cambridge, Mass.: Harvard University Press.

Goodin, Robert E. (1980). "Making Moral Incentives Pay", *Policy Sciences*, 12, 131–145.

Goulet, Denis (2006). *Development Ethics at Work: Explorations 1960–2002*, London: Routledge.

Granovetter, Mark (1985). "Economic action and social structure: The problem of embeddedness", *American Journal of Sociology*, 91(3), 481–510.

Greif, Avner (1997). "Contracting, enforcement and efficiency: Economics beyond the law", *Annual World Bank Conference on Development Economics 1996*, Washington DC: World Bank, 239–65.

Griffith, William B. and Goldfarb, Robert S. (1991). "Amending the economist's 'Rational Egoist' model to include moral values and norms", in Kenneth J. Koford and Jeffrey B. Miller, eds, *Social Norms and Economic Institutions*, Ann Arbor: The University of Michigan Press.

Hausman, Daniel M. and Michael S. McPherson (1996). *Economic Analysis and Moral Philosophy*, Cambridge, UK: Cambridge University Press.

Hausman, Danuel M. and Michael S. McPherson (2006). *Economic Analysis, Moral Philosophy, and Public Policy*, 2nd edition, Cambridge, UK: Cambridge University Press.

Held, Virgina (1990). "Feminist transformations of moral theory," *Philosophy and Phenomenological Research*, 50, Supplement, Fall, 321–44, reprinted in Wilber, Charles K. (ed.), *Economics, Ethics and Public Policy*, London: Rowman and Littlefield.

Heyne, Paul (1995). "Moral criticisms of markets", *The Senior Economist*, 10(4), April.

Hirschman, Albert O. (1970). *Exit, Voice and Loyalty*, Cambridge, Mass.: Harvard University Press.

Hirschman, Albert O. (1977). *The Passions and the Interests: Political Arguments for Capitalism before Its Triumph*, Princeton, New Jersey: Princeton University Press.

Hubin, Donald C. (1994). "The moral justification of benefit/cost analysis", *Economics and Philosophy*, 10(2), 169–94, reprinted in Wilber, Charles K. (ed.), *Economics, Ethics and Public Policy*, London: Rowman and Littlefield.

Johns, Helen and Paul Ormerod (2007). *Happiness, Economics and Public Policy*, London: Institute of Economic Affairs.

Kahneman, Daniel (1999), "Objective happiness", in D. Kahneman, E. Diener and N. Schwarz, eds, *Well-Being: The Foundations of Hedonic Psychology*, Russell Sage Foundation.

Kahneman, Daniel, Jack Knetsch and Robert H. Thaler (1986a). "Fairness as a constraint on profit-seeking: Entitlements in the market", *American Economic Review*, 76(4), 728–41.

Kahneman, Daniel, Jack Knetsch and Robert H. Thaler (1986b). "Fairness and the assumptions of economics", *Journal of Business*, 59(4, Part 2), S285–300.

Kahneman, Daniel, Paul Slovic and Amos Tversky (eds.) (1982). *Judgment under Uncertainty: Heuristics and Biases*, Cambridge, UK: Cambridge University Press.

Kahneman, Daniel and Amos Tversky (2000). *Choice, Values and Frames*, Cambridge, Mass: Cambridge University Press.

Kaldor, Nicholas (1955–56). "Alternative theories of distribution", *Review of Economic Studies*, 23(2), 83–100.

Kamm, Frances M. (1996). *Morality, Mortality Vol. II: Rights, Duties, and Status*. Oxford: Oxford University Press.

Kant, Immanuel (1785). *Grounding for the Metaphysics of Morals*, James Ellington, tr., Indianapolis: Hackett Publishing Company, 1981.

Keynes, John Maynard (1936). *The General Theory of Employment, Interest and Money*, London: Macmillan.
Keynes, John Neville (1891). *Scope and Method of Political Economy*, London: Macmillan.
Kindleberger, Charles P. (1978). *Panics, Manias and Crashes: A History of Financial Crises*, New York: Basic Books.
Kolm, Serge-Christophe (1997). *Modern Theories of Justice*, Cambridge, Mass: MIT Press.
Konow, James (2003). "Which is the fairest one of all? A positive analysis of justice theories", *Journal of Economic Literature*, 41, December, 1188–1239.
Kotler, Philip and Nancy Lee (2004), *Corporate Social Responsibility: Doing the Most Good for Your Company and Your Cause*, New York: John Wiley & Sons.
Kreps, David M. (1990). *Game Theory and Economic Modeling*, Oxford: Clarendon Press.
Krugman, Paul and Robin Wells (2005). *Microeconomics*, New York: Worth Publishers.
Kuhn, Thomas S. (1970). *The Structure of Scientific Revolutions*, 2nd edition, Chicago: University of Chicago Press.
Kymlicka, Will (1991). "The social contract tradition", in Peter Singer (ed.), *A Companion to Ethics*, Oxford: Blackwell, 186–96.
Leibenstein, Harvey (1966). "Allocative efficiency and X-efficiency", *American Economic Review*, 56, 392–415.
Lucas, Robert E. B. (1973). "Some international evidence on output-inflation tradeoffs", *American Economic Review*, 76(1), 131–45.
Machlup, Fritz (1969). "Positive and normative economics", in Robert Heilbroner (ed.), *Economics Means and Social Ends*, Englewood Cliffs, NJ: Prentice-Hall, 99–129.
MacIntyre, Alasdair (1967). *A Short History of Ethics*, London: Routledge and Kegan Paul; Routledge classics edition, London: Routledge, 2002.
MacIntyre, Alasdair (1984). *After Virtue: A Study in Moral Theory*, 2nd edition, Notre Dame, IN: University of Notre Dame Press.
Maital, Shlomo (1982). *Minds, Markets and Money: Psychological Foundations of Economic Behavior*, New York: Basic Books.
Mäki, Uskali (1995). "Diagnosing McCloskey", *Journal of Economic Literature*, 33(3), September, 1300–18.
Margolis, Howard (1982). *Selfishness, Altruism and Rationality*, Cambridge: Cambridge University Press.
Marshall, Alfred (1920). *Principles of Economics*, 8th edition, London: Macmillan.
Marx, Karl (1869). *Capital*, Vol. 1, New York: Vintage Books, 1977.
Marx, Karl and Friedrich Engels (1878 [1974]). *Critique of the Gotha Program*, in English, *Marx-Engels: The First International and After*, Harmondsworth, UK: Penguin.
McCloskey, Deirdre (2006). *The Bourgeois Virtues. Ethics for an Age of Commerce*, Chicago, Ill.: University of Chicago Press.
McCloskey, Donald (1985). *The Rhetoric of Economics*, Madison, Wisc.: University of Wisconsin Press.
Mellström, Carl and Magnus Johannesson (2008). "Crowding out in blood donation: Was Titmuss right?", *Journal of the European Economic Association*, 6(4), 245–63.

Milanovic, Branko (2005). *Worlds Apart. Measuring International and Global Inequality*, Princeton, New Jersey: Princeton University Press.

Mill, John Stuart (1848). *Principles of Political Economy*, in *Collected Works of John Stuart Mill*, Volume 3, Toronto: University of Toronto Press, 1965.

Mill, John Stuart (1863). *Utilitarianism*, London: Parker, Son and Bourn.

Miller, David (1982). "Arguments for equality", *Midwest Studies in Philosophy*, 7, 73–88.

Miller, David and Michael Walzer (1995). *Pluralism, Justice and Equality*, Oxford, UK: Oxford University Press.

Minsky, Hyman (1986). *Stabilizing an Unstable Economy*, Twentieth Century Fund, New Haven, Conn.: Yale University Press.

Musgrave, Alan (1981). " 'Unreal assumptions' in economic theory: The F-twist untwisted", *Kyklos*, 34(3), 377–87.

Myrdal, Gunnar (1954). *The Political Element in the Development of Economic Thought*, trans. by Paul Streeten, Cambridge, Mass.: Harvard University Press.

Myrdal, Gunnar (1972). *An American Dilemma: The Negro Problem and Modern Democracy*, New York: Pantheon Books.

Nagel, Ernst (1961). *The Structure of Science: Problems in the Logic of Scientific Explanation*, New York: Harcourt, Brace and World.

Naim, Moises (2005). *Illicit*, New York: Doubleday.

Nielsen, Richard P. (1983) "Arendt's action philosophy and the manager as Eichmann, Richard III, Faust, or institution citizen", *California Management Review*, 26(3), 191–201, reprinted in Wilber, Charles K. (ed.), *Economics, Ethics and Public Policy*, London: Rowman and Littlefield.

Nordhaus, William and James Tobin (1972). "Is growth obsolete?" in *Economic Growth*, Fiftieth Anniversary Colloquium Volume, National Bureau of Economic Research, New York: Columbia University Press.

Novak, Michael (1993). *The Catholic Ethic and the Spirit of Capitalism*, New York: Free Press.

Nozick, Robert (1974). *Anarchy, State and Utopia*, New York: Basic Books.

Okun, Arthur M. (1975). *Equality and Efficiency: The Big Tradeoff*, Washington D.C.: The Brookings Institution.

Ostrom, Elinor (1991). *Governing the Commons*, Cambridge, UK: Cambridge University Press.

Oswald, Andrew J. (1997). "Happiness and economic performance", *Economic Journal*, November, 1815–31.

Parfitt, Derek (1984). *Reasons and Persons*, Oxford: Oxford University Press.

Plato (360 BC). *The Republic*, trans. Allan Bloom, 2nd edition, New York, Basic Books, 1991.

Platteau, Jean-Philippe (1994). "Behind the market stage where real societies exist-part I: The role of public and private order institutions", *The Journal of Development Studies*, XXX(3): 533–577.

Pogge, Thomas W. (1998). "A global resources dividend", in David A. Crocker and Toby Linden, eds, *Ethics of Consumption. The Good Life, Justice and Global Stewardship*, Boston, Mass., Lanham: Rowman and Littlefield, 501–36.

Porter, Michael and Kramer, Mark R. (2002). "The competitive advantage of corporate philanthropy", *Harvard Business Review*, December, 5–16.

Putnam, Robert (1995). "Tuning in, tuning out: The strange disappearance of social capital in America", *Political Science and Politics*, 28(4), December, 664–83.

Putnam, Robert (2000). *Bowling Alone: The Collapse and Revival of American Community*, New York: Touchstone Books.
Pyke, Frank, G. Becattini and Werner Sengenberger (1992). *Industrial Districts and Inter-Firm Cooperation in Italy*, eds, Geneva: International Institute of Labor Studies.
Rawls, John (1971). *A Theory of Justice*, Cambridge, Mass.: Harvard University Press.
Rawls, John (1993). *Political Liberalism*, New York: Columbia University Press.
Rawls, John (1999). *The Laws of Peoples*, Cambridge, Mass.: Harvard University Press.
Reddy, Y. V. (2011). "Ethics and the world of globalised finance", in Y. V. Reddy, *Global Crisis, Recession and Uneven Recovery*, Hyderabad: Orient BlackSwan, 31–43.
Reich, Michael (1981). *Racial Inequality: A Politico-economic Analysis*, Princeton: Princeton University Press.
Robbins, Lionel (1932). *An Essay on the Nature and Significance of Economic Science*, London: Macmillan, second edition, 1935.
Roemer, John E. (1982). *A General Theory of Exploitation and Class*, Cambridge, Mass.: Harvard University Press.
Roemer, John E. (1998). *Equality of Opportunity*, Cambridge, Mass.: Harvard University Press.
Rorty, Richard (1987). "Science as solidarity", in John Nelson, et al., eds, *The Rhetoric of the Human Sciences: Language and Argument in Scholarship in Public Affairs*, Madison, Wisc.: University of Wisconsin Press.
Sachs, Jeffrey. (2005). *The End of Poverty*, New York: Penguin Press.
Samuelson, Paul A. (1948). *Economics*, New York: McGraw Hill.
Sandel, Michael (1982). *Liberalism and the Limits of Justice*, Cambridge: Cambridge University Press.
Scanlon, Thomas (2003). "The diversity of objections to inequality", in Thomas Scanlon, *The Difficulty of Tolerance: Essays in Political Philosophy*, Cambridge: Cambridge University Press, 202–18.
Schumpeter, Joseph A. (1954). *History of Economic Analysis*, Oxford, UK: Oxford University Press.
Schotter, Andrew (1984). *Free Market Economics: A Critical Appraisal*, New York: St. Martin's Press.
Seabright, Paul (1993). "Managing local commons: Theoretical issues in incentive design", *Journal of Economic Perspectives*, 7(4), Autumn, 113–34.
Seabright, Paul (2004). *The Company of Strangers. A Natural History of Economic Life*, Princeton, New Jersey: Princeton University Press.
Sen, Amartya K. (1973). *On Economic Inequality*, Oxford, UK: Oxford University Press, expanded edition, 1997.
Sen, Amartya K. (1981). *Poverty and Famines: An Essay on Entitlements and Deprivation*, Oxford: Oxford University Press.
Sen, Amartya K. (1983). "Poor, relatively speaking", *Oxford Economic Papers*, 35, July, 153–59.
Sen, Amartya K. (1985). "The moral standing of the market", *Social Philosophy and Policy*, 2(2), reprinted in Deiter Helm (ed.), *The Economic Borders of the State*, Oxford: Oxford University Press, 1993, 92–109.
Sen, Amartya K. (1986). "Adam Smith's prudence", in Sanjaya Lall and Frances Stewart, eds, *Theory and Reality in Development*, New York: St Martin's, 28–37.

Sen, Amartya K. (1993). "Money and value: On the economics and ethics of finance", *Economics and Philosophy*, 9(2), 203–27.

Sen, Amartya K. (1999). *Development as Freedom*, New York: Anchor Books.

Sen, Amartya K. (2009). *The Idea of Justice*, Cambridge, Mass.: The Bellknap Press of Harvard University Press.

Shapiro, Carl and Joseph E. Stiglitz (1984). "Equilibrium unemployment as a worker discipline device", *American Economic Review*, 74(1), 433–44.

Sideri, Sandro (1970). *Trade and Power: Informal Colonialism in Anglo-Portuguese Relations*, Rotterdam: Rotterdam Univ. Press, 1970.

Simon, Herbert A. (1976). "From substantive to procedural rationality", in S. J. Latsis (ed.), *Method and Appraisal in Economics*, Cambridge, UK: Cambridge University Press, 129–48.

Sims, Christopher (1996). "Macroeconomics and methodology", *Journal of Economic Perspectives*, 10(1), Winter, 105–20.

Singer, Peter (1978). "Is racial discrimination arbitrary?" *Philosophia*, 8, 185–203, reprinted in Peter Singer, *Unsanctifying Human Life*, Oxford: Blackwell, 2002.

Skyrms, Brian (1996). *Evolution of the Social Contract*, Cambridge: Cambridge University Press.

Smith, Adam (1759). *The Theory of Moral Sentiments* (ed.) D. D. Raphael and A. L. Macfie, Vol. 1 of *The Glasgow Edition of the Works and Correspondences of Adam Smith*, general editors, D. D. Raphael and A. Skinner, Oxford: Clarendon Press, 1976.

Smith, Adam (1776). *An Inquiry into the Nature and Causes of the Wealth of Nations* (ed.), W. B. Todd, Vol. 2 of *The Glasgow Edition of the Works and Correspondences of Adam Smith*, general editors, D. D. Raphael and A. Skinner, Oxford: Clarendon Press, 1976.

Solomon, W. David (1998). "Normative ethical theories", in Wilber, Charles K. (ed.), *Economics, Ethics and Public Policy*, London: Rowman and Littlefield, 119–38.

Sterba, James (1998). "Social justice", in Wilber, Charles K. (ed.), *Economics, Ethics and Public Policy*, London: Rowman and Littlefield, 187–215.

Sterba, James (2010). "Our basic human right is a right to liberty and it leads to equality, in Charles K. Wilber and Amitava Krishna Dutt, eds, *New Directions in Development Ethics: Essays in Honor of Denis Goulet*, Notre Dame: University of Notre Dame Press.

Stewart, David (1995). *Business Ethics*, New York: McGraw-Hill, 1995.

Stewart, Frances (2008) (ed.) *Horizontal Inequalities and Conflict*, New York and London: Palgrave Macmillan.

Stigler, George and Gary S. Becker (1977). "De Gustibus Non Est Disputandum", *American Economics Review*, 67(1), March, 76–90.

Stiglitz, Joseph E. (1985). "Information and economic analysis: A perspective", *Economic Journal*, 95, 21–41.

Streeten, Paul (1986). "What do we owe the future?", *Resources Policy*, March, 4–16, reprinted in Wilber, Charles K. (ed.), *Economics, Ethics and Public Policy*, London: Rowman and Littlefield.

Tawney, Richard Henry. (1972). *Commonplace Book*, J. M. Winter and D. M. Joslin, eds., Cambridge, UK: Cambridge University Press.

Tickle, Phyllis A. (2004). *Greed*, New York: Oxford University Press.

Titmuss, Richard M. (1971). *The Gift Relationship: From Human Blood to Social Policy*, New York: Pantheon Books.

Tversky, Amos and Daniel Kahneman (1981). "The framing of decisions and the psychology of choice", *Science*, 211, 453–8.
Wade, Robert (1990). *Governing the Market: Economic Theory and the Role of Government in East Asian Industrialization*, Princeton, New Jersey: Princeton University Press.
Walzer, Michael (1983). *Spheres of Justice*, New York: Basic Books.
Weston, Samuel C. (1994). "Toward a better understanding of the positive/normative distinction", *Economics and Philosophy*, 10, 1–17, reprinted in Wilber, Charles K. (ed.), *Economics, Ethics and Public Policy*, London: Rowman and Littlefield.
Wilber, Charles K. (1979). "Empirical Verification and Theory Selection: The Keynesian-Monetarist Debate," *Journal of Economic Issues*, XIII (4), December, 973–982.
Wilber, Charles K. (1984). "Introduction", in *Catholicism, Protestantism and Capitalism* by Amintore Fanfani, Notre Dame, IN: University of Notre Dame Press, vii–xxvii.
Wilber, Charles K. (1998). *Economics, Ethics and Public Policy*, ed., London: Rowman and Littlefield.
Wilber, Charles K. and Roland Hoksbergen (1986). "Ethical Values and Economic Theory", *Religions Studies Review*, 12, 205–214.
Wilkinson, T. M. (2004). "The ethics and economics of the minimum wage", *Economics and Philosophy*, 20, 351–74.
Williamson, Oliver. (1985). *The Economic Institutions of Capitalism: Firms, Markets, Relational Contracting*, New York: The Free Press.
Yuengert, Andrew M. (1996). "Free markets and character", *Catholic Social Science Review*, 99–110.

# Index